The British Administrative System

Principles Versus Practice

Grant Jordan

London and New York

First published 1994
by Routledge
11 New Fetter Lane, London EC4P 4EE

Simultaneously published in the USA and Canada
by Routledge
29 West 35th Street, New York, NY 10001

© 1994 Grant Jordan

Typeset in Baskerville by J&L Composition Ltd, Filey, North Yorkshire
Printed and bound in Great Britain by TJ Press (Padstow) Ltd,
Padstow, Cornwall

British Library Cataloguing in Publication Data
A catalogue record for this book is available from the British Library

Library of Congress Cataloging in Publication Data
A catalogue record for this book has been requested

ISBN 0–415–01550–2 (hbk)
      0–415–01551–0 (pbk)

The British Administrative System

There is a great gap between the principles of public administration in Britain and the way in which policies are actually implemented. Grant Jordan explains and discusses the basic principles and theories before going on to show how in practice Governments tend to make up policy as they go along.

The author finds that organisational theory has failed to engage usefully with practice. There are contending approaches that are used as 'stick-on labels' to endorse change rather than informing it. The book argues that reforms to meet one set of criteria inevitably have adverse consequences elsewhere. Reform has to be about balancing competing objectives and Grant Jordan shows that new initiatives have been enthusiastically introduced without Government properly understanding the results of previous policies. Students will be informed on a wide range of material from the Haldane Inquiry of 1918 to Next Steps and Market Testing in 1994.

Teachers and students of Public Policy and Public Administration will welcome the new approach of this text, which combines an analysis of theory and practice with discussions on recent developments.

Grant Jordan is Professor of Politics at the University of Aberdeen and has taught public administration and policy-making for 20 years.

Contents

Tables

Preface

The theme of this book is that the call to progress is often a dangerous siren: there is much to be said for arrangements that develop through experience and evolution. In Christopher Hood's words the Great Leap Forward is often the Leap into the Dark. So too with technology. The completion of this book was delayed by matters such as incompatibility of computer software systems. These disadvantages were not strongly featured as departments and individuals were encouraged to ever change, ever improve, their word processing systems. That something emerged was due to the rescue work of Hettie Ras and Fiona Cameron.

Gail Nicoll played a singular role in helping sort problems of drafts of different vintages and drafts that seemed adequately footnoted when written, but were thoroughly inadequate years later as the project came to a close. (All Ph.D. students need to avoid this failing as they will not have as effective an aide as I did.) I must also express thanks for general comments on the manuscript by Howard Elcock and on the Judicial Review section by Maurice Sunkin and Cliona Kimber. William Maloney's empirical work on the post-privatised water industry is taking him towards similiar conclusions as those set out in Chapter 6: his support was encouraging in setting out the argument.

To those tempted to criticise the finished book the plea in mitigation is that any particular work is a compromise between the fresh and the necessarily familiar, the specialist and the basic. Writing is a process of disillusionment as what emerges is more prosaic than what was intended. Again, the argument goes, this is like the reform of Government. Potential reform is like the excitement and promise of an unwritten book; reform in practice is the compromise between competing priorities further eroded by defective implementation:

For the defects of the book I accept responsibilty and am only grateful that those mentioned above have saved me from far more. What is not my fault is that much of the theory covered in this book is unconvincing: it is the purpose of the book to underline this. It is for those who think it too critical and negative to demonstrate unfairness and prove that the material here dismissed is more valuable than claimed.

Such a pessimistic set of comments shows why I have such a debt to (in alphabetical order) Alexandra, Grace, Innes and Susan. The study of British public administration is not so rewarding (in any of the usual senses) that one is not grateful of distraction.

Introduction

This book attempts to bring together and discuss different principles, ideas and nostrums that are used in the description of policy-making and administration in Britain. These include collective responsibility, individual ministerial responsibility, arm's-length control, organisation by function, judicial review of administration. Together these ideas represent a large part of the apparatus that a graduate in administration might be expected to have accumulated. The problem for those advancing these concepts – usually teachers – and those receiving them – usually students – is that there is a massive disjunction in what should be the unity of theory and the elements of practice.

Arguably we are attempting analysis in an inappropriate language. If the usual tool-kit of terms did not already exist, and if we were starting an account of British policy-making without an encumbrance of intellectual baggage, would we really find it helpful to use as starting positions labels such as Cabinet Government? Would we really start descriptions of what happens when things go wrong in Government by explaining what *should* happen if Ministers *really* believed in a Back To Basics version of Ministerial Responsibility?

This work focuses on Central Government. It is difficult to maintain this definition of interest as an argument of the book is that the blurring of the boundaries of Government has intensified; it is therefore difficult to justify *not* looking at local government, health administration, and the other elements of the administrative system. The decision is purely pragmatic as it was thought that the scope of the book as it stands was wide enough. However there is also an argument that the same *approaches and attitudes* that permeate these chapters could be legitimately 'read into' these other areas.

The study of public administration is characteristically the study of the process of *unlearning* as ideas with a face appeal and wide accessibility are revealed as fictional rationalisations with little real descriptive or explanatory power (see Hood and Jackson 1991: xii, 161). We expect of students participation in a game in which they must use a set of terms, images, models to get half marks – and prove that they disbelieve these conventional wisdoms to be marked above the minimum pass. We are the unthinking victims of a set of ideas inherited from Victorian constitutional lawyers, and abstract theorists such as Weber. Theory is rooted in intellectual history not observation.

American administrative writing also finds a gap between simple ideas and convoluted practice. Hugh Heclo, for example, describes the relationship between political appointees and career civil servants in the US as follows,

> While the formal categories of people and jobs may seem a jumble, ambiguity is vastly increased by the unofficial arrangements. . . It is not surprising if all this presents a confused picture to outside observers. . . A conventional image of pyramid-like structures in the executive branch, with a neat division of politicians above is badly misleading. Rather than picturing a single, clearly defined boundary line, one should think instead of an erratic smudge that is jagged. . . variable. . . and blurred. . .
>
> (Heclo 1977: 35)

This is the also the tone and expectation required in the study of British Government. Where one might expect bureaucratic rigidity there is *ad hoc* improvisation. British public administration is made up by Governments as they go along. It is characterised precisely by features that might be least expected: uncertainty, inconsistency, disorder.

It is surprisingly difficult to prove this. An account of confusion reads very like a confused account. Since there is no ordered pattern to British administration, the more detailed knowledge that is gathered serves to emphasise the weakness of our understanding. This particular work emerges from the sort of public administration that has been in traditional in the UK: that inheritance has been struggling to absorb conflicting ideas from a business conception of the subject with quite different emphases. This has further twisted the ratchet of complexity.

Ideas 'in good currency' in public administration have changed with surprising rapidity in the past 25 years. The Command Paper, 'The Reorganisation of Central Government', in 1970 set out a case for large, centralised, integrated departments of central Government of the Department of Environment and Ministry of Defence type. The 1980s saw 'reductions in force' as the Thatcher Government exerted pressure to cut back civil service numbers from a high of 734,000 to 559,500 in 1990–1. By 1992 there were again increases in staff, but now the organisational map was transformed by the creation of decentralised 'Next Steps' agencies (and the likelihood of increased 'market testing'). The surge towards nationalisation of the post-war years was reversed in the 1980s: the belief in standardised and central employment conditions and pay bargaining has been overtaken by contrary trends. This instability in the shape and size of Government means that arguments about the best practice of public administration have had to be flexible – where not inconsistent. Only by reviewing the different approaches of the past decades can the insubstantial nature of current thought on Government be appreciated.

Hood and Jackson (1991: 11) record that successful administrative ideas (successful in the sense of being welcomed) are rarely very sound, and that often they are repackaged and relabelled versions of earlier proposals. They say that what makes for winning arguments is *rhetorical power*: the standing of the proponent and the packaging of the argument. The study of public administration is thus to provide confidence for a sceptical reaction to organisational fads which may be based on powerful rhetoric – and surprisingly little else. This book is in tune with that sceptical suspicion in that it leans to the view that the New Public Management (NPM) of the 1980s may turn out to be Fairly Familiar Administration (FFA) as time passes. Hood himself relates NPM to the scientific management movement of the first third of the century. He terms it 'Taylorism with computers'. Delafons (1982) shows that concern with efficiency in administration long predated the Efficiency Strategy of the recent Conservative Governments.

Hood and Jackson (1991: 159) have explained that the 'concrete factual realism' that has permeated the British approach to the subject is an unappealing doctrine for decision-makers and likely to be subordinated by more attractive metaphorical forms of argument. The main example they give is of economics – by public conception the most practical of the social sciences. In fact, as they argue,

> Economics is . . . distinctive in its propensity to reason through explicit fictions, notably in the fiction of the economic person as opportunistic and self-seeking to the exclusion of all else . . . To the extent that the fictions are complex and arcane, they command respect and awe. McCloskey (1985) sees the rise of the 'econocracy' over the past fifty years as a product of the successful use of mathematical metaphor to portray economics as an arcane 'hard science',

establishing for economists a claim to a special expertise beyond the
realm of the laity's understanding.

(Hood and Jackson 1991: 159)

That is to say that the marginality from practical affairs of public
administration is not because of its academic and practical pessimism
but precisely *because it is too practical to influence policy-makers who are more
influenced by theoretical fiction of the economists' type*. The argument of Hood
and Jackson is therefore that the pursuit of concrete facts has marginalised the subject from influencing events: 'The path to influence may
lead through metaphor, the better to understand confused and confusing
reality' (1991: 160).

So the massive irony – as argued by Hood and Jackson – is that the
devaluation of public administration has been because it sought to
challenge

accounts of practice or institutional working which seemed thread-
bare, out-of-date, and deceptive. The thrust and the challenge was to
get out and discuss the true, living 'practice' which underlay the
formal and implausible account of structures and procedures – to
*de*fictionalise, to *de*mystify the way that the administrative system
worked and how it was built.

(Hood and Jackson 1991: 161)

The student reading widely in the literature of the post-war years has to
realise that much of the work is excavating the foundations of culs-de-sac
rather than theoretical highways. Comparative Public Administration,
contingency theory, corporate management, even implementation
theory, have failed to sustain their academic appeal.

The picture so far is of confusion both in the practice and theory of
public administration. Any work that puts forward a more complacent
account should be treated with some suspicion. A major review in the
USA, *Public Administration: the State of the Discipline* opens in similar vein:

It cannot be said that we are self-satisfied. Perry and Kraemer tell us
our research fails to cumulate into greater understanding, is poorly
supported financially, and is little value professionally. Rainey refers
to 'a widely perceived unsufficiency in relevant research'. Studies of
public administration, Caiden advises, are fragmented. Worse still,
efforts to unify the discipline through public-choice theory could well
lead to 'environmental degradation and social disintegration'. Given
to more gentle remonstration, Fried patiently explains, 'why universal
theory remains elusive'. For Nigro, public personel administration is

an impossible subject: Where performance criteria can be followed they are rejected (the traditional model for managers); where they are accepted (the human relations approach by managers), they are too vague to be implemented.

(Wildavsky 1990: xiii)

On a central issue such as the link between politics and public administration have we advanced beyond Norton Lang's comment in 1954?

However attractive [the idea of] an administration receiving its values from political policy-makers may be, it has one fatal flaw. It does not accord with the facts of administrative life.

(Cited in Henry 1990: 4)

The 'bottom line' of this Introduction is not to argue that we retreat 'whipped' from the responsibility of studying public administration. It is to emphasise that the subject is subtle, conceptual and contested. Some students are attracted to the subject precisely because they want to avoid political uncertainty: they are misguided. In 1887 Woodrow Wilson noted that administration was, 'put aside as a "practical detail" which clerks could arrange after doctors had agreed on princples' (cited in Waldo 1990: 74). This was wrong and has 'got wronger'. We need to recognise two main points:

1 We must be sceptical – particularly of those advocates of administrative change who regularly over-sell their wares, and who regard reminders of past failures as 'knocking'. We are allowed to be puzzled when themes of accountability and consistency which have been central to the problems of policy administration for decades are suddenly 'solved' by not being addressed. We must in particular be wary of prescriptions from consultants who have a financial stake in glossing over problems and telling Ministers that their wish list is realistic. Don't ask a barber if you need a haircut. Unless the adviser has the freedom to knock over daft ideas when they deserve it , his or her advice is likely to be of questionable value.
2 We must see much of the writing on the subject not as a step-by-step DIY guide to administration; not as essays on 'how to', but to illuminate the *issues* of administration. In other words, while there is no doubt that consideration of the materials of the academic subjects of public administration (to be old fashioned) or public policy or even New Public Management will produce better informed, more self-conscious administrators, the subject (how are we governed?) is also worth studying for its intrinsic importance.

If this sounds faint praise for a subject we think it fits in with the mood-lowered expectations in economics, psychology and other social sciences. Those who advertise simple and immediately useful solutions are trading in suspect stock. Economics has similiarly retreated in its aspirations to practical influence. Like Keynesianism, monetarism had to acknowledge a failure to cope with reality.

The study of the subject is not practical in the sense that administration is necessarily much improved, in a direct way, by its pursuit. One can be well versed and competent in the literature without being able to 'mind the shop'. Most of the literature on administration is not like a cricket manual giving advice on batting, but is a critique on a match. It is an account of the game – not advice on how to master particular skills. The study of public administration is better able to provide an understanding of issues concerning the provision of public service than it is able to assist individuals to provide these services. As Andrew Gray (1991: 534) has noted, 'the universal truth of administrative analysis is that there are no universal truths of administrative practice'.

Christopher Hood (1990) has set out five functions of research for the subject:

- track and monitor,
- remember,
- explain,
- test,
- criticise.

These, rather than 'reform', 'redesign', 'reorganise' are the practical ambitions of the subject. The academic subject has lurched in the past decade in pursuit of a practical interest in efficiency. To express reservations about this is not to be complacent about the existence of inefficiency but to underline that experience tells us that any remedies should be treated sceptically: a change is not for the better merely because it is well intentioned. Moreover, experience also tells us that reforms to meet one set of criteria often have costs in other valued areas. We need to judge the charges by the light of dimensions that have repeatedly shown themselves to be important – reliability, accountability, fairness (see Elcock 1991). We should hold in mind the complexity of organisations, the contradictory nature of our goals and the lack of political consensus as we receive the reformist agendas that arrive with regularity. What is important is the aggregate of *different* insights and perceptions: there is no 'one best way'.

In so far as the book has a different tone from others in its field it is probably that it shows less confidence in the cumulative body of wisdom represented by the works and approaches reviewed. If we take judicial review as an example, it is less important to grasp the couple of dozen cases cited to show familiarity with the subject than it is to grasp that the bottom line is that the premises of review are so uncertain that they are regularly tested in the courts – with no predictability in outcomes. The Law Society itself failed with an application in 1993.

That it is important to stress the uncertainty in most branches of this subject is further proved by the recent history of non-departmental forms of organisation. The Conservative Opposition of the late 1970s and Government of the early 1980s crusaded *against* the lack of public accountability of, and the number of, 'quangos' (quasi autonomous non-governmental organisations), but by 1993 there was much comment of the type: 'Political patronage is rampaging throughout John Major's Administration as Government allies and Conservative Party donors amass key posts in Britain's burgeoning quangocracy' (*Observer*, 4 July). This article noted that a reduction in the number of quangos (from 2,410 in 1979 to 1,800 in 1992) had been accompanied by an increase in budgets from £13. 9bn to £42bn.[1] By 1994 the tide in favour of such bodies that had reversed so markedly in the middle of the Thatcher years seemed to turn again and there was renewed concern at their lack of accountability. By 1994 there was a mood – justified or otherwise – that any non-Conservative Government would have to do something different as the patterns of the 1980s seemed to be failing to deliver, and had been compromised with partisan association.

If we look at the various approaches to understanding organisational design or behaviour we find a menu of competing truths. We have to concede that these world views are contestable and naturally contradictory rather than pretend that there is a comfortable package of collectively reinforcing knowledge. There is the 'myth of more' that assumes that as we gather more knowledge on administration we move towards certainty. In fact we merely have proliferating and conflicting interpretations. The ultimate benefit of searching in these areas is not that there is a guru available but that the reader might be more aware of the incompleteness of any particular offering. Perrow noted,

> many business and consulting services come equipped with neat packages of nostrums. Not surprisingly they find that every organization they advise needs just what is in their package, whether it is a

1 The British billion – that is, a thousand millions – is used throughout.

better data-processing system, linear programming, human relations programmes or executive development programmes, better central techniques, or a better marketing system.

(Cited in Pitt and Smith 1981: 13)

If this work has a central theme it is that the notion that there is reform or set of reforms that will improve the organisation is fallacious and a search will be fruitless. Reforms tend to attempt to remedy the deficiencies of the last change – and all changes imply as yet unrecognised defects. The various goals that we might wish to set for Government cannot be reconciled.

The British system 'works' – but that is a tautology. This book is concerned not with whether it works or not, or if it could work 'better', but with our understanding of the system. As evidence to the Treasury and Civil Service Committee put it in 1990 (HC 481: 68) 'That's all right in practice, but what's it like in theory?' There is a gap between our practice and the principles which we commonly assert underlie that practice.

The following chapters are organised into two parts. The first tries to indicate the difficulties in comprehending the messy empirical pattern at the centre of Government; the second looks at three of the ways in which it is argued that some democratic control of the administrative system could be achieved. In neither part do the principles that are found take us far in understanding practice.

Part I

Organising without certainty

Chapter 1

Government in the fog

ACCEPTING DISORDER

There are two broad positions to choose between in examining the organisation of Government. On the one hand it is possible to accept some 'givens': that we know (reasonably well) what we understand by 'Government' and to agonise over the concept displaces attention from problems of substance. Richard Rose (1984: 13) has written in such a vein and managed to greatly illuminate the subject – though this aspect of his approach is challenged here. He defined Government organisations 'as formal administrative structures established by the constitution or public laws, headed by officials elected by citizens or appointed by elected officials'. This can be labelled the two-box image. It is reasonably easy in this version to separate out into their boxes, Government (G) and non-Government (NG).

Although for some purposes such a sweeping clarification is useful and necessary, the more the boundaries are examined the less clear they become: certainty dissolves. An alternative view sees Government organisation as messy in design, overlapping in responsibilities. As Rhodes says of sub-central government the metaphor of the 'machine' is inappropriate, 'A maze or labyrinth is a far more apposite image' (1988: 4). If anything that image is still too user-friendly: better perhaps a maze in the fog. As Birkenshaw, Harden and Lewis argue from a different perspective and with a different image (to the same end) in *Government by Moonlight*:

> As to the public/private divide, the British practice has been to preach the distinctiveness of the public and private realms, and perhaps in consequence, has done all it can to obfuscate the reality of the interlocking, the comingling, of those realms.
>
> (Birkenshaw *et al.* 1990: 11)

This alternative disorderly view also underpins an article by Hood, Dunsire and Thompson (1978) in which they asked, 'So you think you know what Government departments are. . . ? They argued that every student (and teacher) should be able to define 'Government Depart- ments', but the task only becomes more and more complex as investiga- tion progresses. The thrust of the Hood *et al.* article was that when one examines the governmental bureaucracy one finds a surprising lack of codification, definition and order. In this chapter the message is ex- tended. Just as there is a problem with the concept of a 'department', there is doubt too about the wider organisational limits of Government.

This second, uncertain perspective was captured in a comment by Brian Chapman (1963: 18). British Government, he said, is a rich Byzantine structure through which few can pick their way with any certainty. In two important senses this interpretation of disorder has become more rather than less powerful and influential. Christopher Pollitt reviewed a major work from the Bielefeld Interdisciplinary Project, *Guidance, Control and Evaluation in the Public Sector* (1985). This, he shows, reflected the views of a large number of leading academics of public administration in the early 1980s. Pollitt summarised their position thus:

> the Bielefeld corpus displays a considerable measure of agreement as to the nature of 'the problem' [of providing a conception of public and private sectors]. From many of these chapters comes a vision of the 'public sector' – in all major Western countries – as multi-centred, only loosely co-ordinated yet increasingly interdependent, fuzzy at the boundaries and exhibiting 'growing entropy' – that is the 'amount of energy that is needed for co-ordination within and between public sector organisations is growing faster than their output in services and society'. Gone are Weberian models of neat, monolithic hierarchies, gone is any clear legal and political separation between public and private sector organisations (PGOs abound), past is the notion that policy formulation is *the* crucial problem, and implementation is a lesser task, safely delegated to ruggedly practical middle-level officials.
>
> (Pollitt 1987: 106)

In brief this perspective is far less confident about finding underlying order in the design of Government. Even the boundary between Government (G) and non-Government (NG) is in doubt.

A second factor leading to the reinforcing of Chapman's message is the 'Next Steps' development of Government executive agencies and other innovations in the late 1980s in Britain. This implied further movement away from any simple pattern of Central Government departments that were easy to delineate and whose status was clear. Instead there was a proliferation of organisational forms that attempted to have some of the qualities of private sector organisations.

Correspondence with the Cabinet Office in 1993 confirmed we have *pragmatic arrangements* largely uninfluenced by consistent principle:

> You will be aware that government and offices and departments owe their establishment and organisation, together with any powers they possess and duties they perform, partly to the Royal Prerogative and partly to Parliament. Sir Ivor Jennings once wrote that, in the absence of general provisions regulating administration, 'there is, in law, only a heterogeneous collection of ministers, officers, and authorities, exercising a mass of apparently unrelated functions'. Confronted by this situation Jennings concluded that it would be wrong to assume that there is a specific number of homogeneous entities called Departments of State. In each there is a central nucleus where decisions are taken by or on behalf of the Minister. But in many cases there are subordinate departments exercising functions pre-scribed by law in the name of the subordinate department. . . for example, the Commissioners of the Inland Revenue are subject to the Lords Commissioners of the Treasury; but on many matters they take their own decisions in their own name. Also, there are connected with many of the Departments of State semi-autonomous authorities who consult the Minister and his advisers only in respect of those matters where it is so provided by law.
>
> I do not know when Jennings wrote that but the situation is not so very different today. It is a complex area where there is, in law, no generally applicable definition of the term 'government department', nor is its use standardised for everyday purposes. Having said that, no difficulties appear to have arisen when the expression 'a government department' has been used in legislation. We conclude, therefore, that the meaning of the term 'department' depends on the particular statutory context in which it is used.

This non-definition of the nature of a department is an indication of the struggle in the centre of government to find a form of words that deals with the fragmented practice. It confirms that there is no regular pattern which might be uncovered by more thorough investigation.

One is reassured when others too are puzzled. Drewry and Butcher (1988: 55) give some figures about the changing size and shape of the civil service but warn,

> We must not forget . . . even the definitional boundaries of our
> subject are indistinct. It is hazardous to try to quantify something
> when a penumbra of uncertainty surrounds the definition of what
> that something is.
>
> (Drewry and Butcher 1988: 55)

The problem of understanding the boundaries between Central
Government and these loosely attached units or agencies (equally a
puzzle in the United States) is considered below (see pp. 32–44), but
first we need to note that Central Government is itself uncomfortably
unclear about self-identity. Basic questions such as 'What is a civil
servant?', What is a department?', What is a Secretary of State?',
cannot be answered without a subtext of reservations. Wettenhall
(1986) looks at Government organisation in several countries, though
mainly Australia. He shows that definitions of 'ministry' and
'department' are consistently inconsistent.

Hood and Dunsire (1981: 37) attempted to record the main features
of British Central Government by relying as much as possible on
published material. The intention was not to uncover any policy
secrets, but to map the organisational structure of the system. However, they soon discovered that different published lists – all with more or
less similar claim to be considered 'official' or authoritative – existed.
There were thus different possible interpretations of what constituted
departments and sub-departments. In *The Civil Service Yearbook* (1975)
they found 787 bodies listed. These were not the same departments as
understood in other governmental publications. Even the main headings
(227) included organisations such as the Women's Royal Voluntary
Service which were not included in other listings. The Treasury
Memorandum on the Supply Estimates for 1976–7 (Cmnd 6452)
picked out 67 'departments'. These were apparently close to, but
not identical to, the 64 units which were counted as departments in
the May 1976 version of HM Ministers and Senior Staff in Public
Departments, or the 61 units which they found in civil service staff
number returns.

Moreover Hood *et al.* (1978: 23) note that 26 bodies were listed as
departments for purposes of the index of Hansard whereas only 24
bodies were considered to be departments for the purpose of answering
Parliamentary Questions. They point out that the Parliamentary Commissioner for Administration ('the Ombudsman') listed 38 in his Annual
Report. Other sources – e.g. the annual list produced in connection with
the 1947 Crown Proceedings Act or the list produced by the Property

Services Agency of departments which could receive free PSA services – produce yet other numbers.

Hood and Dunsire (1981: 40) concluded that the definition of a department was as a deep legal (indeed philosophical) question – 'and there is certainly no single and all-encompassing definition of such a thing – only a variety of lists of agencies called "departments", compiled for a number of different purposes, with a considerable degree of difference between them'.

The 'five-star' departments

Though these issues pose surprising difficulty, none the less all is not completely jumbled; there is a 'core' to Government that would appear on everyone's list. If we look at the departments headed by a Secretary of State then we cover most of that core. We can term these major bodies as 'five-star' departments (based on their importance) or, perhaps, by referring to their outstanding characteristic, we can more clumsily call them Cabinet-Minister-led departments. These are essentially the mainstream departments headed by a Cabinet Minister (see Table 1.1).

While the normal arrangement is one Cabinet Minister (even more precisely one Secretary of State) to each major department – there are (inevitably) deviations from this norm. There is not a tidy and orderly pattern that can be easily grasped: there is an aggregation of exceptions.

The Treasury of the early 1990s has three Ministers in the Cabinet – if the Prime Minister's archaic status as First Lord of the Treasury is included. Realistically however the figure is two: while PMs do have a dominating input into Treasury deliberations this is as Prime Minister and not through their notional place within the Treasury. But even discounting the PM, the Treasury is now 'double banked' in the Cabinet. The Chancellor's position is reinforced by the presence of the Chief Secretary (his Treasury No. 2) who carries the main burden of the public expenditure side of the department. In 1994 Michael Portillo was Chief Secretary, with Kenneth Clarke as Chancellor. The Treasury position is an unusual case in Whitehall where the second in command in the department is accepted as the main authority in an area of business (domestic public expenditure). The participation of the Chief Secretary in the Cabinet is a comparatively new 'norm'. (The Parliamentary Secretary to the Treasury is also sometimes in the Cabinet, but of course – despite the label – the holder of that post is in reality Chief Whip and not a part of the working Treasury.)

In recent years the Department of Employment has also on occasion

Table 1.1 'Five-star' departments*

	Political chief	Bureaucratic head
	Minister	
Ministry of Agriculture Fisheries and Food		Permanent Secretary (G1)
Cabinet Office	Prime Minister	Secretary of the Cabinet & Head of Home Civil Service
Ministry of Defence	Secretary of State	Permanent Under Secreatry of State (G1)
Duchy of Lancaster	Chancellor (Party Chairman)	Clerk of Council
Dept of Education & Science	Secretary of State	Permanent Secretary (G1)
Employment Dept Gp	Secretary of State	Permanent Secretary (G1)
Dept of Energy	Secretary of State	Permanent Under-Secretary of State (G1)
Dept of Environment	Secretary of State	Permanent Secretary (G1)
FCO	Secretary of State	Permanent Under-Secretary of State (G1)
Dept of Health	Secretary of State	Grade 1
Home Office	Secretary of State	Permanent Under Secretary of State (G1)
Lord Chancellor's Dept	Lord Chancellor	Permanent Secretary (G1)
Lord President's Office	Lord President (Leader of Commons)	
Lord Privy Seal's Office	Lord Privy Seal (Leader of Lords)	
Prime Minister's Office	Prime Minister	Principal Private Secretary
DTI	Secretary of State	Permanent Secretary (G1)
Departmental Treasury	Chancellor of Exchequer	Permanent Secretary
Dept of Transport	Secretary of State	Permanent Secretary (G1)
Welsh Office	Secretary of State	Head of Department (G1)
Scottish Office	Secretary of State	Permanent Under-Secretary (G1)
Northern Ireland Office	Secretary of State	Permanent Under-Secretary (G1)
Dept of Social Security	Secretary of State	Grade 1

Source: From 'Ministers and Departments' Section of Civil Service Yearbook, 1990.

Note: * For another, but similar, use of this term see Hood and Dunsire (1981: 42).

been 'double banked' in the Cabinet. This was less due to the importance of the topic than to the fact that the then (1986) Secretary of State,
Lord Young, was not an MP – and hence not available to be answerable
to the Commons. Current convention demands that under these circumstances there should also be a Cabinet-rank Minister to answer for
the department in the House of Commons. Thus, analogously, in 1982
when the Foreign Secretary was from the House of Lords – i.e. Lord
Carrington – there was a supporting Minister in the Cabinet who could
deal with the Commons – i.e. Humphrey Atkins.

The list of 'five-star' departments shows that not all Cabinet members
are styled Secretaries of State. Some Secretaries of State enjoy, by
tradition, alternative titles for their posts – for example, Foreign
Secretary, Chancellor of the Exchequer, Minister of Agriculture. (In
1992 Michael Heseltine resurrected the title President of the Board of
Trade.) These are simply historical terms.

Other exceptions to the normal Secretary of State label are
extravagant Gilbert and Sullivan sounding designations such as
Lord Privy Seal. The inclusion of such Ministers in the Cabinet
gives the Prime Minister some flexibility in the composition of
Cabinet. Not all the Cabinet members head up five-star departments. Some head up none and some of the departments that are
headed by Ministers of Cabinet rank are very minor. These departments
have Cabinet-level heads as the by-product of the PM wanting the
Minister in the Cabinet for political reasons rather than because there
is any administrative rationale.

In the 1986 *Civil Service Yearbook* no Minister was connected with the
Paymaster General's Office (with over 800 staff). Kenneth Clarke's two
immediate predecessors in the Cabinet in that post – John Selwyn
Gummer, 1984–6 and Cecil Parkinson, 1981–3 – held the Paymaster
General title as a means to give Cabinet rank to the Chairman of the
Conservative Party. In 1990 Kenneth Baker was in the Cabinet as
Chairman of the Party through the fiction of the post of Chancellor
of the Duchy of Lancaster. Chris Patten retained this label when he took
over. In 1994 William Waldegrave pursued his functions as Minister in
charge of Citizens' Charters under the label of that office.

The post of Paymaster General is an example of the separation of the
title from real duties. As early as 1852 it began to be held jointly with
other duties and the PMG's office 'was relegated to the back seat, with
day to day control passing formally to the Assistant Paymaster General
(a civil servant) under power of attorney, while the Minister attended to
more pressing duties' (Ulph 1985). Ulph cites a Victorian critic:

The Office of Paymaster General is at present only nominal – a mere sinecure – no salary is paid, but the remuneration is fully equal to the services rendered.

(Ulph 1985: 113)

The PGO has as its main task the payment of civil service pensions and other Government payments. By 1985 it was handling 30 million payments and 1.2 million pensions per year. Ulph, himself a PGO official, noted that,

Strangely enough the Paymaster General has no responsibility for the PGO's banking and pensions policies, which lies with Treasury Ministers. His sole duty with regard to the PGO is to see that the Office meets its obligations as agents for other departments, and although this involves him occasionally in parliamentary questions or correspondence with fellow MPs, it is generally delegated to the Assistant Paymaster [a grade 5/Assistant Secretary level] under the power of attorney which a new Minister signs immediately on taking office.

(Ulph 1985: 114)

Ulph observed that on the four occasions when the post of Paymaster has been left vacant – most recently for a period of 15 months during 1983–4 – the effect on the Office was negligible. In 1992 the Paymaster General was not a Cabinet-ranked Minister.

Other 'floating' posts include that of Lord Privy Seal which in 1987 was held by John Biffen – whose 'real' job was that of Leader of the House of Commons. However, earlier in the Thatcher Administration the title was held by Sir Ian Gilmour and Humphrey Atkins while they, in turn, held the No. 2 Foreign Office job. While Mr Biffen had a staff within the Lord Privy Seal, there were no staff allocated to that office in 1982 when Humphrey Atkins was in the FCO. In 1991 Lord Waddington had the title while acting as Leader of the House of Lords.

In 1994 the Lord Privy Seal was Lord Wakeham. He described his position as,

one of the Ministerial posts without a specific portfolio, and with a grand but completely incomprehensible title, which people find so mysterious. In practice, the main function of the holder of this post within the councils of Government tends to be to chair a number of the committees of the Cabinet.

(Wakeham 1993: 1)

These posts thus exist as constitutional camouflage to accommodate the party political and parliamentary roles of Cabinet members. In passing it can be noted that the holders of the offices of Lord President, First Lord of the Treasury, Lord Privy Seal are usually not 'Lords' but are from the House of Commons. The exception – where facts fit faces – is the case of the Lord Chancellor who is indeed a member of the House of Lords. His panjandrum-like title does in fact relate to a real job as head of the legal system. This contrasts with the other labels which are no more than excuses to 'smuggle' a non-departmental or second in command Minister into the Cabinet.

This discussion of the labels enjoyed by Cabinet Ministers is intended to illustrate the point that there is no regularity at the centre. Moreover the Cabinet is not simply the uncontroversial sum of the political heads of the most important parts of the administrative machine. Who is in or out of Cabinet is a deliberate decision by the Prime Minister. He or she is as much influenced by the list of personalities wished at the Cabinet table as by the need to appoint Secretaries of State to head major departments. There are limits on how many ministerial and Cabinet salaries can be paid (House of Commons Disqualifications Act (1957)) but this restriction can be circumvented by having Ministers who do not draw salaries – or by fresh legislation to raise the relevant ceilings (e.g. Ministerial and Other Salaries Act (1972)). The Prime Minister is mainly influenced by convention and expectations about what a Government should look like – and the practical difficulty of finding suitable candidates on the back benches or a place for those whose political prestige suggests their inclusion.

Smith *et al.* (1993: 569) focus on 61 departments in their study, but again confirm that a range of different options could be selected. They note that 19 of their 61 are headed by Cabinet Ministers. They point out (according to Hogwood 1993) that we have no systematic information about the consequence of whether departments have, or do not have, a ministerial head. They say that this is a key question as non-ministerial departments account for about a quarter of the UK civil service. With the development of agencies that seek to increase the distance between Ministers and the management of departmental administration this is also an issue of growing importance.

The lack of certainty at the heart of Government also extends to the classification of Ministers. The most important politicians in the Government outside the Cabinet have Ministers of State status. For example, in Mrs Thatcher's Government at the start of 1990 (compared with around 22 Cabinet Ministers) there were 29 Ministers of State. As further

Table 1.2 Categorisation of senior civil servants

New grade	Former title
1	Permanent Secretary
1a	Second Permanent Secretary
2	Deputy Secretary
3	Under Secretary
4	Grades between Under Secretary and Assistant Secretary maximum
5	Assistant Secretary
6	Senior Principal
7	Principal

Source: Simplified from *Civil Service Yearbook*, 1990.

terminological complication it can be noted that at that time 10 of the 29 were designated Right Honourable – or in other words were Privy Councillors – a slight nuance of seniority even within the Ministers of State ranks. Below the Minister of State grade is the even more numerous category of Parliamentary Secretary. (Both grades are lumped together by the term 'Junior Minister'.) Parliamentary Private Secretaries are attached to Ministers and even Junior Ministers; they are not technically Ministers but expected to give the full support for Government that is expected of paid Ministers.

The list of top career civil servants in the core departments show that the mainstream departments are headed by a Permanent Secretary to match the Secretary of State: though again for reasons now divorced from any rational explanation, some of these top administrators have the title Permanent Under Secretary (and some have the hyphenated label Permanent Under-Secretary). Since 1984 these senior civil servants have been categorised on a numerical scale (see Table 1.2) that should have, but hasn't, made these older titles obsolescent (also, see Table 1. 1).

Second division or non-Cabinet-headed departments

Not all departments (as listed in the *Civil Service Yearbook*, 1990) are headed by Secretaries of State or their equivalents (see Table 1.3). The impression that these are 'second division' departments is reinforced by a variety of points.

There is no clear explanation of why these activities are not headed by a Cabinet Minister but there is perhaps the implication that these activities are thought to be less politically contentious. This implies,

Table 1.3 Non-Cabinet-headed departments

	Political chief	Bureaucratic head
Office of Arts and Libraries	Minister of State	Head of Office (G2)
Government Hospitality Fund	Minister in Charge	Secretary (G5)
Law Officers Department	Attorney-General	Legal Secretary (G2)
Overseas Development Administration	Minister of State	Grade 1A
Paymaster General's Office	Paymaster General	Asst Paymaster General (G5)

however, that ministerial responsibility exists not just for Cabinet Ministers but for these non-Cabinet political heads.

Bureaucratic–led departments

Table 1. 4 shows that the problem of accountability is greater for a third tier of departments (again as listed in the *Civil Service Yearbook*, 1990). Many minor – and some vital – parts of Government exist in constitutional limbo. A number of bodies listed as departments appear to be headed not by a Minister but by a career bureaucrat – sometimes in tandem with a chairman of uncertain status. There are problems when it comes to operationalising the general doctrine of ministerial responsibility for Cabinet-led departments (see Chapters 7 and 8), but bodies which lack their own political head would seem also to lack a set of principles of accountability. This was confirmed when the Crown Agents lost some £200m in the mid-1970s in a fringe banking debacle. As Christopher Hood concluded in discussing the affair, 'It is easy to dismiss the CA affair as a "one off" problem, but there are over 300 other organisations in the same broad institutional "family" as the Crown Agents in The Directory of Paid Public Appointments Made by Ministers' (1978: 302). The aggregation of minor-sounding exceptions becomes significant.

Some of the bureaucratic-led departments have that status because there seems merit in having them at some distance from Government – where there is, for example, a regulatory function to pursue. However we have no explicit theory to that effect. Their civil servants are interchangeable with any other civil servants. Some of these departments have some kind of qualified relationship to a Secretary of State.

Table 1.4 Bureaucratic departments

	Relationship to politicians	Headed by
Central Statistical Office	'responsible to Chancellor of Exchequer'	Director & Head (G1A)
Charity Commission		Chief Commissioner (G3)
Crown Prosecution Service	'independent Attorney General is the Minister responsible'	Director of Public Prosecutions Deputy & Chief Executive (G2)
HM Customs & Excise	'advises Chancellor of the Exchequer'	Chairman (G1)
Office of Electricity Regulation		Director General
Export Credits Guarantee Department	'responsible to the Secretary of State for Trade and Industry'	Chief Executive
Office of Fair Trading		Director General of Fair Trading/ Deputy Director General (G2)
Forestry Commission	'legal status of & function, as a government department' 'reports directly to Forestry Ministers'	Chairman (part time)/ Director General (G2)
Registry of Friendly Societies	'Government Department serving two statutory bodies, the Building Societies Commission and the Central Office of the Registry of Friendly Societies'	Chairman (G2) Chief Registrar (G2)
Office of Gas Supply		Director General
Government Actuary's Department		Government Actuary
Central Office of Information	'Common Service Department'	Director General (G4)

Organisation	Notes	Head
Board of Inland Revenue	'advises the Chancellor of Exchequer on policy questions'	Chairman (G1)
Intervention Board for Agric Produce	'Responsible to the Agric Ministers'	Chairman/Chief Executive (G3)
HM Land Registry	—	Chief Land Registrar (G2)
Law Commission	—	Commissioners
National Debt Office	—	Comptroller General (G5)
National Investment and Loans Office	—	Director (G5)
Department for National Savings	'reports to Treasury Ministers'	Director (G2)
Ordnance Survey	—	Director General (G3)
Parliamentary Counsel	—	First Parliamentary Counsel
Public Record Office	'under general direction of the Lord Chancellor'	Keeper (G3)
Public Works Loan Board	—	Chairman/Secretary (G5)
Royal Mint	Master of Mint (ex officio) Chancellor of Exchequer	Deputy Master and Comptroller G3
Serious Fraud Office	'under superintendence of the Attorney General'	Director of Serious Fraud Office (G2)
HMSO	Executive Agency	Controller & Chief Executive (G2)
OFTEL	—	Director General
Treasury Solicitor's Department	—	HM Procurator General and Treasury Solicitor (G1)
Office of Water Services	—	Director General

Thus the Board of Inland Revenue, while listed as a department separate from the Treasury, apparently 'advises the Chancellor of the Exchequer on policy questions'. This perhaps implies – but does not state – that the Customs and Excise 'also, advises the Chancellor'. The Department of National Savings 'reports to Treasury Ministers'. The senior civil servants are not only Grade 1, but they have a plethora of titles such as 'Director' that imply a more direct personal responsibility than those with the title 'Permanent Secretary' – which is obviously used to signify an adjunct to a senior politician.

Labels are perhaps not necessarily important but the argument is that these devices signal that the central theory of ministerial accountability is inoperative – without there being any alternative. In 1991, when the Bank of Commerce and Credit International was closed down by the Bank of England, there was an attempt by the Opposition to hold the sometime Chancellor, John Major, to account. But the Bank of England is another of the accountability 'holes' in British arrangements. It is not listed as the responsibility of the Chancellor of the Exchequer.

There is sometimes a false precision on offer. Thus the *Civil Service Yearbook* (1990) presented the (then) Property Service Agency as a part of the Department of the Environment. However, it was headed by its own Chief Executive (Grade 1A). To what extent is there a real difference in accountability from another part of the department? Or how does it differ from the HMSO which appears in Table 1.4 as an Executive Agency headed by a civil servant with the rank Controller and Chief Executive (Grade 2)? How do either really differ from the Agricultural and Food Research Council headed by a Deputy Secretary (Grade 3)? The Council appears in the *Civil Service Yearbook* not as a department but as an 'Other Organisation'.

It is important to emphasise that the categories used in the afore-mentioned tables above are an attempt to hunt for order, and perhaps to impose an arbitrary pattern on the 'departments' listed in the *Civil Service Yearbook* (1990). There seems no theory (other than political convenience) to explain why, say, the Lord Privy Seal's Office sometimes finds its way into Table 1.1. The list of components changes from year to year as the margins are drawn to suit a sort of common-sense demand that the Cabinet be not larger than 22 rather than the fact that there are real differences between smaller, lower profile, departments and those of Cabinet status.

As a separate category the *Civil Service Yearbook* listed 'Other Organisations' which included bodies such as the Advisory Concilia-tion and Arbitration Service, the Audit Commission, Health and

Safety Commission, Sports Council. Why should the Law Commission be a 'department' but the Countryside Commission be an 'other Organisation'? There were also separate categories of 'Libraries, Museums & Galleries', and Research Councils.

The significance of these blurred boundaries is underlined when we note that the essence of the recent Financial Management Initiative and Next Steps programme is to increase management autonomy for all civil service units within the mainstream departments. The Next Steps agencies (see Chapter 5) are claimed to give greater accountability but still within the civil service. These developments presumably further diminish these distinctions between being a department or an 'other Organisation'.

That the distinction between departments and these other organisations is less fundamental than arbitrary is suggested by two points. First, the 1990 *Yearbook* listed all Scottish bodies in the conglomerate category of 'Departments and Other Organisations'. Second, by 1991 the *Yearbook* had a new central category of 'Departments and Executive Agencies'. An entry such as for the DTI says, 'The Secretary of State has delegated responsibility for day-to-day operation of each of the following agencies to their respective Chief Executive within a framework of policy, objectives and resources. . . ' These developments seem to further blur the fences between departments and other organisations.

Political posts have phases of fashion. For example the Attorney-General in 1986 became a spotlight figure as the Westland and Wright/MI5 cases dominated the political agenda. The post was again in the front line during the Scott Inquiry in 1994 into the sale of arms to Iran. Bruce-Gardyne (1986: 100) has described how the Department of National Savings (DNS) lay, 'gently languishing' until 1980. Up until then it was an instrument to borrow money (cheaply) from unsophisticated small savers. However, in 1980 it was given more competitive savings instruments (granny bonds) and a greatly increased target to meet. The DNS thus became a major force in the Treasury's funding programme. Bruce-Gardyne (1986: 75) also points out that the low profile of the Customs and Excise increased dramatically in 1971 with the introduction of VAT. When Customs and Excise won the battle in Whitehall for 'proprietorship' of VAT it increased its size and political exposure.

The boundaries between the sets of bodies in Tables 1.1, 1.3 and 1.4 are less firm than might be expected by those who believe that bureaucracies are rule-bound and strictly ordered by clearly articulated principles or criteria. The proposition to date is that even within the 'mainstream civil service' there is far less uniformity than might be expected. Dunleavy (1989) cites Mackenzie and Grove's (1957) text in which they give their chapter on the main types of Whitehall department the epigraph taken from Burke's Speech on American Taxation,

> an administration, so chequered and speckled . . . a piece of joinery, so crossly indented and whimsically dovetailed; a cabinet so variously inlaid; such a piece of diversified mosaic.
>
> (Dunleavy 1989: 250)

Dunleavy sees this impression of overwhelming complexity as, 'difficulties confronted by empiricist institutional studies operating without a developed theoretical apparatus' (1989: 251). He dismisses the kind of concerns about the unreliability of labels reflected here as 'theoretically trivial methodological problems'. However the assumption in this chapter is that the first step in understanding the organisation of Government is to clear out of the way the common-sense view that reality is captured by a simple organisational map. As Dunleavy has himself complained there *are* problems of understanding if essentially different organisations are lumped into the one category (departmental agencies?) or practices are labelled for public relations purposes. Why, he says, call a fish a dog and then complain that it cannot breathe in air? What, for example, is the case if there is no suitable market available to sustain the so called 'market testing' of civil service efficiency (see Chapter 5).

Dunleavy himself sets out five possible criteria for defining the central state from among the universe of all full public sector bodies:

A   Ministerial and non-Ministerial Whitehall Departments
B   Agencies directly controlled by Ministers, staffed by civil servants, yet not counted as Ministries.
C   Agencies staffed by civil servants but not directly controlled by Minister.
D   Agencies directly controlled by Minister but not staffed by civil servants.
E   Agencies neither directly controlled nor staffed by civil servants.

(Dunleavy 1989: 259)

For his purposes he defines the 'central state' as agencies in A, B and D. Dunleavy says that the matter of deciding which agencies constitute the central state is controversial chiefly because it is not analytically feasible to accept, without modification, the official categories used to classify agencies in publications such as the Estimates, Public Expenditure

White Paper, or the *Civil Service Yearbook*. He shows that while his interpretation of the 'central state' covers 1,016,830 staff, the terrain covered by Richard Rose (1987) would cover less than half the staff (402,600) and nearly half the running cost budget (1989: 265). He thus confirms the lack of system that this chapter seeks to describe.

THE SHAPE OF GOVERNMENT

There are various theories that attempt to provide an understanding of the structure of Government (see Chapters 2 and 3). It has been argued by New Right sources adopted by the Conservatives (such as Niskanen 1973) that Government bureaucracies grow as a consequence of the career enhancement in terms of increased authority and status that growth will give to the civil servants in charge of parts of the machine: it is in their *self-interest* for growth to occur.

Dunleavy rejects this individual-centred Public Choice explanation for the shape of Government. He dissents from the accounts of bureaucracies that see them as tightly hierarchical Weberian line agencies run by rationally self-interested actors committed to maximising their budgets. This means disagreement with Niskanen who suggests that the bureaucrat sees the budget of his bureau as affecting his salary, perquisites of office, public reputation, power, patronage, output of the bureau, ease of making changes and ease of managing the bureau. Niskanen says, 'This effect creates the treadmill phenomenon, inducing bureaucrats to strive for increased budgets' (1973: 22, quoted in Dunleavy 1991: 166).

Dunleavy notes that this argument was supported by the observation that the most distinguished US public servants of recent years substantially increased their budgets. Niskanen claimed that added to the rationality of the wish to grow was the rationality of the need to survive. The sum of these imperatives in the Public Choice view is that there is a tendency in public organisations to over-supply.

Dunleavy claimed that this conventional understanding of the decision-making system of complex organisations rested on the premise that bureaucrats would aggressively propose more activities and higher budgets. He put their requests in a context of Aaron Wildavsky's incremental decision-making. Dunleavy in his alternative *bureau-shaping model* suggests that rational bureaucrats do not necessarily maximise budgets but try to reshape their departments as small staff agencies, removed from line responsibilities and hence more insulated from adverse impacts in the event of overall spending reductions. He says that this assumption explains the tendency in most liberal democracies for welfare state expansion to create a complex decentralised network of sub-central agencies – as opposed to the prediction of 'New Right' approaches that expect the continued growth of large-budget, centrally run, line agencies. Dunleavy says that whereas the Niskanen-type approach would predict opposition by rational bureaucrats to 'contracting out' types of privatisation, the bureau-shaping model would see managers welcome such reshaping of departments. The bureau-shaping model better fits the rapid acceptance in Whitehall of Next Steps type developments in British Government than does the Public Choice expectation.

Dunleavy attempts an analytical classification of the various organisations of Government. On the basis of the characteristics of the budgets of various agencies he distinguished between:

a) delivery agencies which are the classic line bureaucracies of Weberian theory. They directly deliver services through their own staff. They are likely to have a large core budget to pay for their running costs. They also have large programme budgets to fund the implementation of policy.

b) regulatory agencies which are attempting to control other individuals or organisations. They can externalise costs on to the regulated. Thus while they also have a higher percentage of their costs spent on the paper moving activities covered by the core budget, other costs will be low. They will not have a programme budget required by the delivery agencies.

c) transfer agencies are money moving organisations – paying out grants, entitlements or subsidies. As the administration costs are low in relation to the sums dispensed the core budget is small in relation to the total.

(Dunleavy 1991: 183)

He also notes contract agencies, taxing agencies and trading agencies. Such distinctions help with the fuller description of Government but they do not help us simplify the concept of 'Government': they help detail the complexity.

DEFINING THE CIVIL SERVICE

One solution to discussion of this poorly defined territory would be to base the description of Government on elements in administrative life which for reasons of employment law, judicial control, or similar imperatives will necessarily be well calibrated. It might be expected that 'civil service' will be plainly set out for these purposes. Not so. One possible way of defining a civil servant would be as a servant of the Crown (see the following paragrpah, Tomlin Commission of 1931 that starts from this point). However such a style of definition courts circularity – and, more important, would be inaccurate. The concept of the 'Crown' sounds as if it might be a clue in the unravelling of the status of these parts of the 'administrative map'. Unfortunately, it only introduces further uncertainty. It only answers one puzzle by introducing another. To discuss one puzzle in terms of the other is an invitation to circularity – as for example, 'Crown status is possessed by Government Departments' (Bowen 1978: 31).

For example, employees of the National Health Service are Crown servants but not civil servants. A famous definition of a civil servant was given in the Report of the Royal Commission on the civil service (Tomlin Commission, Cmd 3909, 1931), 'those servants of the Crown, other than holders of political or judicial offices, who are employed in a civil capacity and whose remuneration is paid wholly and directly out of monies voted by Parliament'. Hood and Dunsire (1981: 47) show that this definition would include members of the Royal Household staff and, more seriously, would exclude the staff of some departments included in the civil service's own Manpower Count.

Mackenzie and Grove (1957: 10) observed that,

> We are met at the outset by the fact that there are no precise criteria, either legal or historical, by which to determine the scope of the Civil Service. There is a central core which is unmistakeable, but at the margin no sharp drop divides those public servants who are within the Civil Service from those who are not.
>
> (Cited in Drewry and Butcher 1988: 14)

(Drewry and Butcher also reprint the discussion 'Definition of a Civil Servant' from The Eleventh Report of the Expenditure Commitee, HC 535–1, *The Civil Service.*)

The saga of the birth of the Manpower Services Commission (MSC) perhaps underlines the weakness of Crown status as a guide. The MSC was initially conceived of as a non-governmental organisation, trades unions preferring the idea of the MSC being kept from tight governmental control. The Employment Training Act (1973), which set up the MSC, states, 'It is hereby declared that the Commission and the Agencies are not to be regarded as servants . . . or agents of the Crown. . .' The in-house civil service trade unions – dissenting from TUC priorities –

opposed the transfer of the members out of the civil service. The Heath Government and initially their Labour successors, argued against the civil service unions to the effect that it was impossible for statutory creations such as the MSC to employ Crown (civil) servants. However, Michael Foot, when Secretary of State for Employment, eventually conceded full civil service status. After all the claims of 'impossible' the Employment Protection Act (1975) simply amended the above section of the 1973 Act to read, 'The functions of the Commission and of the Agencies and of their officers and servants shall be performed on behalf of the Crown.' Thus political pressure appears to have overcome constitutional reservations.

In 1974 the MSC absorbed 18,000 staff from the Ministry of Employment. They lost their civil service status, but received it back again in 1976. But it wasn't clear that constitutional arrangements were all that important in any case. Successive Secretaries of State emphasised that they retained control of the non-governmental MSC. Maurice Macmillan, in the House of Commons on 13 March 1973 (*Hansard*, col. 1147) claimed that the setting of the MSC was 'an internal matter which in no way lessens the Government's obligations or capacity through their control of funds'.

DEFINING BY CHEQUEBOOK

Another approach used by Hood and Dunsire (1981: 43) to supply some hard data to these 'slippery phenomena' is to assume that the obvious need for financial control has produced its own framework. However, as noted above, the categories used in different financial exercises differ. When Hood and Dunsire were writing in 1981 they found a variety of financial units or blocs in use. For example, they found that the Budget Estimates presented to Parliament referred to 480 bodies but the accompanying annual memorandum from the Treasury contained some 100 blocks for cash control, covering some 70 'departments'. As Hood and Dunsire (1981: 41) say, it is reasonable that for reasons of close financial management that there should be financial blocks smaller than departments, but why should the Ministry of Defence have a single block for a budget? There appears to be no overarching, consistent and rational framework.

A further complicating feature in the machinery of Government has been recurrent wishes to introduce forms of accountable management. About half a dozen pieces of evidence to the 'Fulton' Committee (Cmnd 3638, 1968) were along the lines of that of W.R. Pirie, a Treasury

Assistant Secretary, 'Responsibility should be delegated to subsidiary bodies with well defined functions, wherever possible removed from day-to-day Parliamentary scrutiny.' Certain phrases continually cropped up in the evidence and prescriptive literature of the times – 'hiving off', 'freedom from day-to-day control', 'like Sweden'. Such phases were faithfully echoed in the eventual Fulton Report. For example:

> that large-scale executive operations cannot be effectively run by government departments and that they should be 'hived-off' wherever possible to independent boards. . . The boards or corporations would be wholly responsible in their own fields within the powers delegated to them. Although they would be outside the day-to-day control of Minister and the scrutiny of Parliament, Ministers would retain powers to give directions when necessary. . .
>
> (Fulton Committee Report 1968: paras 147–8)

The consequences of this fashion for 'hiving-off' are more fully described later when we discuss the current Next Steps programme in Chapter 5, but one which had relevance for this attempt to clarify the concept of 'department' was a phenomenon of what can be labelled *de-departmentalisation*. Thus the 1970s saw the proliferation of departmental agencies (e.g. the Property Services Agency). These bodies were not 'hived-off' but 'hived-in' (or in other words internal hiving-off). Such departmental agencies were intended to be,

> an organisational entity under its own executive head either part of a government department or a corporate body within the departmental framework (eg HMSO) acting at the direction of a Minister who is responsible to Parliament for its activities and staffed by civil servants (as at present defined) but distinguished from the conventional pattern of departmental organisation by having its own executive head and accounting officer, and by a large degree of freedom in staff management.
>
> (Cuckney 1972)

Quite apart from the difficult notion that such agencies are somehow both under ministerial control and yet possess day-to-day freedom, they fail to fit any simple departmental template in that one variant of the departmental agency – the Trading Fund Organisation (TFO) – was not funded by the Vote (Parliamentary financial authorisation) but under the terms of the Government Trading Funds Act (1973). Instead of funds from Parliament the TFOs operate a sort of revolving fund, financing themselves from revenue. Bodies such as the Royal Mint, DOE (Supplies Division), HMSO, were expected to finance current expenditure from receipts and capital expenditure by borrowings from the National Loans Fund and from retained earnings. These organisations were not fully hived-off because their customers are (often) mainly within the Government.

THE FRINGE IN THE FOG

The shorthand terms 'G' and non-G' were originally used by Hague, Mackenzie and Barker in their *Public Policy and Private Interests* (1975). Because of the scale of growth of organisations of unclear status Hague, Mackenzie and Barker set out an analytical typology which ran from Government (G), through quasi-Government (QG), and quasi-non-Government (QNG), to non-Government (NG). In the initial formulation the quasi-Government organisation was nearer Government than was the quasi-non-governmental organisation (Barker 1982: 4). Tony Barker went on to coin the term 'quango' to describe the individual specimens of the quasi-non-governmental species. The acronym was based on the fuller version of the term 'quasi autonomous non-governmental organisation'.

While useful in attracting attention to the problem area, the 'coding frame' of Hague, Mackenzie and Barker can be queried. There is in fact ambiguity about the content of their categories. They themselves (1975: 13) modestly advise that their terminology, 'turns out to lack rigour'. Thus as an example, we can note that the Introduction refers to Alan Pifer's contribution on 'The Quasi-Governmental Organisation': in fact his paper printed as an appendix to their volume was entitled the 'Quasi-Non-Governmental Organisation'. But there was a general lack of consistency in their use of examples of the two categories. In his original article Pifer used the term 'quasi-non-governmental', but he none the less asked of his invention, 'Why is it quasi-governmental?' Some of his illustrations appear to be part of the phenomenon of Government performing roles that might be regarded as governmental. It would be preferable to reverse their suggested use of the terms. Whereas they suggest that the concept of 'old fashioned nationalisation' fitted the QG box, it is surely preferable to view the nationalised industries as QNG. In other words what is relevant about them is that they are Government acting 'as if' or 'in appearance only' as non-governmental (i.e., QNG).

To confuse matters further when they discuss the case-study of the

National Research Development Corporation they call it QNG. As it was set up by statute permitting the relevant Minister to 'give to them directions of a general character . . . and the Corporation shall comply . . .', then it is far from clear why in their terms it is not a QG like nationalised industries. Similarly when they label groups such as the Jockey Club or the Royal and Ancient as QNG it might be better to term them 'quasi-governmental'. That is to say they are private bodies which for particular and specific purposes act 'as if' they are governmental. There is no simple (and reliable) guide. The problem is not only nomenclature, however, but in delimiting these categories – howsoever they are labelled. The problem of classifying this diversity may be so profound that inserting a couple of QNG and QG categories does not measure up to the muddle.

In his official *Report on Non-departmental Bodies* (Cmnd 7797) Sir Leo Pliatzky (1980) studied bodies which, 'have a role in the process of government in the United Kingdom but are not Government Departments or part of a Government Department'. He too found difficulties with the quango label. He acknowledged that the term had entered popular usage, but for several reasons Pliatzky avoided it. He pointed out that the special feature of the bodies he was examining was that they were non-departmental and that, 'far from being altogether non-governmental, one of the reasons given for concern about them is that they may represent not only a spread of patronage but a concealed growth of government that does not show up in, say, the size of the Civil Service'.

Jock Bruce-Gardyne – a former Economic Secretary at the Treasury with responsibilities for Customs and Excise – claimed that, like the Inland Revenue, the Customs and Excise might be described as a

'Quago' – a Quasi-autonomous Governmental Institution. They have their own staff, and their own career structure, reporting to a Chairman who may – indeed usually does – emerge from the Treasury mandarinate, but who swiftly goes 'native'.

(Bruce-Gardyne 1986: 74)

Bruce-Gardyne's description of the Customs and Excise as a 'quago' rather than a 'quango' fits in with the distinction offered above. Customs and Excise is Government acting as if it were autonomous (Madgwick 1991: 20, refers to 500 'semi detached organisations').

Between them the three tables (1.1, 1.3, 1.4) cover the bodies which can be considered as *departmental* in character. The terrain we are now exploring introduces further bodies that must be seen as candidates for *governmental* status. An official *Survey of Fringe Bodies* conducted by a retired civil servant, Gordon Bowen, for the Civil Service Department in 1978 contains a list of bodies excluded from the 'fringe' category on the basis that they were departments. Bowen's list has as departments the Law Commission, the Government Actuary, the Public Trustee, Office of the Treasury Solicitor (and Procurator-General) which are not termed such in the sources which produced Tables 1.1, 1.3 and 1.4.

Bowen's efforts to bring some order have been criticised. Chester (1979: 52) conceded that Bowen had found himself in a morass or jungle, but complained, 'Usually . . . those who penetrate jungles leave a track which makes it easier for those who come after.' No doubt some of Bowen's categories and exclusions are arbitrary, but it is difficult to see solutions that would satisfy all potential critics. Bowen's opening paragraph pointed out,

> There have always been fringe bodies although their designation has changed over the years and more recently students of government have been ingenious in their invention of new titles for this form of governmental institution. Even as recently as 1968 the Treasury opted for 'public body' or 'non-departmental organisation'. They justified these ambiguous terms because 'there is a rich variety of these bodies and the possible permutation of their characteristics are almost endless'.
>
> (Bowen 1978: 1)

The Treasury's 'rich variety' is an attractive and optimistic way of saying that they found the population of the 'fringe' unclassifiable. Like others in the field, Bowen was thus starting by claiming, indirectly, that the exercise of satisfactory categorisation was impossible. Richard Wilding, a Deputy Secretary with responsibilities for Machinery of Government matters, started a conference paper with the observation that,

> It is possible, though difficult, to make true statements about an individual quango; the difficulty lies in unearthing the information. I have sadly come to the conclusion that it is not possible to make true statements about them all; the impossibility lies in their bewildering variety.
>
> (Wilding, in Barker 1982: 34)

Wilding, in resisting the temptation to assume 'the mantle of some latter-day Linnaeus', confessed that the temptation was less than compelling since he had grave doubts as to whether any single taxonomy was possible. In other words the complexity of classification has struck a paralysis of hopelessness equally among practitioners and academic commentators.

In explaining his use of the term 'fringe bodies' Bowen (1978: 8) sets out some alternatives (or near synonyms). These included the Haldane Report's 'Administrative Board', a Whitehall use of 'non departmental organisations', a use by Sir Norman Chester of 'semi-autonomous authorities'. No term is perfect but all direct attention to the general area. Perhaps as satisfactory as any – because of the acronym that results – is the term used in a letter in the correspondence columns of *The Scotsman*: the 'semi-autonomous governmental organisation'.

It is significant that when Bowen started his survey for the Civil Service Department no 'master list' existed for his use. His survey was based on returns by departments of a questionnaire, which sought data 'for each of these organisations for which they accepted sponsorship and which they considered to be within the scope of this enquiry'.

As Bowen had no accepted definition to work from he constructed a list of criteria to assist departments decide what bodies should be included in their replies:

a. Fringe bodies are organisations which have been set up or adopted by departments and provided with funds to perform some function which the Government wish to have performed but which it did not wish to be the direct responsibility of a Minister or of a Department. The role of many fringe bodies can be described as government at arm's length.

b. The bodies receive their funds mainly direct from the Vote or by grant or grant-in-aid or through statutorily imposed levies or charges. International bodies to which the United Kingdom Government makes a contribution were not to be a part of the fringe for the purposes of the study.

c. The instrument establishing a fringe body may take a variety of forms: Act of Parliament, Prerogative, Order, Royal Charter, Royal Commission, Treasury Minute or administrative act of a Minister.

d. The Chairman and some at least of the members of the board or council of a fringe body would normally be appointed by the Crown or by the responsible Minister. . .

e. The fringe body should have a measure of permanence. The study would not concern itself with ad hoc organisations intended to be of a temporary character.

f. Advisory committees or working parties which assist departments in the conduct of their day to day work, services by the Department's own staff, would be considered as part of the Department and should not be included as fringe bodies.

g. Fringe bodies are supported by a staff which in some sense is their own, separate from that of departments. Staffing arrangements would, however, in most cases be subject to a measure of control by the Minister responsible for the body and by the Minister for the Civil Service.

(Bowen 1978: 3)

The most significant feature of this list is its non-definitive character: as everyone concedes, the 'fringe' is a very mixed lot. Bowen noted that in setting up the review the Civil Service Department decided that it should not embrace the Royal Household, the armed services, the judiciary, Government departments, the nationalised industries, the local authorities (and bodies controlled by local authorities), the police authorities, Houses of Parliament and the National Health Service. He also remarked that while these exclusions were readily recognisable they were not without their ambiguities. The nationalised industries pose a particular problem. Thus the Department of Industry did not include the British National Oil Corporation (BNOC) in its return – though BNOC had some administrative and regulatory functions. The Scottish Office and Welsh Office included the Scottish Development Agency and the Welsh Development Agency in their responses but the Department of Industry did not include the National Enterprise Board. The United Kingdom Atomic Energy Authority was included in the 'fringe' – but not British Nuclear Fuels which was considered a 'national enterprise'.

Bowen acknowledged this as an area of uncertain boundaries and argued:

It is probably simpler to regard the national enterprises as the constituents of a special category of fringe bodies that have been excluded from. . . this study. The organisations so excluded are carrying out functions for Departments which are responsible for the general policy but the organisations operate as separate institutions enjoying various measures of autonomy, depending on their ability to be self financing but also on the extent to which Ministers decided that they should serve as instruments to further the Government's short-term economic and social policies. Departure from strictly commercial objectives has meant increased dependence on

Exchequer funds. . . Thus the distinction between independent autonomous agencies and dependent departmental agencies has become less marked.

(Bowen 1978: 6)

The thrust of Bowen's point was that – particularly in his study period of the mid-1970s – Government had taken to intervening in the pricing policy of the commercial national enterprises; such intervention made the exclusion of the nationalised industries less justifiable; they were more rather than less 'governmental'. Local authorities were similarly excluded – though as the independence of the latter decreases they also became more fringe-like. These exceptions are not thoroughly argued and defended; they are simply asserted.

Bowen (1978: 7) claimed that a definition of fringe bodies begins to emerge from his exclusions. He said that fringe bodies were not part of a Government department although for the most part they owe their origin to such departments and in a variety of ways draw their funds from them. However no statement in this field stands without qualification and he immediately went on to state that,

Until recently it seemed also possible to say that fringe bodies were not Crown bodies and that the staff were not civil servants. These statements have now to be significantly qualified by exceptions such as the Manpower Services Commission. This with its 2 agencies is a Crown body and the staff are civil servants but they are distinct from the Department of Employment and as for all other fringe bodies the Secretary of State is not answerable in detail for their actions. He has, of course, ultimate sanctions in having power not to reappoint members of the Commission and over the supply of funds which are provided in the form of grants-in-aid. . . All these developments greatly complicate the problem of achieving a definition of fringe bodies and of setting out criteria which would enable them to be identified.

(Bowen 1978: 7)

Bowen ended up his exercise with a list of some 252 bodies. (It might be worth repeating that his was a restrictive and minimalist interpretation of the concept of fringe body.) Alphabetically – and without being misleading as to its character – the list runs from Aberdeen and District Milk Marketing Board and the Advisory, Conciliation and Arbitration Service to the Wool, Jute and Flax Industrial Training Board and the Young Volunteer Force Foundation. When he went on to present the

Table 1.5   Characteristics of fringe bodies

a   Set up by Act of Parliament (174)
b   Probably non-Crown (243)
c   Financed by grants-in-aid (112)
d   Chairman appointed by a Minister (140)
e   Staff are non-civil servants, recruited and employed by the board
    or council of a fringe body (242)
f   Annual accounts submitted to the sponsoring Minister and laid
    before Parliament (158)
g   Annual Report published (189)

Source: Bowen 1978: 34
Note: Numbers in parentheses refer to the number of his list of 252 fringe
bodies possessing these particular features.

core of his findings his reservations on the spread of his survey were
reiterated – e.g.,

> the list contains some bodies of which the inclusion could be ques-
> tions. . . Some of the larger fringe bodies, whether measured by
> employment or expenditure, are not readily distinguishable from
> non-ministerial Government Departments when considered in their
> day-to-day functioning.
>
> (Bowen 1978: 23)

Bowen's basic criteria for considering bodies as 'fringe' are set out
above. These were slightly expanded later in his study when he ended
with seven characteristics (see Table 1.5).

A more dramatic confirmation of the rag-bag nature of fringe bodies
is indicated when Bowen examines the numbers of bodies which had all
or lesser proportions of these characteristics (see Table 1.6). 'Fringeness'
can thus be seen to be a very variable quality.

Table 1.6   Number of characteristics found in a single fringe body

	7	6	5	4	3	2	1	0
No. of fringe bodies possessing that number of characteristics	33	63	71	58	16	11	–	–
Cumulative total of fringe bodies	33	96	167	225	241	252	–	–

Source: From Bowen 1978: 34

The other major source on 'the fringe' is also the work of a senior civil servant. Sir Leo Pliatzky's retirement was delayed to allow him to compile a report on non-departmental bodies for the (then) newly elected Prime Minister, Margaret Thatcher. The motive in setting up the study may well have simply been to 'cull' numbers, but the exercise was more rewarding in terms of illumination than elimination. Pliatzky used the key term 'non-departmental public body' (NDPB). This is similar to the term 'non-departmental organisation' used by the Treasury in 1968 in its *Guide to Setting Up New Public Bodies*. But as appears characteristic of this subject absolutely identical terms are avoided. Pliatzky was clearly in the same territory that Bowen had been in. However his remit was wider.

Pliatzky, like Bowen before him, found definitional problems and conceded (1980: 133) that, 'The boundaries of central government are not easy to define. . . ' He excluded from his field the nationalised industries, other public corporations, major companies in which the Government had a shareholding, NHS bodies/Agricultural Marketing Boards, judiciary (other than tribunals), local government (or its 'fringe'), 'public bodies. . . which are not subject to direct ministerial authority. . .'

His final exclusion was perhaps especially problematic: it might be thought that the absence of direct ministerial authority was the unifying factor of bodies on the list. . . However, the point is not that Pliatzky was 'wrong' but that all attempts at definition in this area are arbitrary. In his Introduction (1980: 4) he accepted that, 'there are no legal definitions to determine what should go in these lists [of non-departmental bodies] or into some other category. There is, for instance, no legal definition of what constitutes a nationalised industry.' For this reason Pliatzky usefully makes explicit his version of the excluded categories. Pliatzky also set out a list of departments and other Crown bodies excluded from his review.

Allowing for alterations caused by the time difference between the Pliatzky review and that of Bowen a considerable variation still exists – again emphasising the non-standardisation within the subject. Part of the difference – but by no means all – is introduced by Pliatzky's notion of 'other Crown bodies'. While the lists have many bodies in common, Bowen had a few not covered by Pliatzky while the latter's list was much more extensive, including bodies such as the Civil Service Pay Research Unit, Council of the Territorial, Auxiliary and Volunteer Reserve Associations, Crown Office (Scotland), staff of the UGC, Forestry Commission, Greenwich Hospital Department, National Insurance Commissioners, Northern Ireland Court Service, etc. The types of bodies listed by Pliatzky are shown in Table 1.7.

Table 1.7 Types of fringe bodies listed by Pliatzky

Type	Number	
Executive bodies etc.	489	Pliatzky said that these carried out a 'wide range of operational or regulatory functions, various scientific and cultural activities, and some commercial or semi-commercial activities. Bodies of this type are commonly described as fringe bodies. . .'
Advisory bodies	1,561	He noted that two-thirds of this total was accounted for by as few as 22 networks of advisory bodies.
Tribunal systems	67	Even more than was the case with advisory bodies, it was difficult to quantify tribunals (with functions of a specialised judicial type). In some cases a particular tribunal system operates through a set of individual panels – for example the 7 Agricultural Land Tribunals in England – or the National Insurance Local Tribunal arrangements under which around 2,000 separate tribunals are set up on *ad hoc* basis. In such cases it is difficult to produce a clear-cut total.

Source: Pliatzky 1980.

Pliatzky gave figures to give a broad scale to the non-departmental public body phenomenon. At the time there were nearly 3 million employees – though privatisation has probably reduced this to half. The label 'the fringe', therefore, is not meant to signify something trivial or marginal.

Though there has been extensive privatisation the common retention of a 'golden share' or the imposition of a regulatory framework means that privatised concerns are not entirely removed from governmental influence. The annual publication *Public Bodies* lists details of public bodies 'for which Ministers have a degree of accountability'. (This concept of partial accountability is not explained.) A summary table in the 1991 edition showed that while there was indeed a reduction in numbers of bodies and staff between 1979 and 1991, the governmental finance involved rose sharply (see Table 1.8).

Hogwood's work (1993) on 'termination' proves that the 'story' of the 1980s was not simply that of a pruning of quangos – as the rhetoric of the early years suggested. While he noted that there had been a

Table 1.8 The changing pattern of quangos

	Exec	Advisory	Tribunals	Other	Total number	Total staff	Total expenditure (£m)*	Govt funded	Other expenditure by departments in support
1979	492	1,485	70	120	2,167	217,000	6,150	2,970	70
1990	375	874	64	131	1,444	117,500	13,080†	10,060	106

Source: From *Public Bodies*, 1991.
Note: * Current prices.
† Excludes English and Welsh Water Authorities from 1984 onwards (expenditure in 1983 = £2,600m).

considerable number of terminations (90), in general the trend was to replace bodies rather than terminate them.

ACCOUNTABILITY IN THE FOG

In discussing the question of the accountability of 'quangos' Richard Wilding put the subject into context by noting, 'The whole question of accountability of all public bodies is a misty one and the mist may be especially thick around some of them.' He pointed out that the problem was not confined to the margins of Government:

> let nobody suppose that it (accountability) is crystal/clear for the departments of central government itself, or that quangos (to change the metaphor) constitutes a unique patch of rough in the middle of an otherwise smooth and well-mown fairway.
>
> (Wilding, in Barker 1982: 34)

Some of the problems of accountability for 'mainstream' departments are discussed in Chapters 7 and 8. There are, however, particular issues raised by accountability in the non-departmental public sector. Wilding sets out the basic and familiar conceptual framework – which operates in the triangle constituted by the Minister/Secretary of State, his department, and Parliament:

> The Minister answers directly to the Parliament of which he is a member for all the things done in his name and of which he is, at least in principle, totally in control; and if Parliament is dissatisfied, there is no obscurity about the identity of the person it harries: it is the Minister whose business it is to act or to defend inaction, Parliamentary democracy is at work.
>
> (Wilding, in Barker 1982: 35)

Wilding asked the question, 'For what part of the fringe body's affairs and in what detail, is the Minster accountable to Parliament?' He pointed out that if the Minister had simply delegated authority to a fringe body then the accountability was as for the Minister's own department. The Secretary of State would have ultimate accountability for the actions of the fringe body. Now this could be as unrealistic as it often is for departments, but in fact fringe accountability is usually even more tenuous than that for the departments. Wilding observes that often an Act of Parliament or Royal Charter or some other founding instrument has caused powers to be vested directly in the fringe body. In that way, or some other, the Minister may have renounced authority over parts at least of the body's decisions – and hence it can be argued that he cannot be held accountable for these matters.

The reasonable compromise that the Minister is accountable in some areas but not in others is difficult to put in practice since the fields of responsibility are often imprecisely defined or difficult to disentangle in practice. Moreover, the Minister normally has the ultimate authority to sack (or decline to re-appoint) the chairman and members of the board or council of the body – and may have some reserve power of specific direction. Wilding claims,

> There is a theoretical inconsistency here. It does not matter as long as Parliament and the Minister are in agreement over where the Minister should interfere and where he should not. But it can begin to matter if they differ.
>
> (Wilding, in Barker 1982: 41)

Johnson (in Barker 1982: 206) recorded that many administrative practitioners and academic students of administration were worried that Britain was witnessing the disintegration of the model of representative and responsible ministerial government. However, like Wilding, Johnson cautions us against comparing the problematic accountability of the 'non-departmental appointed public agency' with an idealised model of responsibility for mainstream departments. He argued (1982: 210), 'We must bear in mind that the traditional methods of securing accountability for the actions of government work only imperfectly and we must beware of setting standards of accountability for these bodies which are not in reality met in Government Departments themselves.'

THE (LACK OF) RATIONALE FOR CONFUSION

Christopher Pollitt examines the changes in the Machinery of Government between 1960 and 1983 and concludes:

> I did look, and looked hard, for evidence of larger determinants of the pattern of departments, both of the 'external', economic/technological kind and the 'internal', ideological kind. My first finding is that they do not appear to exist or, to put it more precisely, such 'determinants' as have been suggested from time to time in the literature on organisations, can for the shaping of government departments, be more fruitfully conceptualised as constraints (and usually fairly loose ones at that). . .
>
> I recall the anxiety with which I began to read Hood and Dunsire's

Bureaumetrics (1981) fearing that the picture of machinery of government decisions I had laboriously put together would have to be
abandoned in favour of some neatly determined model, revealed
through the quantitative, 'objective' methods employed by the
authors. In the event the anxiety was groundless. Hood and
Dunsire's very different theoretical perspective generated many findings which my own approach could not capture: but neither they nor
others have, thus far, identified any set of determinants, 'contin-
gencies' or variables from the settings of which the pattern of
departments can even approximately be 'read off'.

(Pollitt 1984: 2)

As noted above, accounts of the British administrative pattern are linked
by a sense of frustration. Johnson (1982: 209) discusses 'pragmatism run
wild'. Hood (1982: 44) complains of the difficulty in 'gaining any
intellectual bearings on this vast and apparently formless mass of
organisations'.

Some of the detail of the above discussion has been outflanked by the
privatisation programme. Arguably the privatisation was made simpler
and probably encouraged by the lack of consistency and comprehen-
sibility in the foregoing 'system'. Even if privatisation was not specifically
encouraged by the machinery of Government confusion, it meant that
objections to privatisation in terms of its improvised nature, its ambiguous forms of accountability, its uncertain boundaries between 'public'
and 'private' could not reasonably be made. They were not present in
the *status quo ante*. The research for an understanding of the organisation
of British Government is best made by seeking historical explanations of
particular arrangements than for a set of principles that underpin the
complexity. Not only is the subject of Government lost in a fog, we have
no reliable and accessible model or maps to help us through.

Chapter 2

Getting the design of Government 'right'

Looking for the philosophers' stone

In ancient times alchemists believed implicitly in the existence of a philosophers' stone which would provide the key to the universe and, in effect, solve all of the problems of mankind. The quest for coordination is in many respects the twentieth century equivalent of the medieval search for the philosophers' stone. If only we can find the right formula for coordination, we can reconcile the irreconcilable, harmonise competing and wholly divergent interests, overcome irrationalities in our Government structures, and make hard policy choices to which no one will dissent.

(Seidman 1975: 190)

This chapter looks at attempts to increase efficiency and political direction by reordering the organisation of administration. The conclusion of this review of the literature is pessimistic and was anticipated in Herbert Simon's famous observation,

It is a fatal defect of the current principles of administration that, like proverbs, they occur in pairs. For almost every principle one can find an equally plausible and acceptable contradictory principle. Although the two principles of the pair will lead to exactly opposite organizational recommendations, there is nothing in that theory to indicate which is the correct one to apply.

(Simon 1961: 20)

In a review article on the *Crossman Diaries* (1976–8) in 1978 it was claimed that the striking feature of Crossman's contribution to our understanding was his obsession in arguing the need to provide British Government with strategic central control (Jordan 1978). This obsession is not unique to Richard Crossman however. It is *the* theme in the literature by many advocates of reform. They see the main issue as whether Government operates through broad autonomous departments, or whether there is a powerful directing centre providing strategic control. The reformers tend to believe that the dysfunctions of Government are to be remedied by changes in organisational design according to the conscious application of principles. 'More co-ordination' is the constant goal: yet it proves a chimera.

One explanation for this argument for a stronger centre is contained in Kaufman's work (1981: 4). He has written of the 'Law of Perceptions of Power'. This asserts that the power an observer believes another person or a group wields is directly proportional to the square of the distance of the observer from the observed! It certainly seems true that as one becomes involved in any organisation or position 'Power is always somewhere else'. As Kaufman says,

> That is why presidents and the people close to them tend to bewail their inability to get things done, while people far removed frequently talk of the presidency as the strongest office on earth.
>
> (Cited in Lynn and Wildavsky 1990: xvii)

There is undoubtedly a tendency for those who seem to be powerful to be impressed, to the contrary, by the restrictions on their power. Thus those at the centre of Government are not simply being modest in denying their authority: they too are inhibited in their actions.

Blackstone and Plowden (both academics with experience in Whitehall) argue that the tendency to a fragmented Government – to which problem a strengthened centre is the much-touted solution – is not peculiarly British. They say,

> 'Governments', in all forms of regime in all parts of the world, are pluralistic, divided and under-informed, short sighted, only partly in control of their own processes, and unable to guarantee the outcomes which they promise . . . The collective interest is too often dominated and distorted by sectional interests. . .
>
> (Blackstone and Plowden 1988: 12)

They confirm a view of Government as sectorised and divided with departments defining their needs in terms of satisfying their own external clients. This sort of perspective seems a necessary starting point for an appreciation of British Government. Thus the usual complaint about British Government is that there is, in Lee's phrase (1974: 162), insufficient 'central capability' to cope with tendencies to fragmentation. For example – and the example is one of a large pool – in 1987 there was a well-reported struggle in Whitehall over control of the policy area (and funding) for inner cities. This had in the past been primarily a matter for the Department of the Environment, but Mrs Thatcher gave an increased role to the Trade and Industry Ministers, Lord Young and Kenneth Clarke. Under a headline 'Inner city in-fighting' *The Times* had a report which said,

> The departmental sparring is underlaid by serious philosophical differences in the approach to be taken in the inner cities. The prime minister and her two Trade and Industry Ministers . . . believe that the solution to the decline of the inner cities lies with a spirit of enterprise to set up more small businesses and so create jobs, but others in Whitehall, notably at Environment, tend to the view that salvation lies in renewing the infrastructure of the inner cities – imposing a far greater strain on the public purse.

The article quoted a civil servant as saying that,

> There's no question of having vulgar shouting matches, but if Departments are meant to be working together . . . you suddenly find that inter-departmental meetings become very difficult to arrange, people start sending their opposite numbers notes saying: 'I am sorry to be so late in replying to your minute but it raises a number of much wider considerations which will require consider-able thought and consultation in this department.' Things simply stop happening.

The piece revealed that Mrs Thatcher had demanded that there be a more co-ordinated approach: she underlined this by setting up a special unit within the Cabinet Office to advise her on the problem. This small episode shows both the kind of inter-departmental rivalry that is difficult to avoid and the temptation to take a centralising step to curb the friction.

The phenomenon of competition in Government is certainly not restricted to any one administration. In evidence to the Fulton Committee in the late 1960s, one witness with civil service experience said,

> The biggest shock I received [on joining the civil service] was when I learnt that files do not circulate between Government Departments, and that information is not automatically made available to a plan-ning department which is relevant to its work. Departmental rivalries I expected, but I did not expect, in my naivety, to find that British government is merely a United Nations.
>
> (Fulton Committee Report 1968: 993, para. 41)

The former civil servant, Clive Ponting, has made a similiar point,

> Much of the work of Whitehall is institutionalized conflict between
> the competing interests in different departments. Each department
> will defend its own position and resist a line that, while it might be
> beneficial to the government as a whole or in the wider public
> interest, would work against the interest of the department.

(Ponting 1986: 102)

COMBATING FRAGMENTATION BY REORGANISATION

The diagnosis that there is a need for central co-ordination to combat
such tendencies to fragmentation is not novel and can, for example, be
traced back to the Haldane Report (1918) (see pp. 51–5) and in the
contribution by Leo Amery to the topic of the Machinery of
Government. Amery claimed,

> We attempt to direct the affairs of a great nation by weekly meetings
> between departmental chiefs, all absorbed in the routine of their
> departments, all concerned to secure Cabinet sanction for this or
> that departmental proposal, all giving a purely temporary and more
> or less perfunctory attention to the issues brought up by other depart-
> ments. Every Cabinet meeting is a scramble to get through an agenda
> in which the competition of departments for a place is varied by the
> incursion of urgent telegrams from abroad or of sudden questions in
> the House of Commons for which some sort of policy or answer must
> be improvised. The one thing that is hardly ever discussed is general
> policy. Nothing, indeed, is more calculated to make a Cabinet
> Minister unpopular with his colleagues . . . than a tiresome insistence
> on discussing general issues of policy . . . when there are so many
> urgent matters of detail always waiting to be decided. The result is
> that there is very little Cabinet policy, as such, on any subject. . .
> There are only departmental policies. The 'normal' Cabinet is really
> little more than a standing conference of departmental chiefs where
> departmental policies come up . . . to be submitted to a cursory
> criticism. . . But to a very large extent each department goes its
> own way . . . fighting the 'Whitehall War' to the best of its ability. . .
>   The whole system is one of mutual friction and delay with, at best,
> some partial measure of mutual adjustment between unrelated
> policies. . . It is quite incompatible with any coherent planning of
> policy as a whole. . .

(Amery 1935: 443–4)

This theme of the Whitehall 'centre' versus the 'departments' runs through to more contemporary contributions. Heclo and Wildavsky (1974) entitled one of their chapters 'There Must be a Better Way'. The 'better way' which has repeatedly suggested itself to commentators is rational central decision instead of departmental competition and bargained allocation. Anthony Crosland (1971: 167), speaking on his own experiences in Office, observed that a Minister gets resources by 'an endless tactical battle which requires determination, cunning and occasional unscrupulousness'. Crosland goes on: 'in an ideal world it would all no doubt be settled by an omniscient central unit, but this is the way it happens in our crude democratic world'.

One can find comparable discussions implying similar dilemmas between the expertise of the operating departments and the need for integration by the centre in work on Australia, USA, and elsewhere. This problem of weakness in co-ordination appears to be rife in a whole series of different constitutional contexts. Seidman notes in a US context,

> For the true believer, reorganization can produce miracles: eliminate waste and save billions of dollars. . .
>
> (Seidman 1975: 3)

In his book *Governments Under Stress* (1983) Colin Campbell looks at presidential and parliamentary regimes. He addresses the need for what he terms 'executive leadership from central agencies'. He points out how when Prime Ministers in Canada or the UK attempt to upgrade the arrangements for central co-ordination, they are accused of 'presidentialism'. However, Campbell warns against taking too seriously a distinction based on the superficial qualities of the presidential/parliamentary models. He notes that his interviews in Washington in 1979 did not uncover an unparalleled concentration of power in Jimmy Carter's White House. He says 'our Canadian and British respondents often exaggerated the resources available to Presidents while understating the machinery of resources and staffs available to their respective prime ministers' (1983: 5). He observed that his respondents in the parliamentary regimes almost invariably made comments of the type, 'We are a very lean shop here, certainly nothing like what is available in Washington.'

Campbell claims (1983: 56) that this amount of senior staffing in the UK clearly outstrips the comparable complement in the United States. Moreover the British officials represent 'the cream', largely taken on secondment as high-flyers from elsewhere in Whitehall. He says that their US counterparts, although exceedingly bright young professionals, often brought to their jobs no previous experience in the bureaucracy.

It may be that simple numbers are not a sufficiently accurate measure of the point Campbell is seeking to make, but he does at least establish that the matter of relative power at the centre is not by definition closed by the fact that the US has a presidential regime. His second chapter is significantly headed, 'The American Presidency and the *Obstacles* to Strategic Planning' (emphasis added). Campbell convincingly makes the point that presidential regimes may be as weak at the centre as parliamentary. None the less most discussion of weakness in Britain, ignoring Campbell's empirical evidence, recommends a change in administrative design – by further augmenting resources at the centre.

Hood (1979: 6) reminds us that the conventional phrase 'the machinery of Government' is a metaphor – though it is such an accepted phrase. If the similiarity of Government organisation to a mechanical artefact is even subconsciously accepted then there are associated implications. There is, as we shall develop in the next chapter, the implication that if an organisation is a machine then the various component parts should and can be co-ordinated in a planned fashion. Hood (1979: 3) concludes that if Government organisations are machine-like then in this view they are predictable and can be changed in planned fashion: 'we normally expect that the effect of pulling a particular lever or pressing a particular button to be always the same in a machine. . .'

Other perspectives have less confidence in the capacity of reform of structures. Hood (1979: 7–10) considers other propositions:

- that structural change is not a sufficient condition for changed performance;
- that structural change is only of symbolic importance;
- that performance can alter within stable structural conditions;
- that change is crucially determined by the people involved;
- that successful performance is a chance outcome.

This chapter seeks to highlight an unacknowledged dialogue between those contributions which have merely sought to record administrative events and those which have sought to improve performance – usually by the explicit application of some theory-based analysis. Many of the reformers – at least subconsciously – have adopted something of the machine metaphor and the belief that administrative reorganisation will give superior performance.

The difference between the two styles of writing can be seen by different approaches to the creation of the amalgamated Department of Health and Social Security in the late 1960s. The change can be presented as the application of some logical organisational principles (the efficiency of scale), or, alternatively, as merely the response to political imperative – for example, meeting the need to find a Cabinet post of sufficient scale to match Richard Crossman's political stature. In support of the latter explanation William Robson suggested that,

> The desire to give Mr Crossman the status of Secretary of State was presumably the reason for uniting the functions of the Minister of Health and the Minister of Social Security in a new Department of Health and Social Security. . .
>
> (Robson 1971: 87)

Ironically a Conservative MP suggested one reason for the creation of the Ministry of Land and Natural Resources was precisely to take some responsibility *away* from Crossman at the Ministry of Housing and Local Government:

> Ministries have far more often been produced as a result of personal and political factors than by objective need. What is odd about this Ministry is that it is not produced to give somebody a job. It is produced to take away a job from someone else.
>
> (*Hansard*, Nov. 1964, Vol. 703, col. 1575)

Much of the ancedotal memoir evidence we have available seems to support the atheoretical explanation of events. Crossman himself claimed that the creation of the Ministry of Technology and the Department of Local Government and Regional Planning reflected the fact that all Harold Wilson's 'ministerial shuffles are political shuffles' (1975–7: Vol. 3, p. 681). Lee (1977: 49) gives an earlier example of this political explanation of the administrative pattern when he recounts the Whitehall folklore that a new office co-ordinating Transport, Fuel and Power stemmed from Churchill's instruction, 'Leathers is a big man; find him a big job.' Similarly the continuous expansion of the Scottish Office appears to owe more to a need for political placation than to any explicit administrative theory.

THE HALDANE INQUIRY

The 'modern' interest in the design of Government can be seen in the Report of the Haldane Inquiry published in 1918 (Cd 9230). In the terms of this chapter the report was decidedly reformist and theoretical rather than descriptive. The Report discusses two main aspects of the issue of organisational design. One deals with what has been termed *central capability* (Lee 1974: 162). As expressed in the Haldane Report one key issue is, 'the continuous co-ordination and delimitation of the activities of the several Departments of State'. Several remedies for this perception of an absence of central control were advanced including:

- a Cabinet small in number – ten or at most twelve;
- frequent meetings;
- good information supply;
- consultation with affected Ministers;
- systematic method of ensuring departments comply with decisions.

The main means of an improvement at the centre envisaged by the Haldane Committee was, however, through a second theme – the reorganisation of departments. The Report addressed this organisational problem by setting out the famous charge that: 'there is much overlapping and consequent obscurity and confusion in the functions of the Departments of executive government'. Haldane claimed that,

> This is largely due to the fact that many of these Departments have been gradually evolved in compliance with current needs, and that the purposes for which they were thus called into being have gradually so altered that the later stages of the process have not accorded in principle with those that were reached earlier. In other instances Departments appear to have been rapidly established without preliminary insistence on definition of function and precise assignment of responsibility. . .
>
> (*Haldane Report* 1918: para. 4, p. 4)

The Haldane approach to these complaints was to, 'define in the first place the general principles which should govern the distribution of responsibilities in question. . . ' Of course this could all be said more simply – if less elegantly. Haldane was essentially proposing that the organisational problem stemmed from the fact that some departments had been created with no clear definition of scope – and that the boundaries of other departments no longer matched what were now changed circumstances. Haldane suggested that once the departmental pattern was appropriately simplified then friction between departments and the problem of central capability would be eased.

Two alternative principles which would also allow this desirable reallocation of responsibilities were discussed. The first was 'distribution according to the persons or classes to be dealt with'. Under this method each Minister who presided over a department would be

responsible for the activities of the Government which affect the sectional interests of particular classes of persons. The Report gave the
examples – should this principle be adopted – of a Ministry for Paupers,
a Ministry for Children, a Ministry for Insured Persons, or a Ministry for
the Unemployed.

Haldane and his colleagues dismissed this idea in a short order: 'Now
the inevitable outcome of this method of organisation is a tendency to
Lilliputian administration' (para. 18, p. 7). In other words, the argument
was that once initiated there seemed no limit to the number of categories
that can be identified – hence minute departments would result. The
Report in fact came down in favour of the second type of principle
considered – i.e., 'distribution according to the services to be performed'. In this arrangement the field of activity of each department
matches the service which it renders to the community. The Report gives
as an example a Ministry of Education which would be concerned
predominantly with the provision of education wherever, and by whom-
soever, needed. While conceding that some overlap was inevitable (e.g.
between Ministries of Education and Health when it came to the health
of schoolchildren) the conclusion was that distribution of responsibilities
among departments according to the nature of the service to be rendered was likely to lead to the minimum amount of confusion and
overlapping. It argued that,

> It is impossible that the specialised service which each Department
> has to render to the community can be of as high a standard when its
> work is . . . limited to a class of persons (the first principle) . . . as
> when the Department concentrates itself on the provision of one
> particular service only. . .
>
> (*Haldane Report* 1918: para. 18, p. 7)

It went on to suggest that only the application of the latter principle
allowed the development of specialised capacity by allowing officers to
continuously engage in the study of particular questions.

Haldane acknowledged that for some policy areas the departmental
pattern suggested by the principle of 'distribution according to the
service to be rendered' was identical to that suggested by application
of the principle of distribution 'according to the class of persons to be
dealt with'. They gave examples of National Defence or National
Transport – which presented themselves as discrete whether one
applied either of the two principles.

Arguably, as soon as examples are introduced the value of such
grand determining principles is thrown open to question. Does the

identification of defence as a service lead to the creation of one department or separate departments for naval, military and air services? Are roads part of a national Transport Department or should such a department be restricted to canals and railways as Haldane implied? Why should the objection voiced against the 'class of persons' principle – that it leads to Lilliputian administration – be less valid against the 'services to be performed' idea? It too can be indefinitely extended.

The Report, in reasonably conceding the difficulties in operationalising the principles, in effect discredited them as practical aids. Thus, for example, it pointed out that,

> work which is of primary interest to one Department may well be within the province of that Department even when some portion of it is undertaken as a secondary interest by Departments devoted to other ends. If as we suggest, there should be one Ministry of Education, of Health, and of Finance, in which functions relating primarily to these ends should be concentrated, there must at the same time be, within other Ministries, special branches devoted to educational, hygienic, or financial work. . .
>
> *(Haldane Report* 1918: para. 27, p. 9)

The Report thus found that in practice clinically clean lines could not be drawn, and proceeded to recommend standing joint bodies of departments to cover shared interests. The principles, when examined with a view to being put into practice, seemed to recreate the deficiencies being tackled. Even when a primary function such as Health could be widely and uncontroversially accepted, it did not follow that the organisational design issue was resolved. In the 1920s there was much to be said for the argument that a major health factor was housing. Was housing therefore to be part of the responsibilities of a Health Ministry? Similarly health was put at risk by basic poverty: was a wages policy therefore to be part of a Health Ministry?

The Haldane Report has the advantage of looking authoritative. It was produced as a Command Paper and written in the self-confident tones of the post-First World War reformers. Accordingly its arguments have sometimes been accepted uncritically. It is therefore reassuring for those suspicious of its claims to find Professor W.J.M. Mackenzie arguing:

> The Haldane Committee was composed of persons exceptional in ability, in experience and good will, but we can see after 30 years that their conclusions were largely wrong or at least irrelevant.
>
> (in Campion 1950: 82)

This is not to say that the governmental organisation cannot be improved by re-examination every decade or so, but that the sort of tidying up that makes sense at one point in time will itself require re-examination under changed circumstances (see p. 60).

MORE CO-ORDINATION BY ORGANISATION

In the USA Seidman also notes the influence of these reformist ideas that assumed problems of co-ordination could be organised away. He said that the Hoover *Commission on the Organization of the Executive Branch of Government* (1949) addressed:

> The devils to be exorcised are overlapping and duplication, and confused or broken lines of authority and responsibility. Entry into the Nirvana of Economy and Efficiency can be obtained only by strict adherence to sound principles of executive branch organization.
>
> (Seidman 1975: 4)

One specific proposition that followed from the general cast of mind of reformers was Gulick's suggestion in 'Notes on the Theory of Organization' (Gulick 1937) that departmental boundaries could be drawn according to four different criteria: purpose, processes employed, clientele served, area served.

This essay by Gulick started its life as a piece written while he was a member of the Brownlow Commission which was studying the re-organisation of the US Executive branch. It was not dissimilar in purpose to 'Haldane'. Gulick argued that an organisation should be built from the bottom up by grouping work activities so as to maintain homogeneity:

> It will be found that each worker in each position must be characterized by:
> 1. The major purpose he is serving, such as furnishing water, controlling crime, or conducting education;
> 2. The process he is using, such as engineering, medicine, carpentry, stenography, statistics, accounting;
> 3. The persons or things dealt with or served, such as immigrants, veterans, Indians, forests, mines, parks, orphans, farmers, automobiles, or the poor;
> 4. The place where he renders his service, such as Hawaii, Boston, Washington, the Dust Bowl, Alabama or Central High School.
>
> (Gulick and Urwick 1937: 15; cited in Hammond 1990: 149)

This approach is more sophisticated than the twofold distinction by Haldane, but it is possible that this simply aggravates the problem of operationalisation. Many of the same counterarguments that can be put to the Haldane proposals can be recycled. For example, the Scottish Office can be presented as being built on either the area principle (geography) or the client principle (a special electorate). Does the Ministry of Agriculture, Fisheries and Food (MAFF) look after an economic category (farmers as clients) or rural areas?

The process principle is also difficult to interpret. It appears to mean that those engaged in a particular process should be in a separate department – to permit the development of specialisation, perhaps? It is hard to see how, in practice, this would offer an administrative system that would differ from one constructed on the basis of the purpose (or goal) principle.

Chester and Willson (1968: 399) ascribe the four sorts of principles listed above, to 'general experience'. They relate the distinction between the 'clientele' approach and the 'major purpose' (function) approach to Aristotle:

> we have also to consider whether to allocate duties on the basis of duties to be handled, or on that of the class of persons concerned.
>
> (Chester and Willson 1968: 399)

They certainly do not encourage the view that the 'class of person' principle is a sound basis for organisation, but do acknowledge that something of the idea could be seen in past decisions. They argue that,

> the same function can be viewed either as a job to be undertaken by officials, or as work of special concern to a particular section of the community.
>
> (Chester and Willson 1968: 400)

They suggest that in practice departments found themselves dealing regularly with certain individuals, local authorities and their associations, and other interested bodies. They continue,

> Experience shows that there is a tendency for this clientele to look to the department with whom it is in regular contact to provide other governmental services for it . . . links of this kind led to the development of the idea that each department should act as the sponsor of, or as the advocate for, the interests of its particular clientele. . .
>
> (Chester and Willson 1968: 400)

They (inevitably) cite the Ministry of Agriculture as an 'alleged mouth-piece of the farmers', and claim that even if functions are initially distributed without reference to clientele there is a tendency for each department dealing with individuals or associations to try to satisfy that special public.

As Hammond sets out in 1990, Gulick was aware that there were problems in operationalising this idea. Hammond concedes that these four factors may point to different organisational solutions. He uses the example of a New York City doctor who spends his time in the public schools examining and attending to children in the Bronx. Hammond says that Gulick acknowledges that it could be argued,

- he is primarily working for the school system and place him in the department of education,
- say he is primarily a medical man so put him in the department of health,
- say he works with children and put him in youth administration,
- say he is a Bronx resource and put him in the office of the Bronx borough president.

(Hammond 1990: 149)

He argues that because the implications of the principles were unclear Gulick conceded that there must be,

a selection among the items to determine which shall be given precedence in determining what is and what is not homogeneous and therefore combinable.

(Hammond 1990: 150)

Hammond successfully defends Gulick from the charge that he was simplistic and over-optimistic about the ease of these kind of decisions. For example he quoted the disclaimer:

Students of administration have long sought a single principle of effective departmentalization just as alchemists sought the philosophers' stone. But they have sought in vain. There is apparently no one most effective system of departmentalization. . .

(Hammond 1990: 151)

In endorsing Hammond's defence of Gulick it might be worth under-lying the consequence: it is that Gulick is added to the *list of the sceptics* about organisational design. Thus instead of Gulick being a salesman for a 'quick fix' to organisational design (his usual portrait) he actually recognised that,

While the first or primary decision of any enterprise is of very great significance, it must none the less be said that there is no one most effective pattern for determining the priority and order for the introduction of these interdependent principles. It will depend in any case upon the results which are desired at a given time and place . . . it will therefore be found that not all of the activity of any government may be appropriately departmentalized neatly on the basis of a single universal plan.

(Gulick and Urwick 1937: 32)

In his famous attack on Gulick (and others) Herbert Simon argued,

Administrative efficiency is supposed to be increased by grouping workers, for purposes of control according to (a) purpose, (b) process, (c) clientele, or (d) place, but from the discussion of specialisation it is clear that this principle is internally inconsistent; for any purpose, process, clientele, and place are competing bases of organisation, and at any given point of division the advantages of three must be sacrificed to secure the advantages to the fourth.

(Simon 1961: 28)

While Hammond shows that Gulick anticipated that same point, none the less his work was often misinterpreted as giving a simple recipe for administrative reform. If Gulick and Simon are on the same side then who is defending the proposition that administrative principles really help us make difficult decisions? Gulick was not so much wrong as pointing down a blind alley. If a close reading of the text, as by Hammond, shows that Gulick was aware of the problems in operationalising the principles then their attraction disappears.

Peter Self has concluded that,

If there has to be one dominant principle of organisation, it is not hard to show by elimination that major function or purpose should be the one. It is more intelligible, and conducive to goal effectiveness, to base organisation upon output rather than process, ends rather than means.

(Self 1977: 56)

But Self went on, 'Unfortunately this principle is also obscure and inadequate.' He continued pointing out that for the services provided by Government, 'goals are numerous, variable and sometimes conflicting. They do not come in neat, tidy and reasonably durable packets called "major purposes"' (1977: 57).

THE ANDERSON COMMITTEE

The 'Anderson review' of the organisation of Government in the Second World War certainly did not place much faith in the theory-led approach of scientific management. As we will discuss further in Chapter 3, at that date there was a wide support for key elements of the classical approach to design – but the main significance of the classical approach for the work of the Anderson Committee lay in its rejection. The Anderson Committee was firmly uninfluenced. J.M. Lee (1977: 2), quoted Bruce Fraser (who was devoted full time to the machinery of Government matters in the Second World War), making the point that his objective was to maintain, 'a clear view of the abstract principles applicable to a given case *and an equally clear determination not to let theoretical considerations interfere with the practical realities of administration*' (emphasis added).

Lee (1977: 2) claims that for the Machinery of Government officials in war-time Britain, 'The Haldane Committee of 1917–18 . . . enjoyed a prominent place in their demonology.' They thought Haldane's emphasis on general principles to the neglect of current practice had been a cardinal error. Lee noted that the requirements of war production and the apparent demands of national economic survival in the post-war world, 'were much more effective task masters in compelling administrative change than all the elaborate attempts to distil general principles' (1977: 3).

He argues that one reason why the Anderson Committee investigations were not formally published lay in the nature of the discoveries it made about the relationship between constitutional principles and the messier business of practice. Lee said:

> There was a general reluctance to let outsiders know anything about what insiders regarded as personal jockeying for power. Cabinet Government is extremely vulnerable to those Ministers who can 'write their own ticket' or temporary arrangements which 'save face'. There are also important tactical considerations . . . such as keeping the requisite number of ministers in the House of Lords or distributing the parliamentary secretaryships in the House of Commons among its supporters. The claims of different individuals for promotion in the ranks of the higher civil service also play some part in the construction of departments. Neither ministers nor civil servants relish the prospect of . . . public debate on these aspects of machinery questions.
>
> (Lee 1977: 6)

The Anderson Committee therefore developed the practice of central co-ordination of Government – without expressing any belief that this was possible in other than an improvising way. This perhaps reflected a general civil service suspicion of theory. One of the leading (post-war) civil servants in this area, Sir Richard Clarke, remarked that, 'All large organisations need built-in arrangements for change and adaptation; and most will benefit from one major restructuring every ten years or so.' This was a rule of thumb based on experience and not some proven 'law' (cited in Robson 1971: 89).

In his Introduction to Campion's *British Government Since 1918* (1950) Sir John Anderson noted,

> the complex of authorities constituting the Central Government exhibits a continuous process of redistribution of functions dictated not less by considerations of practical convenience than in deference to a priori reasoning.
>
> (Campion 1950: 6)

The Anderson view is thus the practitioners' rebuttal of applied theory: that the pattern of administration inevitably reflects short-term and political pressures and is not to be comprehended through theory.

THE REORGANISATION OF CENTRAL GOVERNMENT (Cmnd 4506)

Pollitt (1984: 79) records that in the late 1960s the Conservative Party in Opposition (in the words of Geoffrey Rippon) harped on the theme of the Balkanisation of departments, 'we have too many Ministers, too many Departments, too much overlapping among them all'. Rippon said, 'I think we need a new Haldane Committee' (*Hansard*, Vol. 757, col. 888).

Edward Heath, the Leader of the Opposition, set up a committee under Sir Edward Boyle to look at the Cabinet system. This, apparently, said little on its remit and specifically (and complacently) defended the No. Ten staff: 'We feel it right that it should continue to consist of a small number of high-calibre young men' (cited in Blackstone and Plowden 1988: 6). Heath also set up teams of businessmen under Ernest Marples, with prominent roles played by David Howell and Mark Schreiber. This side of the investigation was to be far more influential.

Heath also had advice from a working party of retired civil servants on the machinery of central Government chaired by the former Permanent Secretary at the Ministry of Housing and Local Government, Baroness

Sharp. Her attitude was that there was scope for improvement by reorganisation:

> In the particular sphere in which I worked – local government, housing, new towns, land use, planning, etc. – the machinery did not work well. There was a great deal of overlapping between departments and a great deal of friction . . . Sometimes these disputes were taken to the Cabinet for settlement which took up a lot of their time and did not necessarily produce the right result. There was also a lot of chopping and changing on the distribution of responsibilities between Departments . . . But there seemed to be no way of settling the Departmental pattern in the interests of good government. It was nobody's business.
>
> (Cited in Blackstone and Plowden 1988: 7)

These working groups added up to a major examination of the departmental structure in British Government conducted (by internal review) for the incoming 1970 Conservative Administration. The conclusions were published as a White Paper *The Reorganisation of Central Government* (Cmnd 4506, 1970).

In this exercise, influenced as it was by business consultants and Ministers with a pro business persuasion, the efficiency theories of scientific management were resurrected (see Chapter 3). The remedy for the problem of departmental organisation was familiar. The Haldane Report, which had pre-empted the more formal American versions of the argument, had advocated 'distribution according to the services to be performed'. The 1970 White Paper modernised the language while retaining the same ideas:

> the object has been to ensure that the broad framework of the central machinery in terms of Ministerial and departmental functions complies with the Government's strategic policy objectives. In practical terms, this means that the application of the functional principle as the basis for the allocation of responsibilities: government departments should be organised by reference to the task to be done or the objective to be attained, and this should be the basis of the division of work between departments rather than, for example, dividing responsibility between departments so that each one deals with a client group.
>
> (Cmnd 4506, para. 8)

In a fundamental, if predictable, qualification to the thrust of the document, paragraph 10 argued that there could be departures from the functional principle where 'there are strong reasons for moderating its application'. In effect this meant that the functional principle was of limited help in designing the departmental system. Political pressure ensured the continuance of MAFF, the Scottish Office, etc.

The arguments in support of this function-based prescription were that it helped achieve 'economies of scale and avoids the diffusion of expert knowledge and the difficulty which organisation by area or by client group would involve' (para. 9).

The use of terms such as 'client' and 'area' shows that this paper was a contribution to the (unacknowledged) debate between the theory-based designers and the political realists. However the White Paper did not make any attempt to answer the criticisms of the Haldane or Gulick-type analyses which adoption of the terminology necessarily brought to mind. Like the Haldane document, the 1970 White Paper attempts to convince by assertion rather than through supporting evidence. A rather debatable case is wrapped in the authoritative format of a Command Paper. To read it is to be left uninformed that it was discussing an area of some controversy.

The 1970 White Paper was an intellectual gloss put on decisions to create 'giant' departments for Trade and Industry, and of the Environment: decisions that perhaps owed more to a business fashion of conglomerates and loose propositions about the benefits of larger size than from the application of the theories about the importance of function that purported to have suggested the larger aggregates. It was certainly suspiciously convenient that the functional approach (even granting necessary exceptions for Scotland and Wales) gave the sort of number of departments that the reformers thought sensible for other reasons (i.e. a small Cabinet).

One of the Prime Minister's closest aides later commented,

> Because of his justified respect for his senior advisers Mr Heath tended to exaggerate what could be achieved by new official machinery . . . a little more scepticism about machinery would have been wise.
>
> (Hurd, quoted by Pollitt 1984: 93)

The most damaging analysis of the White Paper was made by Nevil Johnson. He noted that,

> one cannot expect an official paper to indulge in any very explicit or extensive theoretical justification of its conclusions. Yet just because the White Paper purports to rest on certain important theories

relevant to the organisation of government, we might reasonably have hoped for a rather more sustained defence of these theories than is in fact offered.

(Johnson 1971: 5)

Johnson demonstrates problems with interpretation of area and client notions and that departments such as Education, 'definable in functional and even clientele terms, can also be characterised as a process. . .' However, his major criticisms concern the weakness of the functional principle which was at the heart of *The Reorganisation of Central Government*. He comments that it is not as if the factual principle is wrong, but that it is banal. He claims (1971: 5), 'The problem is rather that . . . appeal to this [functional] principle may justify a wide variety of organisational conclusions, and one cannot avoid the need to establish a balance of advantage for each particular grouping of functions.'

He points out that if housing, for example, is considered to be a function it would not necessarily follow that there should be a Ministry of Housing. It could be that the best way to ensure a high level of provision and improvement in the housing sector would be to provide a range of incentives through taxation and subsidised interest rates. Thus Johnson concludes that housing as a function could be placed inside a finance ministry or some kind of social policy department.

If one attempts to design the organisation of Government from high-level principles of the 'function' type, it can justify almost any number and nature of departments. Such an approach will confirm the need for the sort of departments that experience has shown that almost any governmental system will devise – Treasury, Industry, Education, etc. But it does not help with the more difficult matter of the precise boundaries.

It fits in with this sceptical discussion of the utility of theory on this subject to note that the assumption in the 1970s that once the 'correct' pattern was devised it would lead to stability in organisational arrangements was ill-founded. The Department of Trade and Industry announced in the White Paper was soon redivided (to be reunited again later), the Department of the Environment soon lost transport to a separate Ministry. Significantly the large 'umbrella' departments lost the label 'giant' and were frequently given the less flattering tag of 'Jumbo departments' with its implication of being unwieldly.

F.M.G. Willson (in Butler and Halsey 1978) argued that a department was too large if it threw up so much political contention as to make representation by one Cabinet Minister impracticable. He says this means that in the period since 1964 defence has been relatively uncontroversial, whereas trade and industry, environmental and welfare matters have been too politically complex to allow their administration in 'giant' departments on other than a temporary basis. This is again a sensible 'rule of thumb' rather than an iron law. The iron law is that political convenience will override any other consideration.

THE CPRS OPTION

Though the Central Policy Review Staff (CPRS) was disbanded by Mrs Thatcher in 1983 it was clearly one means to provide central capability. It was created by the Conservative Government following the 1970 White Paper on *The Reorganisation of Central Government*. The original role was to be an informed but detached evaluator of the Government's progress in implementing its manifesto and sticking to its political principles, but Campbell (1983) describes how over time the CPRS became an arbitrator on contentious policy issues. This could be conflict between departments as when the Ministry of Agriculture was defending its farming clients over land drainage from the encroaching DOE which wanted to handle all water-related matters. It could be conflict between a Minister and his department as when Tony Benn wanted to turn down his officials' advice that Britain should buy American nuclear technology.

The CPRS was a tentative substitute for a strong central department that would adjudicate at the centre. It was small in size, however (around 15 staff), and thus may have been under-resourced to fulfil all the ambitions it enshrined. In a sense the CPRS was a forerunner of other efficiency-centred innovations such as the Financial Management Initiative. It was an attempt to provide a mechanism to evaluate existing policies and policy options for the future.

According to Blackstone and Plowden (1988) in their history of the CPRS, the idea for such a unit came from the Machinery of Government Group of ex civil servants chaired by Baroness Sharp that was mentioned earlier (see pp. 60–1). In the report sent to Edward Heath in 1969 the group noted the Cabinet's preoccupation with the short term and the weak position of the PM who, 'normally had no agency on which to call for objective advice or for help in evaluating colleagues' ex parte statements, other than the tiny personal staff located at No. 10'. The report called for a new Office of the Prime Minister and Cabinet with the roles of 'coordination, planning, research and study, management and organisation services at Government levels'. It would have responsibility for establishing priorities – 'the crucial task of enabling the Government to identify its main objectives, to relate individual decisions to their wider context and, in doing so, to coordinate its own activities'.

Blackstone and Plowden say it advocated a small central staff under a 'Chief Planning Officer' and a permanent research unit which would,

> enable the Government, once its major purposes had been established, to ensure that the means by which these were implemented were compatible with each other; and whether existing activities were compatible with them . . . and to determine whether apparently unrelated proposals coming forward from departments were consistent then, in both the short and the long term. . .

> (Blackstone and Plowden 1988)

Heath, they say, had similar advice from Lords Plowden and Roberthall, both formerly senior civil servants, which noted the need of Prime Ministers and non-departmental Ministers for, 'impartial advice on matters with a high context of expertise which come to Cabinet from Departmental Ministers'. This was essentially a call for the PM to have a 'second guessing' facility to counter the spending departments. Plowden and Roberthall 'talked down' the briefing of the Cabinet Office as too impartial and balanced to be the cutting edge the PM needed. They too recommended a 'relatively small staff of able people who can examine proposals from Departments . . . from the point of view of the whole national interest in the short and especially in the long-term'.

Similar thinking was taking place inside Whitehall. The Secretary of the Cabinet, Sir Burke Trend, and the Head of the civil service, Sir William Armstrong, were also concerned about the lack of any central 'thinking' capacity to offset the centrifugal tendencies of Whitehall under which departments could pursue their own inclinations with no well-informed counter criticism.

The Conservative Party's own proposals in Opposition were leaning towards a 'big bang' 'Central Capability' force based on a large Prime Minister's Office. In the event the more cautious notion of an extra, small-scale, analytical unit was adopted.

The 1970 White Paper argued,

> For the lack of . . . a clear definition of strategic purpose and under the pressure of the day to day problems immediately before them, Governments are always at some risk of losing sight of the need to consider the totality of their current policies in relation to their longer

term objectives; and they may pay too little attention to the difficult, but critical, task of evaluating as objectively as possible the alternative policy options and priorities open to them.

(Cmnd 4506, para. 45, p. 13)

David Howell was the politician most closely identified with the planning of the CPRS and other related changes. His own recollections play down the sort of scientific neutrality with which the CPRS was later identified,

> Frankly some of us actually wanted that to be a staff for No. 10, for the Prime Minister, rather more like today's Policy Unit . . . and less a general body to serve all the Cabinet. We thought that No. 10 was under-equipped to deal with all the great departments of state.
>
> (Quoted in Hennessy 1986: 77)

David Willetts worked in Mrs Thatcher's policy unit from 1984–6. He accepted that in many ways the Policy Unit of 1983 onwards was as much a successor to the CPRS as to earlier policy units. He argued that one reason for the abolition of the CPRS was that in working for the full Cabinet rather than the PM its papers were likely to be circulated widely – giving forewarning to departments and Ministers who were criticised. Willetts concludes that institutional innovations at the centre may have a brief shelf life. He says, 'The grit in the machine is now smooth. Prime Ministers all need arrangements around them with which they person-ally feel comfortable. So perhaps it is a delusion to pursue a "right" organizational answer' (Willetts 1987: 445). (See discussion of policy unit in Chapter 4).

The Central Policy Review Staff was aimed at providing central capability and it reflected a confidence in intellectual analysis that now seems unjustified. One can legitimately query whether the notion of a central analytical unit is not in itself based on an over-optimistic, and flawed, conception of the place of data and rationality in policy-making. Majone (1989), argues that the basic skills of the policy analyst are closer to those of the lawyer than to those of an engineer or scientist. He argues that 'decisionism', the idea that policy can be determined by authoritative analysis, is wrong (cited in Hood and Jackson 1991: 21).

SUMMARY

Hood (1979: 6) has noted the disagreement between those who would (even unknowingly) subscribe to the structure-performance hypothesis and those who would suspect the opposite: that the relationship is no more than an illusion. Hood quoted Leemans (1976: 50) to support the view that the sceptics were perhaps gaining the ascendancy, 'The former excessive belief in the effectiveness of structural change has been thoroughly undermined during the last two decades.' But the structure-performance hypothesis is far from unpopular and has resurfaced in the debate on local government and reorganisation in 1994. Hood notes that even if academics tend to be cautious on such matters, governmental justifications of reform invariably accept the thesis. He cited the 1974 Ryder Report on British Leyland Motors. This had asserted, 'We are convinced that BL's present organisational structure has harmful effects on the efficiency of BL's operations. . .'

However, it is at least arguable that structure is not the casual factor: that success (however measured) legitimates structures. Though there have been periodic attempts to 'tidy up' Whitehall according to some clear principles the day-to-day explanation of change is less 'rational'. As Pollitt noted of the creation of the (short-lived) office of Minister for Science,

> If the government's establishment of the office of the Minister for Science was informed by any specifically *organisational* principles, these were certainly not on public view.
>
> (Pollitt 1984: 30)

As Mackenzie and Grove (1957: 366–7) explained, the arguments for change in the organisation are well worn – as are the counter arguments when further change needs to be justified:

> The debate in these cases follow patterns that tend to recur. A shake up of the organisation will give a chance to get rid of dead wood and to make a fresh start. . . But it is a pity to dislocate existing relations . . . and it will take time for a new organisation to find its feet. . . It is desirable to get rid of small Departments because they are expensive in overheads and make coordination difficult. But large Departments are slow and cumbersome . . . And so on: in isolation, each of the conflicting 'proverbs' makes good sense, but they cancel out. . .'
>
> (Quoted in Hood and Jackson 1991: 18)

Peters and Waterman (1982: 4) relate the idea that structure follows strategy to the business historian Alfred Chandler. This, they said, was the basis for business conventional wisdom and that with the right strategic plan on paper the right organisational structure would pop out. But, they concluded, empirical study showed that strategy rarely seemed to dictate other than vague structural solutions. Moreover, the crucial problems in strategy were most often those of execution and continuous adaption. They endorse (1982: 107) James March's image that organisations are to be sailed rather than driven; that, 'organizational design is more like locating a snow fence to deflect the drifting snow than like building a snowman'.

Arguments based on organisational principle appear as rationalisations called up in support for instinct rather than as diagnostic and determining. The belief that getting the structure right will allow us to escape difficulties in co-ordinating goals that may themselves be incompatible is also identifiable in discussions in the much-altered local government and the Health Service arrangements of the 1990s. Indeed the greater the say in the reorganisation given to consultants from the real world of business the less realistic are the nostrums proposed.

Chapter 3

Understanding organisations
The battle of beliefs

ORGANISATIONS AS MACHINES

In Chapter 2 we identified what has passed for debate in Britain about the organisation of central Government. Parts of the academic literature on theory are considered in this chapter. Some of this provides an underpinning to the arguments in favour of 'designing out' problems from Government: what is really important to note is the *lack* of impact of these approaches on the design of Government.

Rosamund Thomas has summarised a largely American literature as resting on the assumption that organisations can be viewed as machines,

> just as a machine is built by given sets of specifications for accomplishing a task, so an organisation can be constructed according to a blueprint. Classical organisation theory, then, centres upon the formal structure of an organisation and because of this machine like approach to the formal structures it is known alternatively as 'machine theory' or 'formal organisation theory'.
>
> (Thomas 1978: 2)

She presented the classical American doctrines as follows:

1. Government consists of two separate processes; namely, politics and administration.
2. Administration can be made into a science. Indeed, the science of administration necessitates its independence from politics.
3. The scientific study of administration leads to the discovery of principles of administration analogous to the principles or laws of the physical sciences.
4. The principles of administration determine the ways in which the goals of economy and efficiency can be realised.

> (Thomas 1978: 6)

In this chapter it is emphasised that this is one of several competing formulations about the nature of public organisations.

We have looked at the Haldane Report, the 1970 White Paper and other reformist sources that were based on theories of how Government *should* be designed. These ideas for change were based on a (usually implicit) premise that sought to improve performance by clearer allocation of functions to parts of 'the machine'. As Thomas suggests, this analogy is at the core of many theories of organisational behaviour. A machine metaphor relates to a considerable body of writing, though the link to something like the 1970 White Paper is far from direct. The literature seems to have been, at best, a background influence that shaped the thoughts of those responsible for the White Paper.

Naturally the emphasis on organisations as machines has thrown up a counter-analogy of organisations as being *organic*. However, the implications of this sort of conception have proved far more difficult to absorb and, arguably, the machine image is still predominant. (The organic/mechanistic distinction is established in Burns and Stalker's influential *The Management of Innovation*, 1961.)

The machine image

The notion of Government (indeed organisations generally) as a machine is central to the work of Max Weber, though the connection certainly predated him. The contribution of Weber is not easy to understand. Indeed it seems a reasonable guess that its textual density has protected it from criticism.

The thrust of his case was summarised by Morgan (1986: 24) who suggested that Weber was observing the parallels between the organisation of productive industry and the proliferation of bureaucratic forms of organisation. The proposition was that the bureaucratic form routinises the process of administration exactly as the machine routinises production.

Bealey (1988: 61) notes that the machine is Weber's favourite metaphor. We can add the adjective 'formal'. The Weberian image is of an organisation that proceeds by formal rules. (He used the term 'formalistic impersonality'.) Morgan (1986: 378) says that Weber's views of bureaucracy were of an *iron cage*. In this basic image of organisation the bureaucracy is an instrument to attain the goals set by political leaders.

Describing the neutrality of the Weberian bureaucracy, Bealey says 'Civil servants had no goals of their own, for machines do not have goals.' To confirm this apolitical association of bureaucracy, he cites

(1988: 71) the famous proposition by Woodrow Wilson in his article in *The Political Science Quarterly* of 1887, 'administration lies outside the sphere of politics. . . The field of administration is the field of business. It is removed from the hurly burly and strife of politics.'

Robert Haynes in *Organisation Theory and Local Government* (1985) suggests that the Weberian approach is grounded in using structure to impart rationality and efficiency for the attainment of organisational objectives through the means of effective co-ordination and control, consistency and predictability and an emphasis on the depersonalisation of administrative matters. He says of this *classical perspective* that there is a mechanistic view of the organisation that places great reliance on formal structure and authoritarian assumptions:

> For the classicists all organisational ills must be the result of some form of structural inadequacy or some weakness in the formalisation of rules and procedures.
>
> (Haynes 1985: 9–10)

Morgan describes how the machine proposition has taken over our imaginations,

> Increasingly, we have learned to use the machine as a metaphor for ourselves and our society, and to mould the world in accordance with mechanistic principles.
>
> (Morgan 1986: 20)

He notes that the word 'organisation' is from the Greek *organon* meaning a tool or instrument. The organisation is a means to an end. Morgan says:

> This instrumentality is evident in the practices of the earliest formal organizations of which we know, such as those that built the great pyramids, empires, churches and armies. However, it is with the invention and proliferation of machines, particularly along with the industrial revolution in Europe and North America, that concepts of organization really become mechanized.
>
> (Morgan 1986: 23)

In the machine version, organisations exist to implement goals established by political or other leaders. The organisation is the means to attain specified goals. The fact that the comparison between organisations and machines has some appropriateness (they both seek to operate with reliability, responding to controls, etc.) has encouraged other comparisons that might be less legitimate (organisations can therefore be consciously redesigned, they can be made more efficient by planned change, etc.).

Hood and Jackson (1991: 170) argue that the machine metaphor is now being updated by turning away from the Weberian steam-age imagery of cranks, cogs and wheels to the more contemporary version of information-processing machines. Though the image may be updated, it may, of course, still be misleading.

Weber's account

The starting point for most descriptions of bureaucracies is Weber's notion of a rational–legal bureaucracy. This version of the bureaucratic form has become so ubiquitous in discussions that we need to consciously recollect that it was only one of the versions of bureaucracy that he identified. According to Albrow (1970: 39) Weber saw all organisations as consisting of individuals who both gave and received orders in a hierarchy. He distinguished between power – which was found when an individual could enforce his will – and authority which was one source of power but the most important form within organisations. Authority existed when particular commands found obedience. Effective authority existed when there was a belief that orders were justified – i.e. legitimate.

Acceptance of legitimacy could be on several grounds. These different bases led to the distinction between different types of organisation. An order might be obeyed because of the special characteristics – perhaps sacred – of the person issuing the instruction. This is '*charismatic* authority'. Alternatively, it might be accepted because of long-established pattern and precedent. This produces '*traditional* authority'. Finally, it could be obeyed because of the fact that the person issuing the order has a recognised right to do so in a system of legal rules and regulations. Here, orders are accepted as legitimate because the individual accepts the organisational premises.

This final source of legitimacy was '*legal* authority' which was the basis of the legal rational bureaucracy. This form of organisation exists quite independently of individual employees. Individuals come and go while the organisation and the information needed by the organisation remains. (We would say that an organisation was non-bureaucratic if a member of staff took his records, names of customers/clients, with him when he left its employment.) The inevitable metaphor can be applied to say that in the rational bureaucracy the individual is a cog and can be replaced by another cog quite readily.

Employees in the rational–legal bureaucracy thus have a life separate from the organisation in a way that distinguishes the bureaucracy from earlier forms of organisation. Staff are also usually selected for their posts after some particularly relevant training or experience. The organisation tends to fill its senior positions by a system of continuous recruitment and promotion from below. (This promotion seems to be part of the explanation of why staff remain loyal.)

Albrow (1970) has listed the main features of how Weber believed authority was legitimated in a legal authority system. These beliefs were:

(i) That a legal code can be established which can claim obedience from members of the organization.
(ii) That the law is a system of abstract rules which are applied in particular cases, and that administration looks after the interests of the organization within the limits of that law.
(iii) That the man exercising authority also obeys this impersonal order.
(iv) That only *qua* member does the member obey the law.
(v) That obedience is due not to the person who holds the authority but to the impersonal order which has granted him this position.

(Albrow 1970: 43)

Albrow then sets out eight propositions about the organisation of legal authority-based systems that followed from Weber's conception of legal authority:

(a) Official tasks are organised on a continuous, regulated basis.
(b) These tasks are divided into functionally distinct spheres, each furnished with the requisite authority and sanctions.
(c) Offices are arranged hierarchically, the rights of control and complaint between them being specified.
(d) The rules according to which work is conducted may be either technical or legal. In both cases trained men are necessary.
(e) The resources of the organisation are quite distinct from those of the members as private individuals.
(f) The office holder cannot appropriate his office.
(g) Administration is based on written documents and this tends to make the office (bureau) the hub of the modern organization.
(h) Legal authority systems can take many forms, but are seen at their purest in a bureaucratic administrative staff.

(Albrow, 1970: 43–4)

The rational–legal bureaucracy is 'rational' because it is designed to deliver specified goals in the optimum manner and it is legal in the sense that authority is based on accepted rules and processes. For Weber the term bureaucracy did not have the sense of being 'pathology of large organisations' (phrase cited from *Encyclopaedia Britannica*, 1967, by Baker 1972: 34). Indeed though he recognised perversions of the ideal, the ideal rational–legal bureaucracy was advanced as a goal to be attained. Bureaucracy is seen as the response to the complexity of modern society. The caricatured characteristics of bureaucracy – buck passing, slowness in decision-making, empire building by officials – are diseases of Weberian bureaucracy rather than its essence. However Albrow notes that even Weber moved inconsistently from his general version of the phenomenon to the pure and rational type (1970: 42).

Weber himself uses the machine analogy when he says that the bureaucracy is like a modern machine, while other organisational forms are like non-mechanical methods of production (cited in Pugh *et al.*, 1983: 17). The bureaucratic organisation is depersonalised where individuals follow rules within hierarchies rather than their own interests.

Despite the close association in the literature between Weber's discussion and bureaucracy in fact it is quite reasonable when discussing particular organisations to come to the conclusion that many governmental and other organisations have as their outstanding quality noncompliance with the Weberian rational–legal model. Weber offered an ideal type that not only is *not* a description of the British higher civil service but in many respects misinforms us about such real world organisations.

Weber was not the only important source for what is now termed classical theory or scientific management. (It is classical not only in that it was earlier than other theories but because the importance that it accorded to structure seemed to suggest classical architecture.) We will see below that in fact other important sources predated Weber (1864–1920) or at least predated his translation into English in accessible form (Gerth and Wright Mills, *From Max Weber: Essays in Sociology*, 1948), but these other sources had no overt connections with the Weber approach: the Weberian contribution generated its own debate. In summary of the classical school Morgan says,

> When an engineer designs a machine the task is to define a network of interdependent parts arranged in a specic sequence and anchored by precisely defined points of resistance or rigidity. The classical theorists were attempting to achieve a similar design in their

approach to organization . . . by giving detailed attention to patterns of authority, and to the general process of direction, discipline and subordination of individual to general interest, the classical theorists sought to ensure that when commands were issued from the top of the organization they would travel throughout the organization in a precisely determined way, to create a precisely determined effect.

(Morgan 1986: 27)

The essence of the classical school in general, and the Weberian version in particular, was that it suggested a means of delivering pre-determined policies in a controlled and predictable document-based manner by supervision of career subordinates and by division of labour.

Bureaucratic politics?

Despite the deference paid to Weber in the literature there are two major qualifications that need to be noted to his approach. The first is an empirical matter: are the organisations we popularly call (or perhaps unpopularly call) bureaucratic really Weberian in their nature? An important book of the 1980s by Michael Lipsky was called *Street Level Bureaucracy* (1980). As the title suggests the argument was that policy was not simply made by 'top–down' legislators and managers but by the policemen or social workers using their discretion in the delivery of services.

An alternative approach to that of Weber, advanced by Jenkins and Gray, is to regard bureaucracies as political organisations,

Pfeffer suggests that one reason for (an apolitical conception) . . . has been the domination of a rational–legal model or organisation which has its roots in Weber but which has developed through more managerial writings. Such models regard conflict as pathological and hence either to be removed or contained through organisational adjustment; this conflict free model sees bureaucracy as neutral in terms of intrinsic power and values.

(Jenkins and Gray 1983: 179)

They say sources influenced by Weber tend to share a monolithic conception of bureaucracy – a homogeneous structure and process, culture and behaviour (Jenkins and Gray 1983: 179) – but Jenkins and Gray themselves follow Bacharach and Lawler (1980) and Walsh *et al.* (1981) to emphasise that within organisations what happens is con-tested: 'organisations are viewed as aggregates of groups constituting bargaining systems'. This implies a micro approach to policy: outcomes reflect context-specific struggles as different parts of Government and different levels within sub-departments try to shape policy. There is no top–down imposition of policy by politicians. The best example of such an approach is probably Graham Allison's work (1971) on bureaucratic politics.

Perrow (1979: 43) argues that instead of defining organisations as 'conflict free', one might better regard them as arenas in which conflict is endemic. Lewis Dexter (1990) has surveyed a series of studies of behaviour within organisations and concludes that expectation should be of intra-agency conflict. Internal conflict is not an occasional disorder that can be 'cured' – it is the nature of the organisational beast. His perspective is that of Olsen:

> The need for intraorganizational bargaining, the intraorganizational distribution of power, and how this distribution is affected by inter-organizational relationships have often been assumed away. An alternative is to view an organization as a coalition and to assume the members of an organization may themselves be powerful organizations.
>
> (Olsen 1981: 499–500)

Dexter observes that this stress on intra-agency conflict (commonly noted in gossip and description) is underplayed in public administration for two reasons. First, to do so would run counter to the prescriptive character of public administration which stresses command, co-ordination, control, and obedience; second, because senior members of organisations are reluctant publicly to admit this limitation on their powers (1990: 52).

Dexter labels this possibility of sectionalised conflict as 'recalcitrance' or 'contravention'. He says, 'It has the sense of opposing indirectly or covertly, distorting, altering orders, maligning by gossip, foot-dragging, sabotage, etc.' If we accept this perspective on organisational life, the machine is an inappropriate metaphor. The components of the organisation are not cogs available to be connected but wilfully self-orientated tendencies to disorder. Dexter points to 'an inherent tendency to factionalise', even where the subject of the dispute is not terribly crucial.

This sort of approach was earlier mentioned by Philip Selznick in his work on the Tennessee Valley Authority (1949). He argued that sub-units within an organisation might well have goals that were in conflict with the overall organisation and that an attempt to contradict this with co-ordinating departments might only lead to more complex competition. As we noted in Chapter 2, case-studies suggest that these assumptions about endemic conflict within Government seem more realistic than any supposition that there is coherent political leadership and compliant executive staff.

Negative implications of the Weberian model

The notion of bureaucratic politics throws doubts on the empirical utility of Weber. Another set of qualifications to Weber is suggested by Albrow (1970) where he quotes Merton (1940) who argued that the emphasis on precision and reliability, while being attractive, might have self-defeating consequences. He suggests,

> rules, designed as means to ends, may well become ends in themselves. The graded career structure of the bureaucrat may encourage him to an excess of the virtues he is supposed to embody. . . officials develop a group solidarity which may result in opposition to necessary change. Where officials are supposed to serve the public the very norms of impersonality . . . may cause conflict with individual citizens.
>
> (Merton 1940, quoted in Albrow 1970: 55)

Albrow says that the point is that the formal picture set out by Weber fails to relate to the probable behaviour of bureaucrats. Whereas Weber saw merit in the ruled order of rational bureaucracy, other analysts have seen dysfunctional consequences of these same rules. Victor Thompson (1964) has written of *bureaupathology* as a label for the dysfunctions of bureaucracy.

There is an assumption in the literature in support of the notion of the rational bureaucracy that echoes the conservative arguments about the American Supreme Court. This is that the job of the court is neutrally and technically to interpret the law of the Constitution. Critics of this mechanistic view of the court join critics of the Weberian bureaucracy to emphasise that judges and administrators reflect a cultural bias in their (apparently) value-free decisions. Albrow cites Reinhard Bendix's criticism in his *Higher Civil Servants in American Society* (1949) that it is impossible to adhere to rules without the intrusion of general social and political values. Albrow (1970: 57) also cites the criticism of Carl Friedrich (in Merton 1952). Friedrich claimed that the emphasis on authority means that the work, 'vibrates with something of the Prussian enthusiasm for the military type of organization, and the way seems barred to any kind of consultative, let alone cooperative pattern'.

Albrow claims that this appeared to let individual bureaucrats escape all responsibility for their actions.

So there is a considerable body of opinion suggesting that that there are flaws in the rational model as a goal; that it simply is illogical or that it is likely to be dysfunctional in operation and not deliver the benefits predicted by Weber. Albrow cites Talcott Parsons who showed that Weber stressed the importance of professional expertise in his system. Yet there might well be a conflict within the organisation between the views of the most expert and the views of the most senior in the hierarchy. Does position or knowledge prevail?

Haynes cites five categories of dysfunction:

- inflexible behaviour
- reduced incentive for high personal achievement
- goal displacement
- poor internal and external communication
- lack of adaptive capacity

(Haynes 1985: 17)

Others have discussed dysfunctions such as empire building, anxiety of staff members, cost of controls, denial of individual responsibility. There can be conflict between the goals of the staff and the organisation. It might not be rational for the organisation to allow work units to continue in existence after real demand has disappeared, but it might be all too rational a goal for the individuals concerned. Thus their aim might be self-perpetuation in a way that is contrary to the formal goal of the organisation. The individual employee might wish for growth in the number of his subordinates, not because there was useful work to be done but because the salary and status of the senior person is reflected in the number of those he or she controls.

The impersonality of the organisation – seen by Weber as a contribution to fairness and efficiency – might be seen as creating uncongenial environments in which employees are expected to spend their working lives. The organisation may be inefficient because the control rules that are devised are perhaps 'worst case' responses. It might be that sensible discretion can mean that such rules can be waived with beneficial effects. Thus 'working to rule' is usually seen as some kind of industrial protest rather than the efficient furtherance of organisational goals.

Whereas Weber favoured specialisation, most organisations recognise that the costs of rigid specialisation are usually greater than allowing workers to work on a broad range of functions. While the efficient organisation will wish to control staff, control has costs as well as savings. Therefore the call for control has to be qualified to the far less straightforward notion of *cost effective* control (see Hicks and Gullet 1975: 143–52).

Derek Pugh (1991) has included Weber in the school he identifies and labels as the '*organisers*'. They are united in the assumption that, 'more precisely specified plans and programmes, with improved monitoring and control of the behaviour which is intended to achieve them, are necessary for effectiveness'. Pugh contrasts that approach with a school which he labels the '*behaviourists*'. This category is similar to that set out below (see pp. 79–84) as the students of the informal organisation. Pugh says their approach maintains that the continuing attempt to immerse control over the members of an organisation is self-defeating. Increased control, he says, leads to rigidity in functioning where flexibility is required, apathy in a member's performance when commitment and mobilisation are required, and efforts devoted to counter-control through informal relationships to defeat the aims of the organisation.

The debate with the ghost of Weber: the informal organisation

Whether or not Weber provided a very good description of working organisations, he certainly provided the most influential means for the academic analysis of bureaucracy – though the popular interpretation of bureaucracy as a synonym for inefficiency has resisted the Weberian gloss. As Douglas Pitt has said, the subsequent debate has largely been conducted 'with the ghost of Weber' in that alternative means of conceptualising organisations tend to react against the Weberian model.

Even before the rigid version of the bureaucratic form provided by Weber was available in English translation there was a contrary account of organisational behaviour. Opposed to the image of the controlled organisation was the notion developed by Barnard in *The Functions of the Executive* (1938) of the 'informal organization'. This key proposition held that the informal organisation was a system of internal communication and cohesion within the formal organisation – and upon which the formal organisation depended. This contrast between the formal blue-print of the rational organisation and an actual pattern is at the heart of the important debate. This acceptance of the 'informal' is central to the 'human relations' sources discussed below (see pp. 87–92).

Hicks and Gullet (1975: 108) describe how the informal organisation consists of the unofficial and unauthorised relationships that inevitably occur between individuals and groups within the formal organisation.

These are largely immune from management control and serve the interests of the participants. Unless these informal arrangements are satisfactory morale and productivity may be affected. Thus Elton Mayo (1945) showed in his study of a paint factory, production increased when staff were allowed to take rest breaks in the company of others. This appeared to offset the social isolation in the organisation of the work. The informal had to be taken into account. The informal organisation can provide the individual with the status that is denied him by the formal blueprint.

Hicks and Gullet (1975: 111) note Chris Arygris's argument that management's formal power derives basically from making employees dependent on management for their rewards, directions, positions, etc. Arygris claims that in the informal organisation employees are able to win back some control over their working lives, and indeed that this is necessary to allow staff to become mature and well motivated, and self-realized.

Charles Perrow (1979: 40–1) writes that one of the delights of the organisational expert is to indicate to the uninitiated the wide discrepancy between the official hierarchy (or rules for that matter) and the unofficial one: 'The first thing the new employee should learn is who is really in charge, who has the goods on whom, what are the major debts and dependencies – all the things not reflected in the neat boxes in the table of organization.'

There may be a whole series of unwritten rules in an organisation about matters such as tipping, speed of work, duration of breaks. Some of them might suit the management (respect for good workmanship, an informal competition about a 'good' target of bricks to be laid per day, anticipation of orders before they are formally communicated) but usually these are understandings to protect workers against divisive tactics of employers. Thus the argument is that many organisations have features unlike the rational–legal bureaucracy.

The possible inappropriateness of the Weberian framework as an ideal is systematically indicated in Perrow's book *Complex Organizations* (1979). He describes that Alvin Gouldner's study (1954) of a gypsum works in which official rules were rarely enforced revealed that the arrival of a new manager – with a fresh personal style – turned the works from a 'traditional' form of organisation, in which the workers had considerable freedom over their operating practices, to a Weberian-style rational–legal bureaucracy. Perrow claimed that among the features of rational–legal bureaucracy that were consequently imposed on the factory were:

1. Equal treatment for all employees;
2. A reliance upon expertise, skills, and experience relevant to the position;
3. No extraorganizational prerogatives of the position (such as taking home dynamite, wallboard etc.) that is, the position was seen to belong to the organization, not to the person. The employee could not use it for his personal ends;
4. The introduction of specific standards of work and output;
5. The keeping of complete records and files dealing with the work and output;
6. The setting up and enforcing of rules and regulations that served the interests of the organization;
7. A recognition that rules and regulations were binding upon managers as well as upon employees; thus employees could hold management to the terms of the employment contract.

(Perrow 1979: 4)

The shift to a rational–legal structure was accompanied by a drop in morale and, indeed, a wildcat strike. Perrow explains why the 'ideal' of the Weberian bureaucratic model is usually not attained in practice. In line with Barnard's work (1938) on the informal organisation he argued that the employees in the normal organisation have other interests to consider than those of the institution. The work of the institution is often unpredictable, leading to a 'non fit' between the actual pattern and the intended.

Perrow lists the very inconsistent charges that are made of bureaucracies:

that they are inflexible, inefficient, uncreative and unresponsive (the planning attack)

that they stifle the spontaneity, freedom and self realisation of their employees (the human relations attack)

that they hold unperceived and unregulated social power (democratic attack)

(Perrow 1979: 6)

Blau's study *The Dynamics of Bureaucracy* (1963) also finds that empirical study had shown that the most rule-bound and rational organisation was not necessarily the most efficient. Blau begins his study with two quotations from Max Weber, confirming Pitt's point that most of this work is at least in reaction to Weber if not in support. These were,

The fully developed bureaucratic mechanism compares with other organizations exactly as does the machine with non-mechanical modes of production. Precision, speed, unambiguity, knowledge of the files, continuity, discretion, unity, strict subordination, reduction of friction and of material and personal costs – these are raised to the optimum point in the strictly bureaucratic administration.

Its specific nature . . . develops the more perfectly the more the bureaucracy is 'dehumanized', the more completely it succeeds in eliminating from official business love, hatred, and all purely personal, irrational and emotional elements which escape calculation.

(Blau 1963: 1)

Blau addressed that gap between the behaviour of members of an organisation and the blueprint that Weber recognised but did not focus upon (1963: 2). The gist of Blau's work is that informal interpersonal relationships can make an organisation more not less effective. He examined the behaviour of officials in two American agencies – one federal law enforcement agency and the other an employment agency at state level.

Blau found that the introduction of more extensive productivity measures in a job placement agency did indeed increase the percentage of jobs filled. It had other beneficial effects. It helped relations between supervisors and the staff conducting interviews. Performance records meant that the supervisor was relieved of the unpleasant task of assessing colleagues, and that his role became one of offering assistance on how to improve on past performance rather than criticising it. The past performance was self-evident.

However, the extension of the record system also had dysfunctional effects. The major of these was that interviewers would manipulate their work to score better on the records rather than to place more people in work. For example, they would put people assured of a job through the system so that it could be claimed that the placement was a consequence of the processing. Morale in the office fell as the introduction of quotas was seen as leading to a lowering of status, and relations with colleagues became competitive. Interviewers would literally hide notices of job openings from each other. They would rather that one of their marginally qualified clients attended for a job interview than let another interviewer have it. Even if the applicant didn't get the job it was kept open in case the interviewer found a better candidate. Evaluation based on scores also inhibited the assistance that interviewers would give to their colleagues working with the handicapped. It was seen that the special interviewers were 'stealing' openings. Blau was able to show that in comparing the work of two different sections in his first organisation studied 'The group much concerned with productivity was less productive than the group unconcerned with it' (1963: 69). The explanation of this paradox was that in the second group cooperation between the interviewers inhibited the dysfunctional effects of cooperation.

In Blau's second case-study the staff of a federal enforcement agency were required to inspect business premises to ensure the uniform application of federal laws. Statistical records allowed the supervisor to set up production quotas for subordinates: these were a requirement to complete eight cases a month, to find violations in half of them, and to obtain the employers' agreement to make voluntary adjustments in at least two-thirds of these. Blau says that the repeated emphasis on these standards and comparisons of one agent's record with that of another were intended to encourage speedy and effective work, but in fact Blau found that unofficial norms had developed among employees to curb these competitive tendencies. Officials who produced too much were warned by being teased or, ultimately, ostracised. Agents tended to underemphasise their achievements with each other, 'You don't want to seem like an eager beaver.' This strategy was, of course, possible because the work among agents was non-competitive. They were not like the employees in the first case-study who had to share a common pool of jobs.

Other forms of non-compliance with the official style of the agency were actually productive for the organisation. Blau shows that the non-reporting by staff of attempted bribes was based on a belief that it seemed over-zealous to make a big thing of what was simply a pressure of the economy. Agents felt that if they were skilled in their handling of the situation they could discourage the suggestion of bribes before it got serious and thus the reporting of a bribe offer reflected some encouragement (or, at least, non-discouraging behaviour by the agent). (Of course the group norm could also help with the masking of the acceptance of bribes in that agency.) The rationale expressed by agents for this unofficial non-observance of procedures was that having done the employer the favour of not reporting him, the agent met with less resistance in getting the employer to make voluntary changes in the implementation of the regulations. Thus non-compliance with the bribery rule helped agents fulfil their primary function. And any agent reporting a bribe made difficulties for any other agent who later would have to work with the reported man or his acquaintances. However, Blau identified other reasons for non-reporting. There seemed to be a suspicion by agents that threatened prosecution showed 'excessive compliance' by the individual with the superiors in the organisation. In other words the agents in general thought that anyone reporting bribes was out for special recognition or even promotion within the agency. The norm of non-reporting thus protected the agents from other agents seeking special credit.

Blau's work is convincing – which explains its impact on the subject of organisations. But the nature of its lessons about organisations is complex. It is a warning of the difficulties in predicting or even describing behaviour within organisations. What happens in the working operation may not be what happens according to the theory of the formal structure. How employees react to the rules of the bureaucracy are difficult to describe without investigation into the particular circumstances; whether new rules will be worth while or dysfunctional will be difficult to predict from general principles.

Blau's work is very standard management text material. Accordingly it is remarkable that as central Government introduced management by targets in the Next Steps programme in Britain it was not acknowleged that staff are likely to respond with the manipulation of data as reported by Blau. He reports being repeatedly told that, 'figures can't lie, but liars can figure'. In their generally uncritical account of performance indicators, Osborne and Gaebler (1992: 157) even note that when the FBI were given targets they asked local police for lists of stolen cars that had been found in order to claim them as recoveries. They pursued minor felons and military deserters as they were easier to apprehend. By the 1980s US attorneys were declining to prosecute 60 per cent of FBI cases as they were so trivial.

SCIENTIFIC MANAGEMENT AND ADMINISTRATIVE THEORY

The work of Weber did not reach (English-speaking) social scientists until the 1940s. There is thus not a simple relationship in the literature between original publication and the the impact of the material in English-speaking countries. Scientific or classical management theory thus predated Weber.

Some sources attempt to distinguish between scientific and classical management theory: the overlap seems more significant than any distinction. The emphasis of authority and hierarchy in the scientific approach none the less suggests that Weberism was compatible with, if not underpinning, that tradition. The term 'classical' does suggest that the work has now been superseded. However, Baker argues (1972: 23) that other connotations are also smuggled in, 'It is classical in the sense that it attempts to propound simple principles of general application and also in the sense that certain styles of architecture and literature are termed "classical" having characteristics of formality, symmetry and rigidity.'

As Dunsire notes (1973: 92), the title 'Father of Scientific Management' is usually bestowed on Frederick Taylor. In his *Principles and Methods of Scientific Management* he set out that the paper was written,

> FIRST. To point out, through a series of simple illustrations, the great loss which the whole country is suffering through inefficiency in almost all our daily acts.
> SECOND. To try to convince the reader that the remedy for this inefficiency lies in systematic management, rather than searching for some unusual or extraordinary man.
> THIRD. To prove the best management is a true science, resting on clearly defined laws, rules, and principles as a foundation. . .
> (Taylor 1911: 5–7)

Most of the authors discussed in this category were practical administrators and managers rather than academics. Despite Taylor's claims it has been argued that despite the label used what they wrote *lacks* a scientific basis. Baker begins his 1972 survey by describing the work of Fayol whose *Administration Industrielle et Generale* was published in 1916 but the impact of which was again delayed in Britain and the US by the fact that it was not translated until 1949 (Pugh *et al.* 1983: 63). Baker notes that Fayol claims that in any operation of any enterprise there are six functions but the book dwells almost exclusively on the administrative function. The main elements of the administrative function were:

- foresight/planning;
- organisation;
- command;
- co-ordination;
- and control.

Baker also cites Fayol's 'general principles' of administration:

> division of labour, authority, discipline, unity of command, unity of direction, subordination of particular to general interests, remuneration, centralisation, hierarchy, order equity, stability of personnel, unity of personnel, initiative.
> (Baker 1972: 25)

This sort of approach is now commonly criticised for being both self-evident and internally contradictory. Baker (1972: 25), writing from administrative experience, is clearly more sympathetic than some but he notes that a principle such as unity of command (that a man should receive his instructions on one subject from only one chief) is often violated. Often the complexities of the situation mean that such simple principles have to be eroded. Baker comments, however, 'how many managers, struggling with complex interlocking committees and coordinating meetings, long for the simplicity and sense of Fayol's principles. . .'

Baker notes the influence of a mechanical metaphor in Fayol's work, 'he is all the time referring to a very simple straight line diagram with authority and power all emanating from a central point'. Fayol's organisation appears to be a mechanism for giving effect to the wishes of an authoritarian chief. Baker commends him for 'opening up clear straight lines through hitherto not easily penetrable jungles' but also concluded that, 'he was the originator of ideas which were to become later . . . instruments of restriction, frustration and indeed downright oppression' (1972: 27).

Baker assesses the influence of Taylor. Like his classical colleagues Taylor seems to have adopted a simple 'economic man' assumption in his expectations about behaviour. However, in contradiction to Fayol's central idea that unity of command was the main principle, Taylor advocated a system of functional management with development of specialist activities such as planning and clerical work. The foreman's work was divided between gang bosses, speed bosses, inspectors, repairs bosses. Each workman received orders and advice from eight different superiors. Thus within the so-called schools of scientific and classical management there were very basic disagreements.

Taylor's measurements were part of a search to devise the optimum method for arranging work. The approach was seen as being scientific in its neutrality. It was thought that a scheme of arrangements could be devised which would improve production for the employer and which would thus also improve rewards for the employee.

Perrow (1979: 61) finds in this sort of work a form of social Darwinism. This approach lauded the captains of industry as being better endowed than their less-successful competitors and employees. Not only was their success desirable in the pursuit of increased prosperity, in some hands it became a sign of Christian virtue. The ineffective were to be weeded out. One important book was Hubbard's *A Message to Garcia*. The title came from the feat of a lieutenant who managed to carry a message to General Garcia in spite of overwhelming odds against success. Thus, in Perrow's view, the industrial process is presented as a process of continuous selection in which the employer has to constantly protect himself by getting rid of the 'incompetent and the unworthy' and keeping only these who 'can carry the message to Garcia'.

THE HUMAN RELATIONS APPROACH – OR NICE THINGS HAPPEN TO NICE PEOPLE: THE EXTENSION OF THE INFORMAL APPROACH

Whatever the empirical relevance of the scientific management school and its offshoots it offends the liberal values of most contemporary academics and educated managers. It is hard to survive the academic process with a belief in the 'ox-like' qualities of the worker. As Lupton (1971) says of the Human Relations School, anyone critical of the new approach invited the charge of being churlish. After all, it said that participative and non-authoritarian management not only gave the employees the opportunity for self-expression and self-development, it also promised increased productive efficiency.

As with the idea of the 'informal organisation', the Human Relations literature starts with a different, more pessimistic, idea about the 'controlability' of the more complex world it identifies. It also emphasises the need for interaction and cooperation. Perrow (1979: 71) particularly credits Barnard's *The Functions of the Executive* (1938) with influence. He says that the dramatic dichotomies – such as mechanical systems versus organic systems; production-centred versus employee-centred organisations; rigid inflexible versus adaptive, responsible organisations; and authoritarian versus democratic organisations – stem from the contrast between the Weberian and Barnardian models.

The other core of the Human Relations work – certainly the most cited – is the Hawthorne studies reported by Roethlisberger and Dickson (1939) and by Elton Mayo in *The Human Problems of an Industrial Civilization* (1933). The Hawthorne plant of the Western Electric Company was a manufacturing part of AT and T (the Bell telephone group). The studies started in 1924 when the researchers looked at different lighting intensities as a means to improve output. When a test group and a control group were monitored, there was an unforeseen increase in the output of both groups. More elaborate research involving carefully designed studies of the effect of rest periods, hours of work, etc. found the same result. Whether rest was increased or decreased performance improved. Lupton summarises:

After all their carefully controlled changes in hours of work, rest pauses and so on, they were unable to halt a general upward trend in the rate of output, even a lengthening of the working day and a reduction of rest pauses seemed to have no depressing effect. The general upward trend, despite changes was astonishing.

(Lupton 1971: 32)

The suggestion that was eventually put forward to explain this phenomenon has been labelled 'the Hawthorne effect'. It is suggested that all the control groups became more productive (contrary to expectations) because they had been noticed. The fact of having others watch them being 'normal' itself improved their morale and hence productivity.

The Human Relations School does not assume the basic economic man idea; their subjects respond to a wider range of incentives. They also stress the informal organisation that emerges from the relation of the individual to his fellow workers. They would tend to favour partici-pative management in which workers are consulted – unlike the top–down assumptions of Taylor and others (Hicks and Gullett 1975: 200). Perrow notes that Mayo emphasised the desire to stand well with one's fellows, the role of sentiments, and the instincts of human association (1979: 67).

The Hawthorne Effect has entered the social sciences as a warning to consider the impact of observation on any behaviour being observed. Perrow (1979: 94) describes the controversy that followed the conclu-sions. The first sort of criticism that emerged was ideological. The critics (including C. Wright Mills) claimed that the Hawthorne studies made assumptions that conflict was a negative factor and that the workers should be educated to cooperate. The critics claimed that the coopera-tion was on the managers' terms. It was also argued that the managers were presented as rational while the worker was presented as non-rational. Daniel Bell rejected the notion that in a situation of systemic conflict between management and workers, better face-to-face rela-tions at plant level could solve the fact of different and conflicting self-interests.

Perrow suggests that the Hawthorne studies escaped methodological criticism for so long because the academics themselves became part of a human relations industry investigating the relations between morale and production. Perrow sees the Human Relations School as concerning two main themes. The first deals with morale, leadership and productivity. The second deals with similar themes but at the level of the organisation rather than the individual. Of the first approach, he says that it is based on the general thesis that good (i.e., democratic and caring) leadership will lead to high morale. High morale, it is asserted, is connected to increased effort. And increased effort is connected to higher production. This will also lead to lower rates of absenteeism and staff turnover which will also contribute to increased productivity. Unfortunately Perrow has to conclude that the history of research in this area is of progressive disenchantment with the theses and progressive awareness of the complexities of human behaviour. He records how the work was later subject to attack by mainly British workers on the accuracy of the observations.

Perrow (1979) notes that Alex Carey (1967) for example, claimed that, 'The results of these studies, far from supporting the various components of the "human relations approach", are surprisingly consistent with a rather oldworld view about the value of monetary incentives, driving leadership and discipline.' Perrow says

> As a result of nearly thirty years of intensive research, we have a large body of information on what does not clearly and simply affect productivity (or the intervening variable, morale) and a growing list of qualifiers and conditions that have to be taken into account. The size of this list threatens to overwhelm us before we can, with confidence, either advise managers as to what they should do to increase productivity or develop theories that have much explanatory power.
>
> (Perrow 1979: 98)

Thus while much of the incentive to research these areas is to produce conclusions with ready applicability, it is such a checklist of simple rules that has not been possible.

Perrow shows how a survey published as early as 1932 (Kornhauser and Sharp) reported no relationship between productivity and attitudes to work, to supervisors, personnel policies, etc. Perrow says that these negative conclusions were simply ignored as being unacceptable (1979: 99). The belief was that happy employees should be productive employees, but he cites Brayfield and Crockett's (1955) review of some fifty studies of the relationship between attitudes and performance. They too found that waves of research had discovered little evidence that attitudes bore any 'simple or appreciative relationship to performance'. The evidence seemed to suggest that employees who were satisfied with their network of interpersonal relations were less likely to be absent or to leave their jobs but still tended to show no increased motivation as far as production was concerned. Indeed subsequent work by Lawler and Porter suggested that the causal connection might be between performance and attitude – if performance was rewarded. Thus the successful employee who was recognised as such might be happy. In other words high productivity could be the cause of, rather than be caused by, positive attitudes.

Another argument considered by Perrow which throws into doubt the attitude = performance assumption is the proposition that in most modern work there is simply no room for high performance. The individual worker can only do an adequate job as there is no way to increase his pace when he can only respond to the supply of materials from others. Indeed something like a weld of great craftsmanship may be criticised as wasting time or materials; all that is required of the employee is an adequate weld. In this view, productivity is connected to matters such as investment decisions, technological change, or economies of scale.

Of the work connecting leadership to production, Perrow is similarly sceptical. He argues that whereas the human relations tradition considers the important aspect of management to be the process of leadership the non-personal decisions about the market, about competition pricing policy, etc. are probably more important. He points out the phrase that a company has done well because of 'good leadership' is likely to mean that good decisions have been made about these sorts of matters rather than simply about relations with staff. He cited a review by Korman in 1966 which considered a large number of leadership studies and concluded that the variables that had been identified in the studies had little by way of a predictive relationship with performance. Perrow concludes that the relationship between leadership and performance is complex and contingent (different styles might suit different conditions).

The human relations perspective was also found in work by Douglas McGregor (1960) who rejected the scientific management of Taylor and his followers:

If there is a single assumption that pervades conventional organisation theory, it is that authority is the central, indispensable means of managerial control.

(Quoted in Peters and Waterman 1982: 94)

His theory 'X' was that,

(1) the average human has an inherent dislike of work and will avoid it if he can,

(2) people, therefore, need to be coerced, controlled, directed, and threatened with punishment to get them to put forward adequate effort towards the organisation's ends,

(3) the typical human prefers to be directed, wants to avoid responsibility, has relatively little ambition, and wants security above all.

(Summary from Peters and Waterman 1982: 95)

His theory 'Y', in contrast, assumed,

(1) the expenditure of physical and mental effort in work is as natural as in play or rest – the typical human doesn't inherently dislike work,

(2) external control and threat of punishment are not the only means for bringing about effort towards a company's ends,

(3) commitment to objectives is a function of the rewards associated with their achievement – the most important of such rewards is the satisfaction of the ego and can be the direct product of effort directed to an organisation's purposes,

(4) the average human being learns, under the right conditions, not only to accept, but to seek responsibility,

(5) the capacity to exercise a relatively high degree of imagination, ingenuity and creativity in the solution of organizational problems is widely, not narrowly, distributed in the population.

(Summary from Peters and Waterman 1982: 95)

Though there has been such scepticism about the human relations approach, it was none the less successfully revitalised by Peters and Waterman in *In Search of Excellence* in 1982. They say, for example, 'Treating people not money, machines or minds as the natural resource may be the key to it all' (1982: 39). They place their work in descent of Mayo and Barnard who they say,

> In various ways, both challenged ideas put forward by Max Weber, who defined the bureaucratic form of organisation and Frederick Taylor, who implied that management can really be made into an exact science.

(Peters and Waterman 1982: 5)

They said the old rationality that they sought to displace was a direct descendant of Frederick Taylor's School of Scientific Management and has ceased to be a useful discipline. They claim (1982: 56) that most companies take great pride in setting really high targets for people but their exemplars of excellence allowed teams to set their own objectives.

IBM, for example, set quotas so that almost all salespeople could reach them. The tough targets, they say, seem calculated to tear down the staff self-image.

Accordingly it is again ironic – and important for the themes of Chapter 5 – that in discussion of target-setting in Next Steps agencies Sir Robin Butler has argued to the Treasury and Civil Service Committee in 1993 for setting targets that are ambitious: 'Unless you set over ambitious targets you don't get people to achieve more than they think they can achieve . . . all targets should be difficult for people to achieve.' Modern management books are read selectively and different users are prone to ignore the inconvenient ingredients.

Though the human relations/informal approach has the more academic credibility, the scientific approach seems more important in appreciating recent developments in Britain. Pollitt argues that it was paradoxical that in the 1980s, as some management theorists in the business schools were enthusing about the spectacular variations between different organisational cultures, politicians and senior officers in Britain and the US were energetically impressing on British and American public services a traditional model of management which largely ignored their distinctiveness (1990: 146).

Peters and Waterman (1982: 37) complain that business education had been captured by those of a rationalist and quantitative orientation that misunderstood the necessary priorities in practice. They quote Michael Thomas who said of business graduates,

> [They] lack liberal arts literacy . . . need a broader vision, a sense of history . . . I'd close every one of the graduate schools of business.
>
> (Peters and Waterman 1982: 35)

But the Peters and Waterman revival of human relations was more successful as a piece of marketing than as a source of practical advice. Hood and Jackson (1991: 193) point out that more than half the companies identified as excellent by Peters and Waterman collapsed in the decade after publication.

THE OBSOLESCENT MACHINE: CONFLICTING BUNK?

As noted in the Introduction, Hood and Jackson (1991: 184) extended ideas put forward by Mary Douglas (1987) to say that persuasive arguments are usually grounded in metaphor and fiction. They say the 'acceptance factor' is higher when there is perceived to be a symmetry between the metaphor and the phenomenon. They cite

Brown (1978, 1983) who argued that successful administrative analysis, and successful social science generally, lies in the construction of a reality symmetrical with the 'perceived' problem (1991: 26).

As we have seen the machine has been a potent metaphor which, once accepted, smuggles into our thinking assumptions about the possibility of hierarchical, top–down, control in organisations. But this is not really compatible with case-studies of organisation which report a lack of success of directed change.

The literature reviewed in this chapter looks old fashioned if read along with approaches such as contingency theory (which flourished in the 1970s) which proposed that structure followed technological or environmental imperatives and hence sought to avoid the 'one best way' fallacy of scientific management (Burns and Stalker 1961), but the contingency approach proved to have a limited shelf life and academic attention quickly moved on. As Hood and Jackson (1991: 20) observe, the 'contingency approach' has tended to run into the sand. Good administrative practice, they argue, remains deeply contestable. Perrow (1979: 200ff.) describes the basic argument of the contingency approach but he also describes Mohr's study of 1971 that found little to support the approach – this conclusion not inhibiting its popularity in Britain in the 1970s.

By the 1980s 'post Fordism' suggested that organisations would be far more flexible than the Weberian order as represented in early industrialisation. However, notions such as 'post bureaucratic control' or 'formalised informality' (Hoggett 1991) may be more difficult to deliver than their advocates hope. It is premature to abandon the traditional public administration literature as administrative forms may be more resistant to change than those who follow 'restructuring' suggest.

One response to all this is to judge it as 'conflicting bunk'. This phrase was used by Chester Barnard himself about a good deal of the teaching in this field (cited in Lupton 1971). Rose argues the 'explosive' growth in organisation theory to be one of the most extraordinary features of contemporary intellectual life', but a growth leading to a 'shambles' rather than an integrated, theoretical edifice (cited in Pitt and Smith 1981: 1). Depending on one's prejudice there seems to be a range of academic work to support the required point of view. Are workers motivated primarily by money or not? Should power be centralised or diffused? Is there an identity of interest between management and workers? Even the critics can be criticised. Perrow (1979: 87) argues that Barnard glorified management as an activity, 'Barnard's central concepts . . . combine to legitimate and justify what should forever remain problematic – the value of impracticality of co-ordinated systems of human effort.' Thus conflict is inescapable. More research, more reflection has not produced a consensus that can be packaged, learned and applied.

Another response is to question the scale of much of the research in relation to the burden of generalisation it has to bear. Even if the original authors are modest in the conclusions that can be legitimately drawn from a study of twenty-four meat canners in Chicago, the temptation is often not resisted by others. Reflecting on the instability of administrative doctrines, Richard Spann (1981: 14) observed,

> As in fashion, skirts go up and down, ties narrow and widen, so in Public Administration there are alterations – the economics of large scale are preached at one time, to be succeeded by the gospel that 'small is beautiful'; periods of administrative pluralism are followed by ones of integration when semi-independent bodies become suspect . . . ; there is oscillation between the demand for functional rationality and a holistic approach to clienteles; between a desire to politicize and to depoliticize public administration.
>
> (Cited in Hood and Jackson 1991: 18)

An authoritative modern textbook on organisational behaviour – such as Huczynski and Buchanan (1991) – reflects conclusions that follow studies of the literatures on, say, ministerial responsibility or the design of the centre of Government. It argues that the sum of the various approaches reviewed adds to one's understanding of the complexity of organisational life. The literature does not, however, give any mastery of 'how to'. Huczynski and Buchanan catalogue the advantages and disadvantages of various approaches (which resurface regularly). The use of studying 'conflicting bunk' is that it allows criticism of each new organisational messiah. It does not, itself, offer organisational salvation. The wish to have principles of organisation has not meant that these have been accessible.

Hood and Jackson point out that in administrative argument there is a counter thrust to parry every thrust. They advise us to look at the various prescriptions advanced:

> to look for the evidence that has been conveniently omitted from the argument because it does not suit the conclusions, to find the rival proverbs and maxims which will challenge those which have been put

into play, to identify and counter the ways in which disbelief is suspended.

(Hood and Jackson 1991: xii)

Perrow (1979: 58) observes that though classical theory was derived for presenting principles that were really only proverbs, all the resources of organisational research and theory today have not managed to substitute better principles (or proverbs) for those ridiculed. Pitt and Smith (1981: 8) offer a positive interpretation of the multiplicity of organisation theories and cite W. J. M. Mackenzie's (1967: 246) view that we are dealing with a 'sequence of schools gradually enriching thought . . . all sorts of inconsistent theories survive together, for the good reason that no single theory is necessarily the best theory for even a single situation'. But if one endorses their defence of eclecticism, one can perhaps go further. Whereas they say that this is inevitable, 'until a more integrated theory is available', it is probably realistic to concede that no such integration is possible. Of course such a conclusion may be overly pessimistic, but if there is an effective theory that allows us to deliberately increase organisational harmony and productivity it hides under a stone as yet unturned.

Though management or organisation theory sound as if (like economics) they are part of the respectable and practical branch of the social science family they are spectacularly impractical. Not only are these theories not consistent in a way that would encourage their application, they do not have the internal robustness that would have allowed their systematic introduction to large-scale organisations such as Government departments. To attempt implementation is to uncover ambiguities and inconsistencies in the theory. And worse, even where there is a glimmer of consensus about matters such as the morale of staff and the deficiencies of relying on material incentives, such considerations are swept away by the ideological tide in favour of markets and performance pay. Theory is not allowed out of the business schools.

Chapter 4

Co-ordination by political clout
The 'strength at the centre' argument

This chapter attempts to describe what has happened in the organisation of the centre of Government in the absence of suitable theory to apply. Organisation theory plays the role of Conan Doyle's famous dog that 'did not bark in the night': the most significant thing about theory is its silence.

If one line of solution for the problem of conflict within Government has been to adopt a policy of organisational redesign of the pattern of departments on the basis of considered principle (as discussed in Chapter 2), there has been an entirely different pragmatic response that is of more relevance to a debate on constitutional theory. The Constitution appears to tell us that the problem of fragmentation is resolved by Cabinet Government: senior political colleagues meet collectively to discuss and agree solutions to problems on the basis of their shared political philosophy. It is possible however that the *implicit principle* of prime ministerial Government now joins together what the Cabinet fails to unite.

This chapter deliberately uses the memoir evidence of politicians as a resource. By repetition of similiar claims from a wide variety of sources it attempts to sustain generalisations about the centre of Government. It also attempts to indicate that there is less to the claim that we are underinformed about the workings of British politics because of a cult of secrecy than is often asserted. Of course there is much more data that we could utilise, but arguably the main bones of the British system are already clear. The recent wave of accounts of the Thatcher years do not suggest we need to revise the earlier understanding based on the insider accounts of the Labour Cabinets of the 1960s and 1970s.

CROSSMAN AND THE CALL FOR A STRATEGIC CENTRE

The most important of these contributions to our knowledge of the centre of Government are the diaries of the former Labour Minister, Richard Crossman. His argument about prime ministerial power in his *Diaries of a Cabinet Minister* is frequently misconstrued. In his earlier introduction to Bagehot (1963) he had argued that there *was* prime ministerial rather than Cabinet Government. Crossman's complaint was not, however, about the existence of the strong PM, but the failure of contemporary description to capture that change of practice. Crossman was against the persistence of a nostalgic Cabinet Government description of events that did not accord with the actual political world.

Crossman cites support for his Prime Minister-centred description from the Conservative Minister (later Prime Minister) Lord Home, who had said to *The Observer* in September 1962,

> Every Cabinet Minister is in a sense the Prime Minister's agent – his assistant, there's no question about that. It is the Prime Minister's cabinet. . .
>
> If the Cabinet discusses anything it is the Prime Minister who decides what the collective view of the cabinet is. A Minister's job is to save the Prime Minister all the work he can. But no Minister could make a really important move without consulting the Prime Minister, and if the Prime Minister wanted to take a certain step the Cabinet Minister concerned would either have to agree, argue it out in cabinet, or resign.

In *Inside View* (1972: 63) Crossman frankly commented that as a Minister he was aware that he was there at the PM's discretion – and the PM could withdraw that discretion. Crossman's ministerial experience confirmed for him the unrealistic nature of pure textbook Cabinet Government. Thus he criticised his Prime Minister, Harold Wilson, not for failing to fully follow the conventions of Cabinet Government but for failing to use some kind of inner core to provide the strategic leadership which the full Cabinet seemed incapable of providing. The theme is set out more fully in Jordan (1978) but some examples of Crossman's approach, taken from his 1975–7 *Diaries of a Cabinet Minister*, include:

> The strange thing is that the Cabinet would be entirely willing to accept central direction from No 10 because this will make the Cabinet system work . . . [the Cabinet members] feel that they

can't go on muddling through. . . It's at the centre, where strong purpose is essential, that the failure lies.

(Vol. 2: 51)

Of course, it [Cabinet] isn't a coherent, effective, policy-making body: it's a collection of departmental Ministers. . .

(Vol. 1: 201)

Here I think we have to consider how we can persuade Harold to get a policy group around him to consider the government's strategy. . . we must now have some strategic long-term planning.

(Vol. 1: 571)

Policy is now formulated in the various departments and merely co-ordinated by Harold at the last moment, there is no inner cabinet with a coherent policy for this Government; and yet that is what we need more than anything else. . . We must have a clear-cut purpose.

(Vol. 1: 249)

in my view, confirmed once again by this affair, that the failures of the Government are not peripheral failures, not on the whole failures of Departments, but failures of central direction, of the Prime Minister and his personal relations with his inner group.

(Vol. 3: 422)

Crossman sought to be, 'a member of a team determined to substitute central purposive direction for the old easy going muddle through' (1975–7: Vol. 2, 51), but that was his ambition: his experience was as a departmental spokesman. He told Barbara Castle (1984: 117), 'I'm not really a Cabinet Minister any more than you are; I'm a Departmental one.' He repeatedly complained of Wilson's 'functional separatism' (1975–7: Vol. 3, 458). By this he meant the system of bilateral relations between the PM and the key affected Minister – legitimated by a 'group of cypher Ministers who can be reckoned to be compliant'. 'This is the traditional Harold bilateralism of the last five years and it has grown not better but worse' (1975–7: Vol. 3, 458).

Though Crossman does give instances of where a genuine collective discussion takes place at Cabinet, none the less he concluded,

Broadly speaking, the analysis I made in the Introduction to Bagehot is being confirmed. Certainly it is true that the Cabinet is now part of the 'dignified' element in the constitution, in that the real decisions are rarely taken there, unless the Prime Minister deliberately chooses to give the appearance of letting Cabinet decide a matter.

(Crossman 1975–7: Vol. 1, 198)

Contrary to his position in folk memory Crossman was not a defender of Cabinet Government but an advocate of more strength at the centre.

THE PROBLEM OF FRAGMENTATION: BALKANISED WHITEHALL AND DEPARTMENTAL PLURALISM

While the Cabinet is traditionally presented as the means to resolve conflict, the truth appears to be that it is conflict between members that needs resolution and this has to be done outside the formal Cabinet. This section documents that Crossman's prescription of more central control was based on a widely accepted diagnosis that Whitehall is riven by departmental disputes.

It is reasonable and logical to imagine that there is a sort of pyramid of conflicts of different importance that are handled in different ways at different levels; that the Cabinet exists to resolve those issues that cannot be resolved by lesser status methods such as interdepartmental negotiations, Cabinet committees or bilateral relations between the relevant Secretary of State and the PM. There is, however, little evidence that the non-Cabinet procedures act as a filter of the less important issues. If anything the evidence suggests that contested issues are kept off the agenda until there is some solution (endorsed by the PM) that can go to the Cabinet for formal approval. Indeed, Ian Gilmour suggested that in his experience of Mrs Thatcher's administration, 'only rarely were the most important issues permitted to reach the cabinet' (1993: 4). The rules on Cabinet policy-making handed to new Cabinet Ministers as their first Cabinet paper say that,

> Where there is a difference between Departments, it should not be referred to the Cabinet until other means of resolving it have been exhausted. . .

> (Questions of Procedure, May 1992)

Moreover, some matters are not taken to Cabinet simply because the PM so decides. Complaints about Mrs Thatcher's control of the agenda were echoes of earlier concerns. On the matter of the TSR 2 aircraft Crossman, claimed,

> Even on Thursday when we had Cabinet the issue wasn't discussed. I read in the papers that it is being discussed at Chequers this weekend, with George Wigg and his pals present and people like me completely excluded.

> (Crossman 1975–7: Vol. 1, 132)

As noted above Crossman did not object to this management of Cabinet by the PM and accepted that this specialisation was sensible:

> there were some Ministers like Barbara Castle who took up postures of protest. But the rest of us felt that there was nothing we could do and that the procedure under which we were excluded was not unreasonable. Fourteen out of twenty-three members of the Cabinet are members of the Defence Committee. To the preparation of this White Paper these fourteen had devoted nineteen meetings and two Chequers weekends. After all this, it was natural enough that they should expect Cabinet to give formal authorization to the recommendations that they had worked out.
>
> (Crossman 1975–7: Vol. 1, 455)

Crossman's picture of the centre is confirmed by the accounts of a large number of former Ministers and senior civil servants. Sir Douglas Wass, former joint head of the civil service, has also noted that the way in which the Cabinet handles business effectively disqualifies it as a place of *collective* consideration. He notes that the item is always brought to Cabinet by the Minister concerned. If the matter impinges on the affairs of another department that Minister may make a presentation. Thus says Wass,

> the essence of any collective Cabinet is that it takes place on the basis of statements by interested parties . . . where the proposals are contested by a colleague whose departmental interest(s) are adversely affected, the discussion assumes an adversarial character and the Cabinet acts in what amounts to a judicial role. But where as so often happens, there is no adversary, the Cabinet simply hears the case which the minister concerned presents, and this case is inevitably put in terms to suit the minister himself.
>
> (Wass 1984: 120)

Though Lord Hailsham argued that the Cabinet had a veto on policy he accepted that it was not an effective centre of decisions. He said (pre-Mrs Thatcher) that for one thing it is too large and that,

> Although the Cabinet has not gone the way of the Privy Council and become a formal piece of government machinery designed to register and give legal effect to decisions arrived at elsewhere, on many matters of importance it is well on the way to getting there. . . Though the Cabinet remains, therefore, at the seat of power, the

idea that it still sits as the real fountain of policy, like the Cabinets of Disraeli, Gladstone, or Asquith, is misleading.

(Hailsham 1978: 205)

The Cabinet is where the deals are ratified not where they are struck. A key member of recent Conservative Governments, Lord Wakeham, accepted that,

The increasing use of Cabinet as a reporting and reviewing body, rather than a decision-taker is, I think, an irreversible consequence of the complexity of modern Government.

(Wakenham 1993: 12)

Wakeham does not dismiss the Cabinet but he sees it as a place for communication and information: 'the cement which binds the Government together.' (1993: 8). Nigel Lawson (1993: 125) less politely put the Cabinet in perspective. He did not see it as the vital centre of Government and indeed he said, 'Thus, as Chancellor, I used to look forward to Cabinet meetings as the most restful and relaxing event of the week.'

Geoffrey Howe, when Foreign Secretary, was quoted in the press in 1984 on the banning of trade unions at the Government Communication Headquarters,

It was discussed, as almost every government decision is discussed, by the group of ministers most directly involved. There are very few discussions of government decisions by full Cabinet.

(Cited in Doherty 1988: 54)

Lord Young records his experience of Thatcher Government in terms similiar to other recent Cabinet members,

Cabinet turned out to be a far more formal affair than I imagined. Everyone was addressed by the office they held. There was always a set agenda, opening with Parliamentary business, followed by foreign and then home affairs. After some years home was promoted over foreign. Anything else would be dealt with in sub committees and only came to a full Cabinet if it proved impossible to resolve there. As a result Cabinets rarely took more than an hour or an hour and a half.

(*Sunday Times*, 9 Sept. 1990)

One reason why Cabinet is not the place for broad debate is that to participate in these debates requires information and Ministers are so absorbed in their own departmental problems that they do not have the time to invest in other issues. Moreover, the civil service machine exists to brief Ministers on areas relevant to the department, not to arm them for battle on far off topics of which they know little.

Ministers are thus characteristically in competition. Former Labour Minister, Richard Marsh, starts his chapter in his memoirs on 'Life in the Cabinet' as follows, 'The most unwelcome revelation of being a member of the cabinet was the sense of isolation from one's colleagues, and the lack of solidarity, whatever might be said about collective responsibility'. (1978: 87)

In his memoirs (1990: 327), Denis Healey conceded that for his first years as a Cabinet Minister (for Defence) he was so tied up with departmental duties that he played little part in domestic issues where his department had no direct concern. He says 'As I am a newcomer to office, I was both surprised and depressed by the amount of Cabinet in-fighting. But a hundred political memoirs can testify that it has been all too common in Governments of all parties' (1990: 345)

The pressure of departmental life means that Ministers do not have time to prepare to act as informed central decision-makers. A former senior Treasury official, Sir Leo Pliatzky, has written,

> The timetable pressures on Ministers, the deadlines they are expected to keep and the sheer volume of ministerial business are the enemies of rational and considered collective decision making.
>
> (Pliatzky 1985: 59)

Richard Marsh warned,

> It was alarming to sit round the Cabinet table and see a Cabinet Minister so tired as a result of not getting to bed before four in the morning for the previous three days or so. . .
>
> (Marsh 1978: 87)

Edmund Dell, another former Labour Minister, criticised a system of Government that plunges Ministers into Cabinet after Cabinet, Cabinet committee after Cabinet committee. He went on:

> Because of the burdens Ministers carry . . . including the burden of frequent attendance at Cabinet committees, they may not have had time to study their colleagues' papers properly. They may have received them only the previous evening and may have had time merely to skip though them, possibly after midnight.
>
> (Dell 1980: 35, quoted in Pliatzky 1985: 59)

Even briefing is no guarantee of comprehension. In his diary, a Minister in the post-war Labour Government, Hugh Gaitskell, made the same kind of complaint:

> Sometimes Cabinet meetings horrify me because of the amount of rubbish talked by some Ministers who come there after reading briefs which they do not understand. . .
>
> (Gaitskell and Williams 1983: 36)

This version of events that sees the Ministers too busy in their own fiefdoms to worry about the overall mix of governmental policy is verging on being generous in implying that Ministers are prevented by circumstances from carrying on their central role: in fact it appears that role is simply not valued. Ministers, on the whole, do not want so much to be cogs in successful Governments as heads of successful departments. With beguiling frankness Crossman admitted,

> I felt no sense of responsibility for the general Cabinet policy and just pleaded my departmental case as well as I possibly could. In fact I was not the least concerned about the good of the country. I was solely concerned with looking after my department.
>
> (Crossman 1975–7: Vol. 1, 84)

Later he noted, 'We come briefed by our departments to fight for departmental budgets not as Cabinet Ministers with a Cabinet view' (1975–7: Vol. 1, 275) Barbara Castle noted that with her departmental blinkers she only discovered the policy towards Rhodesia by watching television (1984, p. 114). The former Head of the Central Policy Review Department, Sir Kenneth Berrill, observes that in Opposition Shadow Cabinets do perhaps worry about overall strategy but,

> Inevitably things are different when the shadow cabinet becomes the real cabinet and each member moves into his department, for the basis of the system is that each 'fights its own corner'. The regional departments . . . fight for the interests of their areas. Defence, Industry, Transport, Education, Health, etc. do the same. Their job is to fight for their own programmes, their own public expenditure, their own share of the legislative timetable. Inevitably they come to see the world and any proposed action in terms of the possible effect on their particular interests and objectives. So much so that after a year or two's experience at the centre one can predict with a high degree of certainty each department's arguments and views on any topic on the agenda.   (Berrill 1981: 4)

This departmentalism by Ministers can be simply diagnosed as a weakness to be remedied by selecting different, more wide-seeing individuals. But in practice the same phenomenon seems to affect all Ministers, whatever the prior judgement of their abilities. The former Conservative Minister, John Boyd-Carpenter recorded the resignations of Peter Thorneycroft (Chancellor) and his Junior Ministers, Enoch Powell and Nigel Birch from the Macmillan Cabinet in 1958 over failure by their colleagues in the Cabinet to restrain spending. Boyd-Carpenter noted that later, when he was Chief Secretary to the Treasury, Thorneycroft had returned to the Government in the Ministry of Defence,

> I was to be frequently engaged in seeking to restrain his spending as Minister of Defence. Equally Enoch Powell was, as Minister of Health, to show no undue concern at the levels of expenditure incurred by the National Health Service.
>
> (Boyd-Carpenter 1980: 140)

The most spectacular convert as she moved from a departmental to central role is Mrs Thatcher. In 1971 she claimed the success due to a Spending Minister,

> I have done anything possible to show my confidence in the future of higher education. In my monthly battles with the Treasury, I managed to get another £76 million for student grants and last week announced the biggest ever development for further education and polytechnics.
>
> (Heclo and Wildavsky 1974: 136)

The consequence of this departmentalisation is that Ministers would like to see themselves as in business for themselves, and not as the Prime Minister's branch managers (the attitude of PMs may be in conflict). Bruce Headey (1974) surveyed fifty Ministers in the early 1970s and asked them, 'What are the most important tasks a Minister has to perform? In other words, what is a good minister actually good at doing?' Only five gave answers along the lines of 'Contribute to Cabinet decisions on a wide range of issues.' This compared with forty-four who saw the major role as being departmental head. One of his Conservative respondents answered, 'The main thing is the department. This absorbs all your energies. There is not enough time to read cabinet papers.' Headey concluded,

> This tends to confirm the view . . . that in Britain we have departmental Government rather than Cabinet or parliamentary government. Ministers presumably regard their departmental work

as the most important side of their job because they believe that most policy proposals are put into near their final form within departments rather than in Cabinet. In so far as the Cabinet is important to Ministers it is seen as an inter-departmental battleground (by nineteen Ministers) rather than as a forum for collective deliberation on policy (by five Ministers).

(Headey 1974: 60)

The departmental Minister is obviously, in part, judging policies in terms of how he or she will share in the reflected glory of the activist department. But it is not simply a matter of seeking resources for the sake of it. There are problems within his/her field of concern that will respond to attention. To ask the Minister to think collectively to decide on the allocation of resources which might be applied to tackle his/her agenda, is to expect the Minister to act in a way that no head of a department in a university, factory manager or other responsible individual seems to act. The need for resources within one's own area of responsibilities is well established in one's own mind and to allow these resources to go elsewhere without a fight is to neglect one's own duties.

The former Chancellor, Nigel Lawson, has argued that the normal Cabinet meeting had no chance of becoming a grave forum of statesmanlike debate. He says that in a two and a half hour meeting there was time for each Minister to talk on average for six and a half minutes:

Small wonder then that most Ministers kept silent on most issues or confine themselves to brief but pointed questions or observations. . . Given the nature of Cabinet meetings, anyone who was inclined to talk too much would need to have something to say if he was not to forfeit the sympathy of his colleagues and the patience of the Prime Minister.

(Lawson 1993: 126)

For Crossman it was obvious that the Cabinet disintegrated into its separate parts rather than existing as a meeting of 20/22 equals. In describing his relations with Thomas Balogh, he noted that,

We clearly weren't in the same team, this is one of the real difficulties of modern Cabinet government. I had been briefed with one lot of secrets dealing with public expenditure; he had been briefed on the international crisis. Neither of us was informed about each other's sector. . .

(Crossman 1975–7: Vol. 1, 288)

Richard Marsh argued, 'Ministers are surprisingly compartmenta-
lized and separated, not merely from back-benchers . . . but even more
so from each other (1978: 89). He continued later, 'most Members
tended to find they were out of the picture on the major issues'.
(1978: 98)

Jock Bruce-Gardyne who was Economic Secretary at the Treasury in
the early 1980s has emphasised that departmental Ministers see the
support of the PM as the essence of success at Cabinet:

> Under every modern government the wise departmental minister
> seeks to sell his case to the Prime Minister in tête-à-tête. If that has
> been successfully achieved, the argument, except in rare cases of
> acute controversy and political sensitivity, is largely over; and
> another Cabinet member not directly involved who seeks to air his
> implanted wisdom on the subject might as well save his breath.
>
> (Bruce-Gardyne 1986: 239)

An early account of the Cabinet under John Major repeated the usual
comment on the more egalitarian and less cowed discussions within
Cabinet but went on to describe the 1991 Budget decisions as follows,

> But was this really any more an example of Cabinet government than
> Mrs Thatcher's way of running the Whitehall machine? The fact is
> that the central proposal of the reform package, the huge transfer of
> £4.25bn to local government, financed by VAT, was unknown to the
> large majority of the Cabinet. Indeed, when the papers for the
> following day's Cabinet meeting arrived in Ministers' private offices
> on Wednesday, 13 March, they excluded those which dealt with the
> Poll Tax. These were reserved exclusively for members of the cabinet
> sub committee on local government reform.
>
> (*Independent on Sunday,* 24 March 1991)

The picture is thus very much of a system in which Cabinet Ministers
with departments to run tend to be overwhelmed by the departmental
load and rarely see issues in terms other than, 'How it affects my
department.' In 1979 Jeremy Richardson and I described the system
as 'departmental pluralism'. This image of departmental pluralism
appears to have been undiminished under the Thatcher Governments.

As Lord Wakeham suggests, departmental Ministers are in the lead in
developing policies,

> The initiative normally rests with Government departments, where
> the specialist knowledge and expertise is concentrated and whose

Ministers are the holders of executive powers, not 'the centre'. It is just not practicable for the small team in the Downing Street complex of buildings to have the necessary depth of knowledge to drive policy forward over the whole field.

(Wakeham 1993: 5)

But he also notes that there is a sort of 'dynamic tension' between the specialist departments and the 'centre':

The main function of the centre is to ensure that proposals are fully thought through, that they take account of factors which go beyond the specialist concerns of the lead department, and that they are properly considered and subjected to collective discussion by the appropriate Ministers.

(Wakeham 1993: 5)

Clive Ponting says that,

Much of the work of Whitehall is institutionalised conflict between the competing interests of different departments. Each department will defend its own position and resist a line that, while it might be beneficial to the government as a whole or in the wider public interest, would work against the interests of the department.

(Ponting 1986: 102)

Of course, the departmental participants do not see their action as preferring the sectional to the general. They believe that what is best for their clients *is* in the public interest. Where you stand depends on where you sit.

Clive Ponting (1986: 102) observed that unemployment benefit is paid separately from social security benefit and argued that this was because of the self-interest of the Employment Department. Without this basic activity its *raison d'être* would be in jeopardy. He notes that,

Other battles reflect the differing interests of the groups that departments sponsor. Both the shipbuilding and shipping industries are in decline. But if the Department of Industry suggests that British shipowners should buy UK ships in order to support the industry the Department of Transport will, with the strong support of the General Council of British Shipping, fight any such proposal.

(Ponting 1986: 102)

Describing an example of providing for the defence of North Sea oil rigs and of providing fisheries protection vessels, Ponting points out the complex interdepartmental priorities. He concludes that policy emerges,

> not after a careful assessment of the national interest but after a balancing of various Whitehall interests. . . In many ways Ministers are simply acting as arbiters in long running and anarchic Whitehall conflicts that go on regardless of the party in power. . .
>
> (Ponting 1986: 102–3)

This is perhaps the core of the case for a strong central (prime ministerial) presence: the departments need an umpire. The Cabinet fails to provide a coherent centre. Not all Ministers are happy to accept the developing centre: predictably, though, conflict about organisation is sometimes a proxy for other conflict.

THE PM AS THE CENTRAL CO-ORDINATOR

Crossman (1972: 16) argues that in the critical early days of a Government each Cabinet Minister is trying to get hold of his own department. This is one reason he suggests that, 'the crucial decisions tend to be taken by the man at Number 10 who has no departmental responsibilities – along with his Chancellor and one or two Ministers he trusts'. He says,

> *It is the need to provide a central political power which can impose policies on Whitehall that explains and largely justifies the emergence of prime ministerial government in the form we now know it.*
>
> (Crossman 1972: 24; emphasis added)

He argued,

> Perhaps the biggest task of the Prime Minister in any radical government is to stop this fragmentation of the Cabinet into a mere collection of departmental heads.
>
> (Crossman 1972: 76)

In summary the key proposition of this chapter is that the PM acts not to usurp the Cabinet's rights but to provide the central decision-making that the Cabinet cannot deliver.

Former Head of the Prime Minister's Policy Unit under Mr Wilson and Mr Callaghan, Bernard Donoughue, has presented the role of the PM as being, to sustain and coordinate the coherence of government policy-making as a whole. . . A Prime Minister may feel that a department is, understandably, taking too narrow a departmental view, or, even more understandably that a departmental Minister is taking a view that is too politically partisan. The Prime Minister may then intervene to interpolate a wider governmental or national perspective. Conversely. . . Ministers sometimes 'go native' in their departments and the Prime Minister may feel compelled to introduce a degree of party political realism into that Minister's proposals.

(Donoughue 1987: 6)

We can add that Prime Ministers sometimes intervene simply because they think that they know better. Donoughue noted that this is not uncontroversial. He described how there is likely to be resentment when the political centre attempts to 'interfere',

intervention . . . often upset the respective departmental Ministers and officials who believe that Prime Ministers should not trespass on their policy cabbage patches (the Department of Education's reaction to Mr Callaghan's 1976 Ruskin College speech was the worst example. . .) . . . Although the general public may view the Prime Minister as having supreme power in Government, Whitehall certainly assumes and prefers that he or she . . . does not exercise it.

(Donoughue 1987: 6)

He records that when Callaghan intervened in education, 'The Department of Education was shocked. Shirley Williams who had just taken over as Secretary of State . . . was unhappy that the Prime Minister had trespassed on her ministerial territory' (Donoughue 1987: 112).

Donoughue notes that the PM has more scope to intervene in departmental business when there is a crisis;

Routine economic policy does not usually come before the Prime Minister in any systematic or meaningful way. Crisis, however, such as . . . inflation, pay policy, public expenditure, the currency, the IMF and the Winter of Discontent, require the active involvement of Cabinet and provide the Prime Minister with an opportunity to intervene.

(Donoughue 1987: 8)

Donoughue points out that the PM does have hire and fire powers that explain why he or she is normally treated with respect by Cabinet colleagues, yet as he observes there does seem to be an authority intrinsic to the position of PM. He gave the example of Callaghan who was treated very differently by friends and life-long colleagues from the moment that he became PM (1987: 13). Lord Bancroft, former Head of the Home Civil Service until 1981, commented that,

> All leaders of all parties . . . have carried . . . authority and respect – what is called in the jargon the grovel count – and . . . in this particular [Thatcher] administration . . . it was a bit higher than it had been in some others . . . more and more of the levers of effective power have been hauled into the centre of the executive, particularly of No 10 and the Cabinet Office.
>
> (Quoted in Young and Sloman 1986: 45)

But the deference to the PM is long-standing. Simon James points out that in 1879 Gladstone had observed that,

> Nothing of great importance is matured or would even be projected in any department without his cognizance, and any weighty business would commonly go to him before being submited to the Cabinet.
>
> (James 1992: 114)

Waltz (1968: 36) reminds us that in the nineteenth century George Carslake Thompson, thinking of Palmerston and especially of Disraeli, identified tendencies that would cause the Constitution 'of its own accord to slide, involuntarily, almost imperceptibily, towards a Caesarism'.

James quotes George Mallaby who served as a civil servant under every Prime Minister from Chamberlain to Macmillan,

> The deference accorded to every British Prime Minister by his Cabinet colleagues is very striking indeed . . . they will accept his reproofs. They will hurry, like schoolboys, to do his bidding.
>
> (Mallaby 1965, cited in James 1992: 94)

He also quotes John Boyd-Carpenter (1980) who emphasised that only those who had served in Government fully realised the gulf between a PM and even the next most senior colleagues.

Richard Crossman (1972: 47) claimed that Ministers were all too aware that they served at the PM's whim. He said that, 'it is far more difficult to drop a member of the Russian Presidium than a British Cabinet Minister. . .' Nicholas Ridley in *My Style of Government* (1992), agreed that Mrs Thatcher made 'sure she got her way'. While failing to see much wrong with the practice, he confirmed that the Cabinet was a sort of rubber stamp.

Margaret Thatcher saw the cabinet as very much a formal body. She did not see it as a body to take decisions, except for decisions of the greatest importance. She saw it as the forum in which all important activities of government were brought together and reported upon. She saw it as the body to approve individual ministers' policies.

(Ridley 1992: 28)

She didn't believe the Cabinet should decide on contentious issues; she never took matters there to a vote.

(Ridley 1992: 25)

He accepted in a way that many previous Ministers would reject (1992: 28), that the Prime Minister carried the full responsibility for the activities of all Ministers and so, 'Cabinet ministers have no status or independent positions: that they are there to help the Prime Minister, and at the Prime Minister's pleasure.'

According to Ridley, Cabinet was the 'court of appeal' to which any Cabinet Minister could take a disagreement with his Cabinet colleagues and have it decided. He said that he recalled this happening only twice. The first occasion resulted in Heseltine's resignation. The second concerned Hailsham's disagreement with his colleagues on a Cabinet committee over the breaking of the monopolies of barristers and solicitors.

She was the Prime Minister, she knew what she wanted to do and she didn't believe her policies should be subject to being voted down by a group she had selected to advise and assist her. Just as an American President would never allow himself to be outvoted by his Cabinet, so too did Margaret Thatcher believe she had every right to retain the initiative as head of Government. Anyone who did not like her policies could resign. Indeed she had the power to dismiss those who were not likeminded. I can remember only one occasion when a formal vote was actually taken in Cabinet.

(Ridley 1992: 30)

This confirms that collective responsibility was the duty to agree with the Prime Minister. This point will be argued in more detail in Chapter 7. However, this description does not add up to a totally dominant PM but to one that has particular strengths in the event of disagreement. Donoughue, too, remarks that most policies start somewhere else:

Policies are not generally born in No 10; it is more usual for them to be finalised there. Many begin with party programmes. . . Other

policies are generated in the relevant Whitehall Ministry; every
department has its inherited history of views . . . individual Ministers
do themselves have policy preferences. . . Outside pressure groups
gtalso have a major influence. . .

(Donoughue 1987: 5)

The thrust of this section has been to argue Crossman's proposition
that the PM has taken a policy lead not to undermine the collective
Cabinet but to *substitute a collective capacity because Cabinet itself was not
performing that role.* This interpretation is unambiguously confirmed by
Nigel Lawson. He argued,

Why did the colleagues allow her to govern in the way she did? While
spinelessness or careeerism may be adequate explanation in the case
of some, it will not do for all. And belief in her infallibility was even
more narrowly shared. . . But beyond this, *her method of Cabinet
Government was accepted because in many ways it was highly convenient to her
colleagues.* Most Cabinet Ministers, particularly after a longish period
in government, tend to be preoccupied with fighting their own battles
and pursuing the issues in their own bailiwick, and lose interest in the
wider picture. . . I suspect that any Prime Minister so long in office is
likely to develop along the lines she did – which, to repeat, was far
from inconvenient to individual Ministers most of the time. . .

(Lawson 1993: 129 emphasis added)

ORCHESTRATING THE CENTRE: PRIME MINISTERIAL CO-ORDINATION

Power drained (further) from the Cabinet under Mrs Thatcher. Cabinets
met under an average of once a week – half the previous average. But as
we have noted this did not increase the significance of the Cabinet
committees under Mrs Thatcher. Hennessy reports that Cabinet papers
were down to 60–70 per year – one-sixth of the flow in the 1950s.

Instead of using the formal Cabinet committee system – with its
expectation that all relevant views are represented, Mrs Thatcher
seemed to prefer less systematic meetings with a carefully selected group
– or even one-to-one sessions with the Minister in question. Hennessy
(1986) describes these latter meetings as follows,

She further syringes the collective marrow from the bones of Cabinet
government by engaging in what one official calls judge and jury
sessions (in which she acts as judge and jury in her own cause). A

minister is invited to prepare a paper to her, not the Cabinet, he then appears, plus departmental team, at No 10 before Mrs Thatcher and her team. Such occasions are not the highlight of ministerial lives. . .

(Hennessy 1986: 142)

In this system the Cabinet is not the focus of collective decision-making; it is the forum where the PM might occasionally be told 'of things which we will not put up with,' but the last resort examples of the Cabinet's reluctance, post 'Westland', to sanction the British Leyland sale are not the stuff of generalisations about the normal practice.

Sir Frank Cooper has argued that, 'The collective activity of the Cabinet as a whole has diminished.' He also notes that the influence of No. 10 has grown over the whole of Government and even over the Cabinet Office. Colin Campbell's interviews found a very similiar picture,

Under the last administration, we had a committee . . . that looked at incomes and this wretched committee used to meet about twice a week and they used to get into the most incredible, mind blowing detail . . . so [now] you don't have any of that. It is true that the prime minister does have ad hoc meetings with ministers directly concerned. . . Then . . . if this is of any importance, she will take it to cabinet or to a cabinet committee.

(Campbell 1983: 73)

One of Peter Hennessy's civil servant sources complained,

Does it matter that temporarily we don't have cabinet government? Does it matter in Parliament that the Minister is the monkey?. . . we have a form of presidential government in which she operates like a sovereign in her court.

(Hennessy 1986: 99).

Francis Pym wrote,

She would ideally like to run the major Departments herself and tried her best to do so – not just in terms of overall policy, but in strategic detail. This is neither practical nor desirable. Policy and decision-making require a full and careful understanding of many facts and considerations . . . she cannot know enough to dictate the policy of each Department . . . her response has been to expand the Downing Street staff to include experts in every major area, thus establishing a government within a government . . . no one can object to having a

well-informed Prime Minister, but I object to a system that deliberately pits Downing Street against individual departments, breeds
resentment amongst Ministers and Civil Servants and turns the
Prime Minister into a president. . . I do not like the growing
tendency for ministers (and Civil Servants) to be accountable to
Downing Street, and only accountable to Parliament as agents of
the Prime Minister.

(Pym 1984: 16)

There is perhaps a logical difficulty in the picture in the Wonder
Woman version of the PM – dashing from crisis to crisis, looking over
the shoulders of all the Ministers at once. As the job of PM becomes
more time-consuming, as he or she is involved in international affairs,
humouring the British media, appearing in Parliament, acting as chief
export salesperson, being head of party . . . there is not the time for the
PM to be very effective at interfering in departmental affairs.

There are in fact at least three options when considering the position
of the Cabinet and the PM. There is romantic collective responsibility in
which the colleagues discuss all important business; there is caricature
prime ministerialism in which the PM has an absolute power. Obviously
neither of these is sustainable, but there is a third position – what we
might label the Inner Circle approach. It is clear that all Cabinet
members are not equal. This is a fact that is confirmed by the attention
paid to the order in which the names in the Cabinet are announced. Mrs
Thatcher's former minister, David Howell, claimed that five or six
people tend to be all important,

five or six is what you need and that's what any prime minister tends
to form around them.

(in Hennessy 1986: 96)

Cabinets tend to have a top tier. If perfect Cabinet Government
doesn't exist, it does not automatically follow that the system is prime
ministerial. If the PM can square the inner core there is no basis for
successful challenge, but the PM is not unfettered. (Though the PM can
– eventually – determine who is in the inner circle.) The Prime Minister
thus needs the acquiescence of other 'big hitters' in the Cabinet, but it is
true that as the case of Mrs Thatcher shows, even those big hitters seen
as rivals can be marginalised.

The Prime Minister cannot be involved in everything but he or she
can be involved where they choose. In a *Dispatches* programme (Channel
4, 24 April 1991) Kenneth Clarke noted that the increased prominence

of Prime Minister's Question Time in the Commons in recent decades had greatly enhanced the role of the PM *vis-à-vis* departmental colleagues. As there is now virtually no topic on which the PM will decline to answer, the PM's staff has the right and need to be briefed by departments in all areas. The idea that departments run their independent policy domains is thus now subject to the possible intervention of the PM's staff under the real (or fabricated) need to brief the PM on a likely question.

Similarly, in his memoirs, Jim Callaghan pointed out,

> To a large extent the Prime Minister marks his own pace. It is the Prime Minister himself who takes the initiatives, who pokes about where he chooses and creates his own waves.
>
> (Callaghan 1987: 403)

But is is not necessarily the case that a strong Prime Minister is imposing him or herself on a relevant Cabinet. The central argument of this chapter is that the Prime Minister is obliged to act as a central co-ordinator.

Thus the PM – *and the central institutions associated with him or her* – seems to be vital in shaping such central policy as is made in Britain. This is the basis of the complaint that there is prime ministerial Government. However, while the PM is criticised on that flank, ironically (as considered at the end of this chapter) the other major discussion point on these matters is that there is none the less insufficient central strategic thinking.

THE ORGANISATION(S) AT THE CENTRE

Campbell's book on *Governments Under Stress* is a very useful comparative source. As noted in Chapter 2 its message is that political systems of different constitutional types have to face similar issues in the management of policy-making. His book focuses on 'the operation of central agencies' in Britain, the USA and Canada. He says, 'these departments, agencies and offices perform the functions essential to coordination and control of bureaucracy throughout government'. He goes on,

> The growth of central agencies and the consolidation of executive authority appear to be inextricably linked. This phenomenon has given rise, in each of the three countries, to recurrent concerns that improved central agency resources will concentrate power in the hands of the chief executive or an inner circle of the cabinet.
>
> (Campbell 1983: 3–4)

The argument in this section is that the organisations at the centre are the support needed by the PM in his or her attempt to exert control over the tendencies to fragmentation and departmentalism: this is the source of the so called 'presidentialism'.

Writing generally about the issue of bureaucratic control, Hoggett has noted that one response to the inevitable development of organisational segmentalism or departmentalism has been a tradition of centralisation,

> Centralized units devoted to development of corporate strategy grew like Topsy, budget making processes became geared to undermining the dysfunctional autonomy of the corporate sub units, the culture of mistrust necessitated the enforcement of the principle of 'delegation upwards', and so on.
>
> (Hoggett 1990: 10)

Hoggett (1991: 247) notes that in general the centre of bureaucracies adopt a policy role that seeks to combat disintegration. The development of the PM and his central machinery needs to be examined in such a light.

Campbell warns against taking too seriously a distinction based on the superficial qualities of the presidential/parliamentary models. Campbell thus takes a very different line from that argued by Clive Ponting, who complained that,

> There is a hole in the centre of British government. The institutions at the centre of Whitehall are small scale and act not as strong central policy makers but as co-ordinators of the powerful Whitehall departments.
>
> (Ponting 1986: 104)

On the Ponting side of the argument are other sources such as Sir John Hoskyns (former head of the Policy Unit under Mrs Thatcher) who characterised Whitehall as a 'headless chicken'. Indeed, as will be discussed in a later section (see pp. 134–6), the bulk of insider comment on Whitehall by former Ministers and civil servants is in line with the Ponting view that Britain is weak at the centre and should be strengthened: this near unanimity is, however, balanced by Campbell's arguments in 1983 which were derived from a comparative focus.

Campbell claimed that the concentration of executive power is a consequence of a necessary response to problems. It is a reaction to complexity rather than a gratuitous degradation of the traditional procedures and constitutional proverbs. He records the drift in different political systems towards an enhancement of resources reporting to the chief executive. He does admit (citing Richard Rose and Peter Self) that there appears to be a law of diminishing returns; that staff at the centre can become part of the problem rather than the solution.

He provides estimates of the number of senior staff at the centre of the three systems:

- USA 385
- UK 481
- Canada 221

It is impossible to read these figures as a definite statement that Britain has more senior staff at the centre than does the US but it at least gives cause to doubt the conventional wisdom that would place the US as the best staffed centre. Campbell describes how the Cabinet Office and the (then) Central Policy Review Staff (CPRS) existed as a highly developed machinery for assisting the Cabinet and its committees in mapping out strategy (1983: 50). J.M. Lee (1974) in his pioneering chapter on central capability noted that between 1966 and 1971 the number of senior administrative staff in the Cabinet Office increased almost threefold. He presented the increase of those ranked Principal and above from seventeen in 1963 to sixty-two in 1973.

PRIME MINISTER'S OFFICE (i.e. No. 10)

The most obvious candidate for the job of centrally organising policy is the PM's Office or No. 10. The terms cover a series of small organisations, but most importantly the Private Office.

Private Office

Campbell describes the PM's Office as a staff of seventy crammed into No. 10 Downing Street. He claims that many British respondents made much of the fact that No. 10 falls far short of the White House both in size and accommodation.

> They overstate the reality. In Washington, the most vital segment of the presidential staff uses quarters in the west wing of the White House that are almost as cramped for space . . . in looking at No 10 one should remember that much of its compactness relates to a tendency among staffers who must be close to the chief decision-maker and one another to bunch up in the nooks and crannies of hopelessly congested facilities.
>
> (Campbell 1983: 50)

This is to make the point that the apparently hopeless congestion at the centre of the British machine is functional in that it prevents dangerous gaps in information; everyone is aboard the same ship.

The Private Office is headed by a Deputy Secretary/Grade II civil servant (normally) with the title of Principal Private Secretary to the Prime Minister. Campbell points out that in a mainstream department a Deputy Secretary is entitled to a large room with a large desk, a sofa, and a large table for meetings. He recorded that in No. 10 he/she shares two small rooms adjacent to the PM with four other private secretaries, the personal assistant to the PM and a duty clerk. The Deputy Secretary screens all material that converges from Whitehall. Three of the private secretaries (at Principal or Assistant Secretary level) cover specific areas of governmental business:

- one seconded from the FCO (normally for roughly two/three years) superintends overseas matters;
- one seconded from the Treasury watches the economy and industry;
- one (usually from a relevant department) concentrates on home affairs.

The fourth private secretary devotes his or her attention to delivering and preparing briefings for the PM's twice-weekly Question Time in the House of Commons.

Until 1992 the Foreign Office representative in the Private Office was Charles Powell – although his secondment dated back to 1984. This seemed to reflect his extraordinary closeness to Mrs Thatcher, and shows how at the 'centre' exceptions are nearly the rule.

Campbell argues that the members of the 'mainstream' Private Office perform a threefold function. The first is intelligence gathering – for which their pre-existing knowledge of the subject matter and the networks of relevant officials prepares them. He quotes a respondent who made the point that the congested working conditions help translate the intelligence of the individual into common property.

> Since we all live, work, in two very overcrowded offices . . . then in the course of the day one thing after another will be the subject of discussion between us as to whether we should get some more advice on this, what's going on on that, what we think about this.
>
> (Campbell 1983: 52)

George Jones similiarly stresses the way in which the physical proximity of the private secretaries encourages co-ordination by the Office;

Each has his own main concern, but is not limited just to sticking to his range of responsibilities. . . They overhear conversations, they chat together about business, and they dip into each other's work trays. When work has been finished it is put in a tray, the 'dip', and each secretary can go along and 'dip' in and see what the others have been doing. . . this need to interchange with each other is reinforced by a rota system for the evenings and holidays so that one of them is always available to take over the work of the others.

(in King 1985: 77)

This 'dipping' needs to be underlined as quite contrary to a general Whitehall concern that departments keep off the turf of their neighbours. The second function identified for the Private Office is to organise the PM's advice filling the red boxes that organise the PM's work pattern.

Third, the Private Secretaries act to transmit the PM's views to the departments. Campbell (1983: 52) says that this often is more than the circulation of information as the Private Secretaries have to be prepared to provide interpretation for the departments and to 'read the PM's mind'. The former Ambassador to the US, Sir Nicholas Henderson, has described how the Prime Minister's Private Office communicates with the Private Offices of the other Ministers.

A Minister may often wish, before considering some new policy or some proposals for eventual submission to Cabinet, to know how it will be viewed by one of his Ministerial colleagues and the latter's department. He may, of course, have a chance to ask the Minister himself. But often he will leave it to his Private Office to find out how the wind sits in other quarters of Whitehall, particularly at No 10.

(Henderson 1984: 113)

He noted slightly later:

the Private Office network throughout Whitehall is, therefore, of value to Ministers in helping them to know what to expect from their colleagues when it comes to meetings.

(Henderson 1984: 113)

He described the status of the staff in the PM's Private Office as greatly exceeding their nominal rank,

Seconded from their different departments of Whitehall and known for their competence and adaptability, it is amazing how quickly the Private Secretaries, once they arrive at No 10, come to adjust themselves to their new altitude. The senior ones manage to throw off all former diffidence of manner, the hallmark of the civil servant. They succeed effortlessly in rising above the narrow horizons of their parent departments. They often appear to find no difficulty in discarding the official mentality altogether and in identifying themselves with their political master, cursing the various ministries and their entire staff as dry as dust neutrals.

(Henderson 1984: 114)

Statements about two-year secondments to the Private Office perhaps underplay the extent of continuity at the centre. In fact there tends to be a cadre of civil servants with a 'homing instinct' that sees them return to the centre in different guises. Robert Armstong was Principal Private Secretary from 1970–5. He moved to departmental work before returning to Downing Street as Cabinet Secretary to Mrs Thatcher in 1979. Sir Kenneth Stowe was Under Secretary and then Deputy Secretary at the Cabinet Office from 1973–9, ending up as Principal Private Secretary. Burke Trend was Deputy from 1956–9 to Norman Brook who was Cabinet Secretary from 1947–63 – and succeeded him in 1963. John Hunt was Brook's private secretary for two years in the 1950s and succeeded Burke Trend as Cabinet Secretary – after serving as Deputy to Trend (Hennessy 1986: 19–21). There is a constant temptation by Prime Ministers to prefer known faces and working habits and accordingly to erode the temporary rotation principle.

Many senior mandarins serve in No. 10 or the Cabinet Office without later serving large chunks of their career there, but the *possibility* that they might be selected to return perhaps colours their relations with the senior staff at the centre. The fact that the Cabinet Secretary has latterly also been in a vital position with regard to promotions as head of the civil service, has been another minor increment to the power of the centre.

The Political Office

As discussed in detail by Jones (in King 1985), the Downing Street map is unreliable to the extent that a great number of *ad hoc* arrangements have been made. Harold Wilson had Marcia Williams as Political and Personal Secretary (paid by Harold Wilson) whereas Mr Macmillan had John Wyndham who was unpaid but listed as a private secretary like the other civil service private secretaries. Mr Heath had Douglas Hurd as his Political Secretary. There is no clear line saying which appointments in this area are civil servants, which temporary civil servants paid by public funds, and which are to be paid by party or other outside funds (Jones, in King 1985: 81) The personal assistant looks after the PM's diary. There is also a fringe of special personal advisers. For example Mrs Thatcher had David Wolfson as political 'chief of staff' (Jones, in King 1985: 91) and advisers such as, for some time, Alan Walters on economic policy and Sir Percy Cradock on foreign affairs.

Parliamentary Private Secretary

This post held by a junior politician in the Commons is usually seen as being a very useful stepping stone to full Ministerial Office and is usually held by a Member of Parliament identified as loyal and able to represent the PM's views effectively and informally to back-benchers.

The Press Secretary

This position has moved into prominence; it has a word-of-mouth importance that greatly exceeds the importance of the post in terms of formal powers. The recent appointments of Joe Haines (for Harold Wilson), Tom McCaffrey (for Jim Callaghan) and Bernard Ingham (for Mrs Thatcher) all have been credited as key policy advisers as well as having a formal position as being in charge of the orchestration of relations with the press. Donoughue (1987: 25) suggested Joe Haines was, 'possessed [of] remarkable political insight and judgement and for most of the 1974–6 period he was effectively the Prime Minister's main political adviser'.

The fact that the PM has a skilled disseminator of news – from his or her point of view – is a useful way to diminish opposition in the Cabinet. Crossman observed that the PM has a personal control of Government publicity. He said the press relations means,

> we have a daily coherent, central explanation of what the Government is doing an explanation naturally in terms the Prime Minister thinks right

(Crossman 1972: 67)

Francis Pym complained that,

> All Governments want a favourable Press. . . but this Government [Thatcher] goes further than most. Increasingly, Ministerial and Departmental press releases are channelled through Downing Street

and suppressed or modified as necessary. The notorious leaks have emanated as much from Downing Street as from anywhere else. The Press receives a very good service from Number 10, which is perhaps why much of it is so uncritical.

(Pym 1984: 18)

When Bernard Ingham assumed the role of Chief of the Information Service this was held by critics as increasing his capacity to influence 'the line' in the operating departments. Gus O'Donnell, who succeeded Bernard Ingham, was in his time seen as a less active 'voice'. According to Sir Frank Cooper (1986), commenting on the Ingham years,

The aim now is the management of the media with a very much higher degree of central control from No. 10 Downing Street . . . there is now public relations which I would define as biased information. I suggest that the post of Chief Information Officer at No. 10 Downing Street is in fact a political job in a party sense and is not a job which it is proper for a civil servant to fill unless he, or she, resigns from the Civil Service on appointment.

(Cooper 1986: 23)

Policy Unit

This part of the Prime Minister's Office was created by Harold Wilson as a means to provide a more orderly location on the wall chart for the special advisers the PM had accumulated. It acts as the French-style Cabinet for the PM (Hennessy 1986: 82). The main weakness of the Policy Unit appears to be its small size and a potential for the career civil service to freeze it out of deliberations if it is seen as too political. When Campbell was doing his fieldwork the Unit was headed by Bernard Donoughue, a former politics lecturer from the LSE, and a small number of policy specialists: in 1993 there were seven members of the Unit under Sarah Hogg. The press release that announced the creation of the Policy Unit in 1974 said that, '[it] would assist in the development of the whole range of policies contained in the Government's programme, especially those arising in the short and medium term'. According to Donoughue (1987: 31) this was an attempt to distinguish it from the CPRS which had longer-term horizons (see Chapter 2). The Policy Unit appointments are more obviously partisan than those of the CPRS, which seemed to strive for detachment in a way that worried some Prime Ministers.

An internal memorandum approved by Mr Wilson said,

> The Unit must ensure that the Prime Minister is aware of what is coming up from departments to the Cabinet. It must scrutinise papers, contact departments, know the background to policy decisions, disputes and compromises and act as an early warning system.
>
> (Cited in Donoughue 1987: 22)

Donoughue says the Unit also picked up the role of 'guardian of the manifesto' that had been reduced in importance within the CPRS,

> The Prime Minister has assumed responsibility as custodian of the Labour manifesto. The Unit must assist in that role, making sure that the manifesto is not contravened not retreated from, without proper discussion and advance warning . . . the individual Ministries must not become isolated from the Government as a whole and lapse into traditional 'departmental views'.
>
> (Donoughue 1987: 22)

Donoughue obtained the right to attend most official committees, Cabinet committees with the PM in the chair, many other Cabinet committees, some full Cabinets, and the meeting of the 'future business' committee chaired by the Cabinet Secretary. He was required to give an undertaking not to show papers of official committees to the Prime Minister or to report the views of individual officials to him. Apparently this was,

> not just to preserve the freedom of official discussion of issues at a preliminary stage but more importantly to respect the position of departmental Ministers. . .
>
> (Donoughue 1987: 23)

An example of the way the PM could use the Policy Unit to support him against members of the Cabinet is recounted by Peter Hennessy:

> Tony Benn, his Industry Secretary, was wedded, in a fashion that the Prime Minister found highly inconvenient, to the manifesto pledges on greater public ownership and planning. Wilson used both his Policy Unit, which contained a special 'Benn watcher', the economist Richard Graham, and the Cabinet machinery to geld Benn's favoured strategy. Industrial policy was effectively hijacked from the Department of Industry to No 10 and the Cabinet's Public Enterprise Committee. . .
>
> (Hennessy 1986: 86)

This unusually clear case of a PM who did not back his Minister obviously caused divided loyalties for the departmental civil servants. Tony Benn felt that the civil service failure to actively promote his views was evidence of some anti-socialist bias. The simpler answer is that the civil servants preferred to take their cues from the PM. (For a fuller discussion see James 1992).

THE CABINET OFFICE

The Cabinet Secretariat is housed next door to No. 10. Though in theory the No. 10 staff work directly for the PM and the Cabinet Office serves the Cabinet as a whole, given the dominance by the PM of the Cabinet there is no fundamental difference in function apparent in the roles. Indeed, different PMs will find certain personalities more attractive to work with and hence whether the Cabinet Secretary or the (technically more junior) Principal Private Secretary is the PM's main adviser need not be consistent (see Donoughue 1987: 218–19).

Jones (in King 1985: 79) remarks that the Private Office is likely to select and annotate papers that go to the PM, 'From their central vantage point, they might spot something. . . neglected by departments that might be somewhat blinkered. . .' He says,

> There are basically two streams of paper to the Prime Minister, those from the ministers' departments directly and those channelled through the Cabinet Office. The Cabinet Office itself is also performing a filtering, commenting, co-ordinating role, and the Private Office feels less need to comment on their submissions.
>
> (Quoted in King 1985: 79)

Jones makes the vital point that,

> At the top in politics, sharp distinctions do not count. All is ambiguity and shading. . . At Number 10 distinctions are blurred. It is hard to sustain sharp divisions between official, political and personal roles.
>
> (Quoted in King 1985: 86–7)

Campbell says one could not quarrel with assertions that the Cabinet Office is busy but one rejects that it is small. He says that in 1981 the Cabinet Office housed 'a Permanent Secretary, 3 Deputy Secretaries, 5 Under Secretaries, 10 Assistant Secretaries, 27 Principals, 6 military advisers' (1983: 56) – making a total of fifty-two personnel. By adding in the eighteen staff of the then CPRS he arrives at a total of seventy for the Cabinet Office. As recorded earlier, Campbell says that Jimmy

Carter had a Domestic Policy Staff with some twenty-six appointees, mostly youngish and new to Government. He contrasts this with the pattern in Britain where,

> In the UK Cabinet Office, for instance, some 48 senior career officials run secretariats for the cabinet and interdepartmental committees and provide briefing material for the prime minister. Another 5 career officials working in two rooms right next to the prime minister in 10 Downing Street operate an intelligence system geared to assuring that she keeps her hands on the most important levers in Whitehall. A further 18 senior professionals, seconded from government and the private sector, advise the cabinet and prime minister on issues that require longer term analysis. . .
>
> (Campbell 1983: 5)

Campbell's suspicion that the central capability of the US system is exaggerated outside the US is endorsed by insider accounts such as by Reagan's former Head of OMB, David Stockman (1986). He describes a shambolic amateurism in the worst sense as a new President tried to put new appointees into place. For example Stockman notes of himself, 'As I started work in my new office, I began fully to comprehend how ill-prepared I was for the job ahead' (1986: 107). He describes how they ended up taking vital early decisions without staff in place, '[the] personnel operation was overwhelmed with several thousand slots to fill. As a result there were empty desks all over Washington. Most cabinet secretaries hadn't even got their top policy deputies approved. There was a vacuum in their outer offices' (1986: 107). In his first week in post he reached the very British type conclusion:

> It'll be the people in the Executive Office versus the cabinet departments like it always is. The cabinet secretaries are getting domesticated by their people, by their permanent bureaucracies.
>
> (Stockman 1986: 110)

The British Cabinet Office is organised into six secretariats under their own Deputy Secretaries (see Seldon 1990: 107).

- Overseas and Defence;
- Economic Affairs;
- Home and Parliamentary Affairs;
- European Affairs;
- Science and Technology;
- Security and Intelligence.

These secretariats expanded in the 1970s. Lee (1990: 237) argues that this expansion allowed them to perform a different role. Senior officials came not simply to run the procedures of interdepartmental negotiation at Cabinet level but also to be knowledgeable about particular policy communities. In other words the central staff became something of a counter-bureaucracy to challenge the departmental expertise. The secretariat serves the Cabinet committees of Ministers (and the shadowing official committees) that cover 'their patch'.

It is the provision of a Cabinet Office support that essentially defines a Cabinet committee and distinguishes it from another interdepartmental meeting. The Cabinet Secretary acts as adviser to the PM and chairs official committees on matters regarded as especially important by the PM. He chairs the weekly meetings of permanent secretaries in his capacity as Head of the Home Civil Service.

One of Campbell's British sources claimed that,

> The Cabinet Office doesn't and oughtn't sort of develop its own policies. . . But there is very often a role for us to do, knocking departmental heads together.
>
> (Campbell 1983: 56)

Seldon concludes that the Cabinet Office is not very significant. He quoted from interviews,

> I never thought [Cabinet Office] officials had any influence at all. I was constantly surprised that such clever men were content to preoccupy themselves on such pedestrian tasks . . . throughout my years in the civil service, I always thought the importance of the Cabinet Office was greatly exaggerated.
>
> (Seldon 1990: 121)

J.M. Lee (1990) argues that perhaps this accepts too readily the official self-image that Seldon's respondents were deliberately or unselfconsciously projecting. He says that senior officials all wish to be remembered for their procedural efficiency and to deny that they exercised personal influence. Lee simply does not believe the homogenised version of the Cabinet Office role that accepts statements such as 'the agenda largely decides itself'.

Donoughue claimed that apart from its basic role as the administration centre for the civil service the Cabinet Office *has* acquired an independent policy-making role.

In practice, led by an ambitious Cabinet Secretary, backed by a swelling staff of over 500, and particularly aided by the CPRS, the Cabinet Office clearly exercised policy influence. . . the increase in the policy influence of the Cabinet Office caused displeasure to some departmental Ministers who often complained to me about the intrusion of this extra policy arm.

(Donoughue 1987: 28)

Donoughue wrote that,

The Cabinet Secretary is, of course, supposed to serve the whole cabinet but, in practice, where there is a conflict between the Prime Minister's interests and a Cabinet Minister's interests, he is always tempted to give priority to his final master and centre of power, the Prime Minister. . .

(Donoughue 1987: 29)

Another of Campbell's respondents tiptoed around the issue of the degree to which the Cabinet Office is a *de facto* PM's department,

In this country. . . we haven't got a Prime Minister's department, in theory the Cabinet Office serves all Ministers; in practice it serves the prime minister a good deal more than anyone else. He has, at No 10, very efficient private secretaries who can deal with his daily life. . . But, they, when they want advice, almost always look here. I don't want to pretend we are a prime minister's department . . . we haven't got that position yet . . . but we are the department that services him.

(Campbell 1983: 58)

Donoughue says that as PM Jim Callaghan contemplated the idea of a permanent Prime Minister's department as a tidier alternative to the administratively confused non-system of units at the centre of Government, but he concluded,

You know, I can pull all the levers I want and it does not matter too much whether the signals go into No 10 or into the Cabinet Office, or into the Lord Privy Seal's office or whatever.

(Donoughue 1987: 31)

COMMITTEE NETWORK

It is necessary to look at the Whitehall and Cabinet committee systems for two reasons. First, it appears to be where the bulk of decision-making takes place and hence it is as important to look at the Cabinet committees as it is to look at the Cabinet itself. Seldon (1990: 111) claims that although the Cabinet was the critical decision-making body as late as 1973, by the time John Hunt left as Cabinet Secretary in 1979 the principal standing committees had virtually replaced it as the principal axes through which decisions were made. Former Minister, Kenneth Baker has argued that,

> Under Thatcher, much of the debate on major governmental issues was held in cabinet committees: for particularly critical issues, she took the chair herself.
>
> (*Sunday Times*, 5 September 1993)

This was confirmed by Nigel Lawson:

> The imprimatur of the Cabinet was taken seriously, and there were occasional Cabinet meetings that really mattered, such as those that concluded the annual expenditure round. But in general and for good reason, key decisions were taken in smaller groups – either the formal Cabinet committees, of which the most important (such as the Overseas and Defence Committee, and the two main economic policy Committees . . .) were, like the Cabinet itself, chaired by the Prime Minister; or at still smaller informal meetings of Ministers which she would usually hold in her study upstairs. The Cabinet's customary role was to rubber stamp decisions that had already been taken, to keep all colleagues reasonably informed about what was going on, and to provide a forum for general political discussion if time permitted.
>
> (Lawson 1993: 125)

There is a second reason, however, for looking at the committee system. The core argument here is that the move to handle business outside the Cabinet has been a means to increase prime ministerial influence as he/she can, in effect, choose the pitch and the players. Seldon says (1990: 111), 'Mrs Thatcher's preference was for taking decisions outside full Cabinet in subordinate bodies over which she has felt, . . . she had more control.' In 1986 Mrs Thatcher herself commented along lines we have already seen from Nigel Lawson,

> The idea that you could run things competently by [taking] everything to Cabinet is nonsense. There are 21 Members of Cabinet. On one issue if they all speak [for] two minutes that's forty two minutes. Most things are done in Cabinet committee and reported to Cabinet.
>
> (Cited in Doherty 1988: 55)

The former Permanent Secretary at the MOD, Sir Frank Cooper, gave a lecture in 1986 with the title 'Changing the Establishment'. In this he argued that,

> The Cabinet committee system plays an increasingly large role in Government, largely, . . . for convenience and essentially practical reasons. For example, it is unrealistic to suppose that the full cabinet can be assembled frequently enough to discuss the many matters which theoretically could come before it. Furthermore, bringing more than 20 people together to discuss issues in which many cabinet members do not have the time to play any useful role – even if they had the inclination – is not a sensible way of using that scarce commodity, namely Ministerial time. Hence, the great majority of issues are disposed of in Cabinet committees.
>
> (Cooper 1986: 16–17)

Cooper observed that while there was nothing constitutionally wrong with this practice, what was objectionable was that the existence and composition of these bodies were 'secret'. He termed this camouflage of the operations of Government as 'bizarre'. He contrasted the position with that in Parliament and local government and concluded that such secrecy about the existence and membership of committees simply cheapened the notion of secrecy and security.

The significance of the committee system was underlined when Crossman complained,

> I became more and more aware of how fictitious Cabinet government really is. The big issue to be decided concerned . . . Rhodesia . . . So at this point the Cabinet is sent out of the room and the Chiefs of Staff come in. It's the Defence Committee who manage Rhodesia. But at least that consists of half the Cabinet whereas the committee which is secretly preparing the budget consists of only Harold [Wilson], George [Brown] and Jim [Callaghan]. So the two main decisions to be taken in defence and finance are lifted entirely out of the hands of the Cabinet. . . I feel a sense of anticlimax . . . with the idea of just carrying on as a departmental Minister. I have had enough of it and now I want to be a Cabinet Minister. . . [This is] more and more a fictitious Cabinet, where none of the real issues are discussed. . .
>
> (Crossman 1975–7: Vol. 1, 499)

The widespread breaching of the secrecy of the existence of the main committee led Mrs Thatcher to announce the name and chair of the

Table 4.1 The four major committees, 1979

Title	Chair
Defence and Overseas Policy	PM
Economic Affairs	PM
Home and Legal Affairs	Home Secretary
Legislation	Lord Chancellor

Table 4.2 Main elements of the committee system, 1992

Ministerial committees	Ministerial sub-committees
Econ. & Dom. Policy (EDP)	
Def. & Overseas Policy (OPD)	European Questions (OPD(E))
Gulf (OPDG)	
	Eastern Europe (OPD(AE))
Nuclear Def Policy (OPDN)	
	Terrorism (OPD(T))
European Security (OPDSE)	
Hong Kong & Other Dependent Territories (OPDK)	
Northern Ireland (NI)	
Science and Technology (EDS)	
Intelligence Services (IS)	
Industrial, Commercial & Consumer Affairs (EDI)	Public Sector Pay (EDI(P))
Environment (EDE)	
Home and Social Affairs (EDH)	Health Strategy (EDH(H))
	Drug Misuse (EDH(D))
	Urban Policy (EDH(U))
	Alcohol Misuse (EDH(A))
	Women's Issues (EDH(W))
Local Government (EDL)	London EDL(L)
Queen's Speech & Future Legislation (FLG)	
Legislation (LG)	
Civil Service Pay (EDC)	

four major committees in 1979 (see Table 4.1). The composition and existence of a sub-committee of the Defence and Overseas Committee (labelled OD, i.e. overseas and defence matters) was revealed at the time of the Falklands war when the existence of the war Cabinet and its tag – OD (SA) – was made public. ('SA' stood for South Atlantic.) In 1992 the main elements (then) of the committee system were revealed (see Table 4.2). By 1994 an extra committee on Regeneration, Chaired by Lord Wakeham, was in place. Its remit is 'to consider regeneration policies and their coordination'.

There are committees of two main types: the first (including those we have just been discussing) are the permanent standing committees (which, though 'permanent', change title and substantially alter their patterns of sub-committees) and *ad hoc* committees to deal with one-off matters. The barrier between the two types often seems insignificant with a sub-committee of a standing committee being functionally interchangeable with an *ad hoc* committee. The initials used to identify permanent committees varies by Prime Minister to help distinguish the papers of different administrations. Thus the Economic Committee is EDP under Mr Major, was EA (Economic Affairs) under Mrs Thatcher, but was EY (Economy) under Mr Callaghan. The *ad hoc* committee series alternates between MISC (Miscellaneous) and GEN (General).

An example of the Miscellaneous type was a Committee MISC 127 chaired by Harold Wilson into a system to allow council tenants the right to buy leases of their homes for themselves (and perhaps for a second generation). Donoughue complains that under Harold Wilson there was no rationale for the allocation of business to overlapping committees – such as the Economic Strategy Committee (then termed MES – Ministerial Economic Strategy), PIO (the official's committee on prices and incomes) and MISC 91 (an *ad hoc* committee on pay). Similarly Mrs Thatcher could have chosen to deal with the replacement of Polaris by a sub-committee of Overseas and Defence rather than the MISC 7 actually used.

In 1993 there was an *ad hoc* committee 'Refugees from Former Yugoslavia' (Gen 24) with the terms of reference:

> To consider whether a visa regime should be instituted for citizens of former Yugoslavia in the context of the Government's overall policy towards that region and to review the practical arrangements for the reception and subsequent support of those arriving in the UK from the area taking into account the implications for the treatment of refugees from other parts of the world, and to report to Cabinet.

Peter Hennessy (1986: 99) says that in 1985/6 there were at least 160 specimens taking standing and *ad hoc* committees together. Ministers, on average, sit on five committees spending 6–8 hours per week in attendance (Seldon 1990: 114). The initials by which the committees and their sub-committees are known are a sort of jargon for the initiated.

Though in theory Cabinet committees come together at Secretary of State level, in practice Junior Ministers often represent their political bosses – except on the high status committees such as on Defence and the Economy. 'Scotland and the Union' (Cm 2225) not only lists all standing ministerial committees where the Scottish Office has member-ship, but distinguishes between those where the representative would normally be the Secretary of State and those where a Minister of State or a Parliamentary Under-Secretary of State is a member.

COMMITTEE COMPOSITION AS A PRIME MINISTERIAL POWER

It has been argued by Patrick Gordon Walker that the existence of these Cabinet Committees does not detract from the essence of Cabinet Government in that it is a means of organising the business of the Cabinet more conveniently – that it is after all only a means of 'the relevant Ministers meeting' (Walker 1972). Thus, in this light, it is sensible for the Ministers connected with (say) water to meet without colleagues with no departmental interest being present. However the composition of these committees is not so mechanical as that sentence suggests. As Sir Frank Cooper proposes,

> It is difficult not to believe that the final argument to sustain the status quo is the fact that membership of these committees is in the gift of the Prime Minister of the day . . . the weighting of the compositon can ensure that particular courses of action are more, rather than less, likely to be followed.   (Cooper 1986: 19)

A confirmation of Cooper's claim is perhaps the episode in 1981 when the PM convened an *ad hoc* group to look at the problem of the inner cities. According to Hennessy (1986: 102) she stacked the committee against Michael Heseltine who was known to favour an interventionist approach. There was apparently an increase in the urban programme but nothing on the scale sought by Heseltine.

Crossman noted that the Cabinet committee system was part of the explanation of the power of the PM,

> What committees exist, how they are manned above all, who are the chairmen – all this is entirely a matter for the Prime Minister.
>   (Crossman 1972: 63)

Hennessy claims that there was a decrease in the number of Cabinet committees as Mrs Thatcher took more and more business into even smaller forums where she and her advisers could grill individual Ministers. He documents that under Mrs Thatcher there were 30–35 standing committees and about 120 *ad hocs* in six and a half years. Callaghan in three years created about 160 *ad hoc* committees. Wilson in his final two-year term created about 120 *ad hocs* and in his first four years created 236.

Nicholas Ridley noted that Mrs Thatcher extended the committee system by use of small groups. He said that when the decision concerned spending money, the composition was usually the PM, the Chief Secretary and the Spending Minister. Though some Ministers would object to this further centralisation of decision making, Ridley argued that this was sensible: as Environment Secretary he saw no need to attend Defence business. This confirms the sectorisation of the Cabinet (1992: 29).

Richard Crossman's diaries also recorded how real power seemed to have drained to more informal settings,

> As I sat there first at the EDC [Economic Development Committee] and then at home affairs, I reflected on the way that Cabinet committees as well as the cabinet itself are becoming part of the dignified element of English [*sic*] constitution.
>
> (Crossman, 19 July 1965).

In 1987 Lord Hailsham also noted an informal 'core' to the Cabinet that was under prime ministerial control. He said that decisions were often taken, 'Not by the regular structure of Cabinet committees, but by groups of ministers chaired by the Prime Minister. Sometimes I think it has been growing towards a semi formal status, but they are given rather extraordinary names and they exist sometimes in theory as sub committees of the Cabinet committee structure and sometimes under a designation which indicates their miscellaneous character' (Hailsham 1987). In 1993 Lord Wakeham cited Hailsham's comments and concluded that in recent years the balance had probably swung back to more work going through the standing committee option.

Even if Cabinet committee and other less formal committees effectively increase the power of the Prime Minister it is the argument of this chapter that this is not to over rule a jealous Cabinet. Echoing Nigel Lawson (see p. 128) Ridley said that,

> All decisions of importance were reported to the Cabinet, except those that were market sensitive, or just plain 'sensitive' . . . There

was thus opportunity for anyone who wanted to do so to reopen a question if he didn't like a decision. It did sometimes happen, but only rarely. *For the most part, Cabinet ministers were so busy that they were only too thankful that other people's complex problems were sorted out without their having to be involved.*

(Ridley 1992: 30; emphasis added)

THE WEAKNESS OF 'STRENGTH AT THE CENTRE'

This chapter has broadly accepted that the PM *is* the force for central capability, but there is a large literature that suggests that this central co-ordination is still inadequate. In his Stamp Memorial Lecture in 1981, the former Head of the CPRS, Sir Kenneth Berrill, called for a Prime Minister's Department. The arguments are similar to those in favour of the CPRS that were rehearsed earlier. The complaints for which he is offering a remedy should at this stage in the argument be familiar. Berrill claimed that the longer Ministers hold a particular portfolio the more likely they are to see the country's problems through the eyes of their department and less in terms of the strategy of the Government as a whole. He observed that the sum of the spending department's interests can be a long way from adding up to a coherent strategy. Accordingly he argued for more strength at the centre, 'to hold the balance in the decision between the requirements of strategy and the cross pulls of the interests of the different spending departments'.

Other voices have echoed this current version of the need for a stronger centre, these have included the Bow Group, the former head of the Policy Unit, Sir John Hoskyns, the former secretary of the Cabinet, Lord Hunt, and the former joint head of the civil service, Sir Douglas Wass. At the Institute for Fiscal Studies in October 1983, Sir John Hoskyns called for a greater use of political appointees but his broad diagnosis was that Governments were failing to set realistic policy objectives – and lacked a strategy to reach objectives. Because Whitehall was a 'headless chicken', Hoskyns advocated a reconstructed Cabinet Office, 'A small new department, responsible for the developing and overseeing of the Government's total strategy, across all departments into a single whole.'

Sir Frank Cooper in 1986 pointed out that – contrary to the argument at their inception – the creation of large departments in the 1970s created a more demanding role at the centre 'because their very existence sharpened up boundary problems'. He made the point that no structure can eliminate such boundary problems but if the Cabinet

Office is to make the attempt, 'can it rely mainly on administrators seconded from other departments for a two year stint. Can it do without a CPRS?'

The best publicised of these calls for greater central capability came from Sir Douglas Wass in the Reith lectures of 1983. He talked of central analytical staff to look at the 'balance of policy', the way the Government programmes fitted into its strategic objectives and the way it ordered its priorities. He asked that policies should be rigorously evaluated and their effects set against their objectives. He endorsed Amery's picture of Cabinet as, 'a score of overworked departmental Ministers . . . quite incapable of either thinking out a definite policy or of securing its effective and consistent execution'.

Sceptical reservations are needed to qualify these authoritative and persuasive views. The first is to argue – as Campbell and others do above – that the existing resources at the centre are not to be under-estimated. As an extension we can note that earlier generations have noted the disease of departmentalism and that the current procedures are themselves a response to the identification of that weakness, in *Portrait of a Profession* (1950) the then head of the Home Civil Service, Sir E. Bridges, recognised that the 'fragmentary character' of the civil service was a danger. He recalled how on one occasion two Ministers engaged in a heated controversy changed places while the battle was at its height, they reconsidered the question and promptly found that each now held entirely the opposite conclusion to that which they held in a previous post. However, Bridges thought the tendency to fragmentation was combated by 'early and frank consultation' between interested departments. Thus the consultation is a means of co-ordination.

Second, there seems to be something of a breakdown of 'professional memory'. In advocating such reforms their value should be tested against the experience of the CPRS that seemed to be a partial pre-cursor of what is now advocated. The 1970 White Paper on *The Reorganisation of Central Government* heralded a new system, 'to give rigo-rous analysis of existing and suggested Government policies, actions and expenditures . . . to test whether such policies or activities accord with the Government's strategic aims'. Third, the uniform assumption appears to be that co-ordination equals coercion; that co-ordination means more power to the centre. Advocates tend to ignore the indirect co-ordination that already exists.

Co-ordination already takes place by the consultation identified by Bridges. There is also the co-ordination that comes from having staff that shift between departments (especially from the Treasury to the spending departments). Those who want to reform the centre of Government appear to require a tidy pattern that might be more logical than the arrangements that currently exist, but the current system fits the main requirement (which is flexibility) however ill it fits notions of clear accountability, systematic allocation of functions and the like.

In looking at the centre of Government, we find little clarity over how to depict practice. A principle like Cabinet Government no longer seems tenable, but prime ministerial power suggests far too simple an alternative. We need to recognise that the discussions of change at the centre are attempts to impose some order. But the problems are so rapidly changing that a rational and orderly solution would soon be inappropriate. The complex redundancy at the centre may look untidy but it has its own rationality.

As argued in Jordan and Richardson (1987) at the centre of British Government there is a Cabinet system that goes far wider than the formal Cabinet itself. Campbell (1993: 39) has argued that to compensate for a weakening of collective government Prime Ministers have augmented the co-ordinative apparatus at the centre. There is now a multiplicity of bodies, under the general control of the PM, which seek to provide some set of central co-ordination. In 1965 the Conservative former Deputy Prime Minister, Lord Butler, argued,

> if you take the Cabinet as covering the Cabinet committees and the committees of Ministers under it, you get a rather better conception of what the Cabinet is. If you just take the Cabinet meeting itself . . . much of the decision has already been taken before it reaches them.
> (Herman and Alt 1975: 207)

We now need to broaden that image further and see that there is a wide range of bodies, from the PM her/himself, through the Policy Unit, the Cabinet Office, the Private Office, etc., that exist to manipulate a workable, if imperfect, order.

Chapter 5

'Next Steps' into the fog

THE SCALE OF CHANGE

At first sight at least the most spectacular change in civil service structure in the United Kingdom in the twentieth century has been the creation of 'Next Steps' agencies. Announced in February 1988, the Next Steps programme has introduced executive agencies which are essentially the operating arms of Government departments. Old-style departments are being divided into small policy-making 'cores' with the operational effort being transferred to a clutch of satellite agencies which implement policy. In April 1991, in launching the Benefit and Contribution Agencies of the Department of Social Security (DSS), Prime Minister John Major argued:

> What we are seeing at the moment . . . is, frankly, nothing less than a revolution in management . . . that will make it more responsive, more open, more effective, more rewarding for the clientele of the Civil Service's operations . . .

In his Introduction to the *Next Steps Annual Review* (Cabinet Office 1991) the Minister of State, Tim Renton, described the 'quiet revolution' that saw:

- Chief Executives put in charge to see that the job is done properly; and
- Making Chief Executives accountable to a Minister for the Agency's performance.

Despite the low public awareness of these changes, the Treasury and Civil Service Committee (1990: para. 6) described Next Steps as 'the most radical reform of the public service in this century.' In 1994 Ministers were talking with enthusiasm about a return to a Victorian scale civil service with a core of 50,000 staff in the central departments.

By late 1991, 97 per cent of staff in the Department of Social Security were in executive agencies. By November 1993, 92 agencies were in operation employing 268,970 staff (262,965 of them civil servants). Furthermore, there were 31 HM Customs and Excise Units (25,135 staff) and 33 Inland Revenue Executive Offices (61,555 staff) which are usually described as 'operating on Next Steps "lines"'. (As they have 'Boards', there is not a direct relationship between the agency chief executive and the Minister: this technicality – and perhaps some Treasury dissent from the policy – has exempted them from the full Next Steps status.) About 60 per cent of the civil service staff now work in agencies or the above units or offices (Next Steps Briefing Note, 9 December 1993).

Ministers claim that the Next Steps developments are compatible with the Citizen's Charter approach that was established in 1991. The First Report (1992) claimed that this provided six Principles of Public Service:

- setting, monitoring and publication of standards;
- information and openness;
- choice and consultation;
- courtesy and helpfulness;
- remedies;
- value for money.

The 1992 Report recorded that 28 charters have been published in the main public services, but despite the assertions by Ministers, it seems unlikely that this movement reflects fundamental change in public administration control. Whether Next Steps agencies are seen as desirable or otherwise, by either judgement they are likely to be seen as more significant in their potential.

THE ORIGINS OF THE NEXT STEPS CHANGE

At the end of 1986, Mrs Thatcher asked Sir Robin Ibbs of the Efficiency Unit to look at the next generation of organisational change in Whitehall. This form of words presents the Next Steps proposals as the incremental extension of policy. More cynically, it can be seen as a gambit to try to revitalise a reform that seemed to have fallen flat – the Financial Management Initiative (FMI). The Public Accounts Committee, in looking at the FMI in 1987, noted the need to stress 'the importance of keeping the momentum of the major shift in management attitudes represented by the Initiative' (HC 61, 1986–7, paras 20–43, cited in Fry 1988: 430). Arguably, there was a sense that it had lost direction.

The terms of reference of the Ibbs Inquiry were:

> to assess the progress achieved in managing the Civil Service; to identify what measures had been successful in changing attitudes and practices; to identify institutional, administrative, political and attitudinal obstacles to better management and efficiency that still remain; and to report to the Prime Minister on what further measures should be taken.
>
> (Jenkins *et al.* 1988: 33)

The Report (*Improving Management in Government: the Next Steps*) followed the pattern for efficiency scrutinies and the study took 90 days and cost £50,000. However, it can be argued that the speed and economy of the policy development is a weakness rather than a strength. Instead of implementation after reflection we have seen an aggressive marketing of the merits of the changes by the civil servants involved that has failed to connect this exercise with the difficulties experienced in the past. To read the Next Steps Government literature is to enter a doubt-free zone.

One does not need to read far below the surface of the semi-official history of the creation of the agencies by Goldsworthy to discover an admission that the thesis of the Report was really an assertion rather than an argued case:

> Its persuasiveness lay not in the presentation of detailed evidence but in its description of a state of affairs which many readers said they recognised readily from their own experience; and in an analysis with which most of them instinctively agreed.
>
> (Goldsworthy 1991: 8)

This is to admit that acceptance of the benefits of change has had to be an article of faith. Goldsworthy claimed that:

> although the Government was firmly committed to implementing Next Steps, the policy itself was not publicly set down anywhere in any detail. Indeed Sir Robin Ibbs' Report had described an ideal, and sketched out – but no more – how it might be put into effect, so the policy had to be developed in the light of progress.
>
> (Goldsworthy 1991: 34)

It is only marginally unfair to translate this as 'we made it up as we went along'. That said, it is surely neither unexpected nor unwarranted for there to be criticisms from those looking for a coherent rationale.

There is a remarkable degree of variation in types of agency. The Project Manager for the Next Steps programme, Peter Kemp, informed the Public Accounts Committee that,

> the thrust of the Next Steps was that Government activities were infinitely variable. We have coastguards, we have vehicle services, we have prison officers . . . they are all different activities and should be treated differently.
>
> (Cited in Flynn *et al* 1990: 172)

This rather smacks of 'it doesn't matter as long as they are called agencies'. As Flynn *et al.* wrote in 1988, with no clear idea of what agencies are to look like, those most centrally involved seem to be championing the virtues of organisational plurality or indeed organisational design by instinct.

THE DIAGNOSIS CONTAINED IN THE IBBS REPORT

The Ibbs Report had seven main findings:

(i)   those 95 per cent of Civil Service staff involved in the delivery of Government services were generally convinced that the developments towards more clearly defined and budgeted management were positive and helpful. However, it was claimed that there was frustration at what were felt to be unnecessary controls and the intervention of ministers and senior officials in relatively minor issues.

(ii) civil servants were aware that senior management was dominated by those with a background in policy formulation. . .

(iii) civil servants responded to the pressure of Parliament and improving performance in delivery of policies tended to be neglected. . .

(iv) ministers were overloaded and hence the task of management had to be taken up by civil servants.

(v)   pressures on departments tended to emphasise expenditure reduction rather than effective use of resources.

(vi) though the Prime Minister [Margaret Thatcher] favoured improvements in performance there was a general lack of pressure on departments in this area. . .

(vii) the scale of the Civil Service was too large (600,000 employees) to manage as a single entity.

(Jenkins *et al* 1988: 3–5)

The Report claimed how the freedom of an individual manager to manage effectively was circumscribed. It said that s/he was controlled not only on resources and objectives (which it conceded was necessary) but also in the way in which resources could be managed – recruitment, dismissal, choice of staff, promotion, pay, hours of work, accommodation, grading, organisation, the use of Information Technology equipment. All this was attributed to the fact that rules were established centrally.

THE PRESCRIPTION IN SUMMARY

The major recommendation that followed on from this analysis was that

agencies should be established to carry out the executive functions of government within a policy and resources framework set by a department.

(Jenkins *et al* 1988: para. 19)

The civil service should be restructured so that as far as possible the delivery of services is separated from policy work and executed by agencies operating under business-style regimes. The Ibbs Report said that such an agency could be part of Government and the public service or 'it could be more effective outside government'. In practice, to date, the agencies have been retained as part of the Government: though some of those close to the reforms certainly favour 'busting the system open'.

The Report claimed that the term 'agency' was not used technically but to describe any executive unit that delivers a service for Government. The vagueness is enough to cause some concern in trade union circles that the ultimate intention was privatisation of the agencies – though this was not acknowledged as an original goal of the agency operation – and, indeed, it was argued by some that the agency idea was a civil service ploy to avoid wide-scale privatisation. By December 1992, however, a Next Steps Briefing Note was proposing,

It is not ruled out that, after a period of some years, Agencies, like other Government activities, may be suitable for privatisation.

By 1994 each new agency (or agency being re-examined) needs to meet the 'prior options' test that asks whether the activity is needed at all or whether it should be privatised, contracted out or market tested (see pp. 160–4).

The core idea underlying the agency arrangement is management by *pseudo* contract. Each agency is run by an Agency Chief Executive (ACE) and publishes a framework document which prescribes goals. This sets out the policy, the budget, specific targets and the results to be achieved. The Ibbs Report said that the frameworks must specify how politically sensitive issues are to be handled and that the management of the agency must be held rigorously to account by the departments for the results they achieve.

FULTON MARK II?

There seems to be an irresistible connection between the thrust of the Fulton Report of 1968 and the Ibbs Report of 1988. It would be all too easy to pass off the following passage from the Fulton Report as a Next Steps manifesto:

> It is not easy in the Civil Service clearly and distinctly to allocate to individuals or units the authority to take decisions. . . we believe. . . that the work of departments can be so organised as to enable responsibility and authority to be defined and allocated more clearly than they often are at present. Individuals and units could then be called to account for performance which it measures as objectively as possible . . .
>
> (Quoted in Butler 1990: 365)

Peter Kemp, has argued that:

> There is a gap in the market for those activities which fall between activities suitable for privatisation and those carried out by the traditional 'Whitehall' Civil Service. This gap can be identified and filled – by Next Steps.
>
> (Kemp 1988: 5)

This shows how closely the discussions since 1988 have reflected the issues raised in the setting up of the departmental agencies as recommended by Fulton.

Reference to the Fulton Report is double-edged for the Next Steps advocates. On the one hand it confirms the diagnosis that something is wrong, and that agencies might be part of the solution. On the other hand the post-Fulton experience raises some questions that seem to have been being ignored.

At that time it was found that very few functions were suitable for hiving-off (activities to be undertaken outside mainstream departments – or even in the private sector) as Fulton had expected. Instead a 'hiving-in' arrangement was developed which created separate units within the overall umbrella of a department. By 1976 over 172,000 civil servants were in post in these departmental agencies (Jordan 1976: 37). Progress in the hiving-off sense was most fundamentally inhibited by the account-ability issue: it was thought impossible to reconcile real freedom and real political control and responsibility.

The connection to Fulton was conceded by Sir Robin Butler in his Redcliffe-Maud Memorial lecture in 1990, and he reminded his audience that Next Steps was built on a whole series of delegated arrangements: he seemed to be resisting the black and white imagery of the Next Steps advocates that present 'their' agencies as the definitive attempt of change rather than as another tilt at old windmills. Sir Robin went on to make a point that further diminishes the significance of agencies as an arrangement:

> But over the devolution of responsibility, and accountable and efficient management, the Fulton report has much to say that reads as convincingly now as when it was written. Moreover, great progress was made in both the 1970s and the 1980s which it would be wrong to ignore. A number of trading funds were set up, and many civil service organisations spectacularly improved their service and perfor-mance. For example the Driver and Vehicle Licensing Centre did not have to become a Next Steps agency before it converted its reputa-tion for notorious delay into that of an organisation so much more efficient that every Member of Parliament will tell you about the reduction of this source of complaints in their postbags.
>
> (Butler 1990: 4)

This quotation draws attention to the possibility that performance and structure may be very loosely connected. When one looks at the lists of claimed improvements in performance in the agencies, one wonders if agency status was necessary. For example, descriptions of Companies House and the Driving Standards Agency, present innovations such as 'roadshows and exhibition stands', 'New Central Enquiry unit . . . Premium service . . . Credit cards accepted. Courier delivery.'

It might as well be the case that all these desirable innovations are more easily introduced in the context of agency status, but it is hardly the case that only agency status allows the introduction of a fax service or the explanation of faults to failed driving candidates. In other words the justification of the agencies needs to be more realistic. What is required is an argument about how agency status facilitates change rather than a stereotyping of staid Whitehall department bureaucracies and thrusting agency entrepreneurs.

If, as this account suggests, the Next Steps programme is a throwback to the ideas of the early 1970s, the advocates must show why the current attempt will succeed where Fulton stagnated. There were major arguments put up against too much hiving-off (and hiving-in) in the 1970s on the grounds that accountability was infringed and their autonomy was bogus. These remain valid until they are countered: they simply cannot be ignored.

For advocates to now claim, as they do, that there is greater corporate identity and commitment under agency status may be perfectly valid, but since we were persuaded by civil service sources that the post-Fulton changes had already induced such improvements in the 1970s we need now to be told of the specific added benefits of Next Steps agency status. If we are told that the managerial culture has changed and that managers now think more boldly than in the past about operational objectives, does this mean we now discount all the post-Fulton claims that hived-in agencies were delivering such benefits?

THE CREATION OF THE AGENCIES

In her statement to the Commons about the Ibbs Report on 18 February 1988, Margaret Thatcher summarised the main features as being:

(a) executive or service delivery functions of Departments (as opposed to policy work) should, to the greatest extent practicable, be carried out by units [agencies] clearly designated within departments;

(b) agencies would be run by chief executives who would be responsible for delivering management within a policy and resources framework set by the responsible Minister, in consultation with the Treasury;

(c) staff would be properly trained and prepared for the resulting changes; and

(d) that a 'project manager' (at Second Permanent Secretary level) would be appointed to ensure a programme of change takes place.

On the same day the then Minister for the Civil Service Richard Luce, held a press conference. This identified the first tranche (12) of potential

candidates for agency status – ranging from HMSO to the Metereo-
logical Office, to the Passport Office and the Queen Elizabeth II
Conference Centre.

The 1989 *Annual Report* on the Initiative indicated that three agencies
were in place: the Vehicle Inspectorate, Companies House, and HMSO.
Such speedy implementation is an indication that these operations were
already out of the departmental mainstream. Terming them Next Steps
agencies was a relatively simple matter. Arguably the change was in *label*
as the bodies already had many Next Steps qualities.

The way in which early agencies very much concentrated on the
margins of departmental duties has been viewed sceptically by some.
Such cynicism was justified since previous attempts at the reform of
(Programme Analysis and Review, Central Policy Review Staff, etc.)
have, after bright starts, 'run out of steam'.

In fact, experience has shown that the Next Steps programme has not
failed in the sense of numbers. Scepticism is not now about the percentage of departmental staff affected, but centres on the possibility that the
organisational change will have less operational impact than predicted
by advocates.

NEXT STEPS AND ACADEMIC UNDER-ENTHUSIASM

There has been some scepticism by civil servants – at least by retired civil
servants. For example, in his memoirs the former Permanent Secretary,
Sir Antony Part, described the Ibbs document as,

> a report by three junior members of the Cabinet Office putting
> forward a superficial proposal that most executive functions should
> be transmuted into agencies with more or less unfettered freedom of
> action. . .
>
> (Part 1990: 190)

But on the whole there has been an unceasing flow of endorsements
from the (serving) civil service about the significance of these changes.
There is an obvious difference in tone between the depiction of the
Next Steps programme by those involved and by academic
commentators.

The academic under-enthusiasm about the lasting importance of
these changes was perhaps a reasonable response among those who
had been obliged to track, describe and assess a succession of other
efficiency reforms in central and local government. Peter Kemp con-

ceded that the 'bones of previous Civil Service reforms litter the wayside' (Treasury and Civil Service Committee 1990: 17).

The academic community may have been over-suspicious in their 'seen it all before' response, but they were motivated not by some malice towards the goal of reform but by an awareness of the difficulty of reform. Moreover, and ironically, this lack of academic enthusiasm for change in the civil service is not proof of an anti-public service mood but the reverse. Perhaps the academic community's confidence was misplaced, but it broadly accepted that the British civil service was held in the highest regard internationally. Because they did not recognise the civil service as ailing, they were unwilling to endorse changes which might undermine those established virtues which were part of the mixed package of the traditional service.

A further type of academic unease is really directed not at the idea of agencies or even at the implementation of the ideas – it concerns the 'story' advocates have told about the idea. No doubt it is naive to expect those in charge of change to underline weaknesses in their schemes, but the Next Steps programme has been presented in a particularly one-sided manner. For example, a 'Briefing Note' dated 31 October 1991 briskly begins:

1. Next Steps is a programme which is delivering better quality central Government services, within available resources, for the benefits of tax payers, customers and staff.
2. The Government machine is too big and its activities too diverse to be managed as one unit. The solution in most cases is to set up free standing agencies to carry out specific activities. Each agency is headed by a Chief Executive directly accountable to a Minister. Chief Executives are set tough financial and quality of service targets and have financial and management freedoms tailored to help them do the job better.

Such an account (or rather series of assertions) cannot be expected to be accepted without reservations, qualifications and criticisms. Where is the evidence that services are better; that taxpayers and customers and staff all profit in this arrangement? Where is the evidence that old-style management was 'too big'? Did it really operate in the homogeneous manner implied or was there not, in reality, a federal system? What theory justifies the new units when the scale runs from 30 staff in the Wilton Park Conference Centre to the 65,000 of the Social Security Benefits Agency? How is the description 'free standing' reconciled with ministerial accountability? Who judges the targets to be tough? Where is the proof that this freedom increases effectiveness? In other words, even if one goes along with the diagnosis and the prescription, one can legitimately say that the case for the reforms is under-argued. The comments of the former civil servant Sir Leo Pliatzky – who is by no means hostile to the notion of agencies – expressed the same unease that the new agencies were not placed in any context. In 1979 Pliatzky conducted a review of what he termed Non Departmental Public Bodies (NDPBs) (published as Pliatzky 1980). At the time Government had deemed these to be 'a bad idea' and was seeking ways to restrict their number. He noted,

> In contemplating, as one of its options, a whole raft of executive agencies which might be outside government, the Next Steps report ran completely counter to the 1980 report and the thinking which led up to it. Theories of organisation do tend to go in and out of fashion. The fashion had changed between the Fulton Report and Mrs Thatcher's review. The authors of the Next Steps report may conceivably have thought that the time had come for it to change again. But it does seem curious that, in its appendix on 'Previous Reports on the Civil Service', the Next Steps report does not even mention the 1980 report on non-departmental bodies.
>
> (Pliatzky 1992: 557)

That agencies were 'good' for Fulton (but difficult to put in practice), 'bad' in the Thatcher review of quangos, but 'good' again for the Ibbs Report, was surely worth a comment. One reason why such a sense of context is not available might be the practice of seconding civil servants to the centre or importing secondments from business to staff such projects. Not only do they reinvent the wheel they can reinvent less useful things that experience has discredited.

Some have criticised the Next Steps as too radical. We need be careful not to be railroaded by the revolutionary rhetoric of the advocates of change. Sir Peter Kemp was ousted from Whitehall in 1992. Once out of post he was able to vent his frustration that the changes had been too limited.

> There are welcome breakthroughs but they do not add up to a revolution. At the centre, in Whitehall, old attitudes and the old guard prevail. The only heads that have rolled have been among the revolutionaries themselves.
>
> (Kemp 1993: 8)

Sir Leo Pliatzky has also suggested that the most significant feature of these bodies might be the *modesty of the change* that they represent. He underlined that, 'The agencies will generally be *within the Civil Service*, and their staff will continue to be civil servants' (Pliatzky 1992: 558). Pliatzky's argument seems to be that Next Steps changes, despite the 'hype' by their supporters, were a quite minor reorganisation within departments. As Pliatzky points out (1992: 558) the Next Steps agencies kept the activities within the Government and retained parliamentary scrutiny. This improved the political acceptability of the initiative;

> In the absense of fresh legislation, so it seems to me, ministers cannot abrogate responsibilities placed upon them by existing legislation. What they can do is delegate authority for operations, but without surrendering ultimate responsibility for them, and that is what is resolved in the Next Steps agencies.
>
> (Pliatzky 1992: 558)

NEXT STEPS AND THE FMI

Officially Next Steps is a development of the Financial Management Initiative but it can be argued that if the FMI was a success then there would have been a need to search for the next generation of change. Flynn *et al.* point out that there is little explicit mention of the FMI within the Ibbs Report:

> Indeed, the report's criticisms of existing systems and the claims that its recommendations involve fundamental changes appear to place distance between agencies and the FMI.
>
> (Flynn *et al.* 1988: 440)

The Ibbs Report had to be phrased delicately when dealing with previous efficiency changes; if the past was so good why did there have to be change? In deference to the much-trumpeted FMI, the Report had to go on to say that 'where accountability on the lines we suggest is in place, substantial and quantifiable benefits are coming through' (para. 48). This eroded the scale of benefits that could be expected from the new agencies.

The advocates of the Next Steps do seem caught in a dilemma of both wanting to wave a banner saying that the changes are important and possible and wanting to enter footnotes of reservation. Thus, while heading up the project, Peter Kemp noted: 'No manager in this world is free from some kind of constraints and controls, and I think that there are some unrealistic ideas in the Civil Service of the flexibilities enjoyed in the private sector' (1988: 8). The Appendix to the Next Steps Report said that all departments now had top management systems intended to force management at all levels to take clear decisions about the direction of activities in a department. It noted however that some headquarters and policy divisions doubted the value of Top Management Systems as they were being operated:

> in many departments it was not clear how far the use of management systems had become an integral part of the policy divisions, rather than a one-off form filling exercise. A number of people commented on the weight of paper surrounding the systems and the number of forms to be filled in – or as one person said 'typical civil service: management has been bureaucratised'.
>
> (para. 11)

It is as reasonable to see Next Steps as a replacement for the FMI – reflecting disillusion about FMI – as it is to have the cosier view of it as a logical extension.

A CONSTITUTIONAL FUDGE?

There seems a determination on the part of those involved in the public presentation of the agency case to deny the existence of problems. A case in point is perhaps the matter of accountability. As part of the 'fudge' that Next Steps agencies are new and innovative – without affecting traditional responsibilities – a compromise was devised whereby replies from agency chief executives that would previously have been given by Ministers were to be available from the House of Commons Public Information Office (PIO). In November 1991, after complaints that replies were difficult to track down, the Government agreed that the replies in the PIO would be published. In July 1992 it was finally agreed that the answers could be printed daily as part of *Hansard* (*The Independent*, 27 July 1992).

The Treasury and Civil Service Committee (1988) argued that the traditional system of accountability was not consistent with the increased delegation of responsibility to individual civil servants in the Next Steps programme. It called for Chief Executives to appear personally before Parliamentary committees to be questioned on the activities delegated by the framework document. The Government's response was that Chief Executives could appear in order to answer on behalf of Ministers.

Flexibility is undoubtedly 'a good thing', but when the Treasury and Civil Service Committee rehearses (1990: para. 66) the different versions of the accountability principles found in different framework documents one suspects that flexibility is also a synonym for the less attractive quality of irresolution.

According to Peter Hennessy, the original version of the Ibbs Report proposed

> A change in the British constitution, by law if necessary, to quash the fiction that ministers can be genuinely responsible for *everything* done by officials in their name.
>
> (Hennessy 1989: 620)

This version of events means that the authors of the published report are innocent of the charge that has to be laid against the final version – that it ducks the vital issue that it identifies. If Hennessy is correct, the civil service, even in an era of open Government, has disguised the nature of the reforms by refusing to acknowledge that contentious matters are involved. As Richards (1988) represents the Next Steps programme, it is,

> *the lowest common denominator* for all the parties involved . . . the management radicals and the Treasury consolidators.
>
> (Cited in Davies and Willman 1991: 18; emphasis added)

The civil service has tried to internalise legitimate debate and present a single face to the outside world. This has in reality discredited the reform process by implying that those in charge were ignoring what they were in fact suppressing. Neither is it a particularly desirable trait.

Instead of accepting that Next Steps was transforming administration, the official view was that everything had changed but nothing was different. Somehow the operations were to be fundamentally new, but no constitutional or legislative issues were raised. As Pliatzky points out (1992: 558) the Next Steps agencies kept the activities within the Government and retained parliamentary scrutiny. This seems to have helped the political acceptability of the initiative:

> in securing the favourable reception given to the initiative by the Select Committee on the Treasury and the Civil Service, I guess that members of Parliament are quite happy to see a shake-up in cosy civil service regimes . . . provided that their own locus is not affected.
>
> (Pliatzky 1992: 560)

It is not to be against the notion of reform to be concerned that the changes have no very satisfactory system of accountability, or to point

out that the fragmentation of welfare responsibilities among a multiplicity of single-purpose agencies might be the least desirable development if one wishes to develop a 'whole person' integrated package of
ways of responding to individual need.

There appears to be a wish to claim that agencies are autonomous
but, as we have noted from Pliatzky above, the fact that these are *intra*-
departmental developments has meant that no new theory of accountability is required. In a lecture to the First Division Association (a trade
union for senior civil servants), Sir Robin Butler reiterated that the thing
that civil servants had in common was that 'they are all accountable
through Ministers to Parliament, so that they are in the realm of
politics'(1991: 3). He said:

> I believe that line of accountability has to go through Ministers
> because in a democracy the ultimate sanction on a Government is
> that they are not re-elected; and Ministers are the only people in
> Government who are subject to that sanction.
>
> (Butler 1991: 6)

Sir Robin's remarks need to be decoded because he is in fact taking part
in a debate about the purpose and goals of the Next Steps changes. He is
taking something of a traditionalist line:

> It is now very widely asked whether, if delegation takes place in this
> way and different operations of the Civil Service are allowed to go
> their own way in devising terms and conditions for their own opera-
> tions, anything will be left which is recognisably a single service? Is
> the Service in the process of disintegrating and, if so, does it matter?
> Can we live up in practice to the manifesto which I and others issued
> when Next Steps was launched, that the Service would remain
> unified though not uniform?
>
> (Butler 1991: 8)

Butler is, in fact, articulating a more conservative view from those
agency advocates who see the end game as involving distinctly separate
agencies with their own staffing arrangements.

If there was an internal battle over the nature of the independence
to be allowed for the agencies the advocates of radical change seem to
have lost as, as noted above, Sir Peter Kemp was replaced as Permanent Secretary at the Office of Public Service and Science in July
1992. He was given no alternative post. (But see comments on market
testing on pp. 160–4 that suggest that Next Steps changes have been
'out-radicalised'.)

The official line that agencies are both free-standing *and* part of the integrated civil service is a formula to satisfy both the Butler forces for unity and a more zealous line that fragmentation would be no bad thing. By failing to admit there is a debate, far less resolving that debate, the advocates of Next Steps have invited upon themselves the charge of 'constitutional illiteracy' (term used in Hood 1990: 15).

The Next Steps concept is sometimes seen as emulating a Swedish style of administration of core policy-making bodies and executive departments, but, as Fry (1988: 434) points out, the Swedish situation is not complicated by the British obsession with ministerial responsibility. He says: 'The most striking difference between Britain and Sweden is the absence of a concept of ministerial responsibility.' He cites Elder's (1970) point that Swedish Government's relations between Ministers and boards were to be compared to those conducted in the twilight zone of Minister–public corporation relations in Britain (Fudge and Gustafsson 1989). Agency advocates may be correct when they point out that ministerial responsibility is a bankrupt and unworkable formula but they seem to have no coherent ideas with which to replace it. They say that moving from ministerial responsibility only recognises reality and depicts ministerial responsibility as a fiction, and yet there appears an unwillingness to really assert some new mode of accountability or to concede that so little has changed that no new theory is needed.

There is clearly scope for a comparison between British and New Zealand experience. The lack of an explicit comparison by those responsible for British developments is presumably because they do not wish to follow the radical precedents that involve changes such as making the Agency Chief Executive the employer of staff, and the ending of tenure for Chief Executives of departments (Boston *et al.* 1991).

The Next Steps approach is presented in a constitutional vacuum. Where there should be the delineation of new arrangements (or the admission that little has changed), there is a bold empiricism that the detail can be worked out later. There is no sense in the propaganda of change that this is a controversial area. It has been argued that such arrangements could not be better crafted to facilitate blame-avoidance and a confusion of accountability.

UNCRITICAL OPTIMISM?

The Ibbs Report said:

The framework will need to be set and updated as part of a formal annual review with the responsible Minister, based on a long-term plan and an annual report. But main strategic control must lie with the Minister and Permanent Secretary. But once the policy objectives and budgets within the framework are set, the management of the agency should then have as much independence as possible in deciding how those objectives are met. . .

The presumption must be that, provided management is operating within the strategic direction set by Ministers, it must be left as free as possible to manage within that framework. To strengthen operational effectiveness, there must be freedom to recruit, pay, grade, and structure in the most effective way as the framework becomes sufficiently robust and there is confidence in the capacity of management to handle the task.

(para. 21)

Annex A of the Next Steps Report explicitly cites the nationalised industries as examples of arm's-length administration. The confident 'see no problem' tone of the Ibbs Report in commending agencies seems to be invoking precisely the arrangement that prevented the nationalised industries confronting their problems on pay, prices and investment, free from ministerial interference. Why do advocates of agency theory not dwell on British Rail as an example?

CENTRAL CONTROL OR REAL AUTONOMY?

A central issue is whether decentralisation is indeed 'a good thing'. Again, this is an area that is insufficiently explored in the public presentation of the proposals. Instead of allowing that there is an issue as to whether central control is too loose or too tight, we are led to believe that in all examples, under all circumstances, control is, 'just right'. Will the Chief Executive of the Vehicle Inspectorate be able to close a vehicle inspection station without political interference?

The usual response to putting this sort of dilemma is to suggest that Chief Executives will be politically sensitive and that they will consult and clear any important initiatives. But this only solves the easy cases. Consultation does not cover the cases in which Ministers and Chief Executives hold different views. The formula on offer is useful in fair weather. It says that when things are straightforward the Minister will give strategic direction and the Chief Executive will run the day-to-day operations.

Such a relaxed 'play it by ear' approach cannot avoid the criticism that there is uncertainty over 'doomsday scenarios'. If the worst comes to the worst, there is little doubt that the buck ends back at the department. If, for example, there were a major financial problem at an agency, the Treasury would be required to act as banker of last resort.

The Treasury and Civil Service Committee recommended:

> Departments should maintain a self-denying ordinance to ensure that . . . review arrangements [for frameworks] . . . should be used only strategically and not as a vehicle for interference within the running of the agency.
>
> (Treasury and Civil Service Commitee 1990: para. 19)

This is sensible, but it is also an aspiration rather than a guarantee.

Hennessy (1989: 81) notes:'If implemented in full, The Next Steps would undo Warren Fisher's revolution of 1919–1922 which created . . . for the first time a genuinely unified civil service under tight Treasury control' (cited in Painter 1991: 81). But as O'Toole has argued:

> The evolution of a unified and career bureaucracy was a slow, at times piecemeal process, but nevertheless it was a process accompanied by considerable thought, energy and vision on the part of those who were responsible for its development.
>
> (O'Toole 1989: 51)

O'Toole justifies his call for a Royal Commission on the civil service by noting that the revolution proposed in the Ibbs Report was advocated without the consideration put into the unified and uniform model.

The reformist Next Steps literature arguably fails to give sufficient attention to the merits and demerits of relaxing central control – or how to ensure that this relaxation is not merely rhetorical. There were still undoubted tensions late in 1990 with an agency advocate sourly noting 'that the Treasury have got enough controls, but try to tell a child that he has got enough chocolate'.

The reservations by the Treasury are signalled by Nigel Lawson in *The View From Number 11* (1993: 390). He starts his discussion with the heading 'Stumbles on "Next Steps"'. He recounts how that in the first years in office the Thatcher Governments had reduced civil service staffing by 20 per cent and in 1982 created the FMI. Lawson describes how when Robin Ibbs took over the Efficiency Unit in 1983 a split emerged between the Unit and the Treasury. As described by Lawson, Ibbs was too ready to accept the argument that departments could attain savings by investment. Lawson argued that as long as public services existed, and they were insulated from the market place, Treasury control was needed. He argued that as there was no price mechanism at work there had to be Treasury discipline or none at all. That he argued that the chaotic consequences of the collapse of the Soviet Union showed what happened when market disciplines did not replace a command system shows that Lawson (and the Treasury) was out of sympathy.

His description of the introduction of Next Steps agencies was decidely cool,

> With this background, I was inevitably suspicious when, towards the end of 1987, I and other Cabinet colleagues were informed by Number 10, out of the blue, of a new Ibbs initiative, which apparently had Margaret's enthusiastic support . . . the main burden of which was a recommendation that the executive functions of Government should be hived off into separate agencies, to be run like businesses by chief executives . . . it was clear that Ibbs had not addressed either of the two principal problems involved in a change of this kind, however attractive the concept may have been. The first was the question of parliamentary accountability. . . But even when this was solved there remained the second problem, that of main-taining effective control of the agencies' expenditure, in which Ibbs showed no interest . . . a long battle ensued, resulting in a lengthy concordat negotiated by Peter Middleton on behalf of the Treasury and Robin Butler on behalf of Number 10. . . The main practical advantage I see is that by creating accounts, boards of directors and saleable assets, future privatization may prove less difficult.
>
> (Lawson 1993: 393)

NEXT STEPS TO WHERE?

A specific example of the ambiguity in the direction of Next Steps – whether a unified service is envisaged or whether a patchwork of civil services will result – is detectable in the tone of the discussions over pay arrangements. It is not clear if flexibility – or disintegration – is the message.

Some of the recommendations for agency freedom met with resis-tance within Whitehall. The Treasury was concerned that freedom on pay would indeed mean freedom to pay more. In evidence to the first Treasury and Civil Service Committee inquiry into the Next Steps Sir Robin Butler said:

I think you are right in saying that the Treasury have had reservations. When the report was being discussed the Treasury were very
anxious . . . that this approach to delegation should not weaken the
overall controls of public expenditure which are necessary for
macro-economic purposes and control over the pay bill.

(Treasury and Civil Service Committee 1988: 57)

Pay flexibility seems an important ingredient of the Next Steps package.
But as noted by Sir Robin Butler (1990: 2), there are already agreements
with the civil service unions giving a more flexible and varied pattern of
civil service pay related to geographical locations, and the market for
individual skills and merit.

The assumption appears to be that the development of agencies
would reduce wage bills outside London – but the possibility of wage
and grade drift appeared to worry the Treasury. Indeed, another thread
in the Next Steps approach envisages rewards for performance. This has
the implication of a higher pay bill. The Ibbs Report noted the development of performance-related pay within the service but it did say
that the experimental performance bonus scheme introduced in 1985
had not been successful. The major constraint here is the traditional
expectation of a Government department that common conditions
should apply to all its staff and the wish that staff should be freely
transferable to work anywhere in the department. This is seen not only
as a protection for staff but as allowing flexibility for the employing
department. As things stand staff are still technically civil servants with
full transferability into and out of agencies.

There has been some concern that agency salaries – high by civil
service standards – are not competitive enough to attract the attention of
top flight private sector applicants. Some forty-one of the first sixty-three
Agency Chief Executives (ACEs) were appointed after open competition. (Fifty-five of the first eighty-five appointments or designate appointments were already serving civil servants.) Open competition has meant
paying rates above the departmental scales. This will make it very
difficult to absorb such appointees into the mainstream department. If
there is not transferability of staff, there will be a real problem of the loss
of 'the common culture' that facilitates policy-making.

THE INTRODUCTION OF MANAGERIAL PAROCHIALISM?

A general Treasury worry about lack of control sometimes leads to a
more particular worry that the creation of agencies will create backwater

administration: that the agencies will not have the policy work and interest to attract the high-flyers and that the lack of staff mobility will have very negative consequences. This 'backwater' notion is rejected by those involved in agency development, but civil servants have often taken unexciting postings precisely because there was a prospect of a move in two or three years.

In an interview with Colin Campbell a former Treasury official argued,

> In departments like the Treasury as well as operational departments, after returning from going out and running something people would say, 'He's actually gotten his hands dirty, he's not one of us' . . . the problem is that Treasury controls key policy posts . . . deputy and under secretary posts go to those with Treasury and Cabinet Office favor . . . the central departments would say, 'Who's he, we haven't heard of him' . . . hiving off operational agencies will give the people back in the department a chance to run the divisions and keep policy jobs clean. . . It's the policy jobs that command the premium and the real high fliers who want these jobs. . . you don't breed them from running a railroad. . . Your best chance of reaching the very top will still be to stick to the pure, 100% traditional mainline jobs in the Treasury.
>
> (Campbell 1993: 39)

ARE TARGETS REALLY A SUBSTITUTE FOR MARKETS?

Financial and quality of service targets are set (and published) for each agency. Reports and accounts have to show how far these have been met. A general review of progress across all agencies is published annually around October (Cabinet Office 1991). The UK Passport Agency for example, is required to process correct applications within twenty days in January to July and ten days at other times (1991/2 target). The Social Security Benefits Agency is set a target of same-day service for crisis loans, five days for income support and seven days for community-care grants.

It is possible to be unfashionably sceptical about the central notion of target-setting as a means of holding agencies accountable. For one thing we do not know whether the target was set at a correct level in the first place. It is one thing to claim (Cabinet Office 1991: 6) that targets are 'demanding'; it is another to supply evidence of that judgement.

Does this tell us about the quality of the performance or the realism of the targets? Elizabeth Mellon (1991) has written,

> What tends to happen is that the agency asks for targets it feels safe with, the department adds some more, and the agency aims for the ones it can achieve.
>
> (Cited in Hogwood 1993: 18)

Dopson's conclusions about the HMSO were,

> This small-scale study does not permit firm generalizations, but the results of the field work stand in sharp contrast to Peter Kemp's comment that,'in terms of fun, the place to be is the Agency' . . . The more negative comments (from staff) . . . seem to be a consequence of the subsequent restructuring exercise in the HMSO and a profound disillusionment with the stark contradictions in Government policy which on the one hand advocates freedom and initiative, yet, on the other, seems set on producing rigid guidelines . . .
>
> (Dopson 1993: 23)

The advocates of agencies would readily admit such criticisms but respond by saying that these indicators are the best that is practical. However, as we have noted, the mood after experimenting with such approaches after Fulton was that such attempts were only 'playing at shops': that the exercise was distracting participants into targetmanship rather than aiding management.

There is, to date, little empirical work on the impact of these changes, but Mellon's evidence to the Treasury and Civil Service Committee (July 1991: 108–11) is, at best, worrying for advocates:

> Evidence submitted by the same author in June 1990 looked at five executive agencies from the point of view of strategic management . . . The broad conclusion was that the executive agency status was 'not really a structural attempt to bring a market or competitive market to bear in the public sector' . . .
>
> (Treasury and Civil Service Committee 1991: 108)

> One could argue that the Agency model is inadequate because it brings only marginal change. However, this subsequent research shows a much more interesting finding. This is that while Agency status on its own is not sufficient to bring about significant change, significant change can be achieved if other tactics are used to bolster the small changes which Agency status on its own implies
>
> (Treasury and Civil Service Committee 1991: 110)

It is a strange irony that a Government apparently with an ideological commitment to the market could endorse such an ambitious planning framework as implied by the FMI and the Next Steps. The Conservative Government asserts that it is borrowing from business. As Nigel Lawson suggested it is not clear that in depending so much on performance indicators the Government is not borrowing from the discredited planning regimes of Eastern Europe. If one has indicators, fulfilment of these targets can distort behaviour. If one believes in markets, and genuine markets are seen as unattainable, one might draw the conclusion that pseudo-markets are not so much second-best arrangements but antithetical to the genuine article.

DOES THE SUSPECT FIT THE DESCRIPTION?

The language used to describe Next Steps is a political language: political in that it is selected because it will help 'sell' the arrangements, whether or not the image invoked is appropriate. The impression is given that those developments are part of a modern managerial mood. It is just possible that the current model is rather old-fashioned, and at least it is a matter of debate as to whether we are dealing with the latest generation of managerial thought.

Pollitt (1990: 56) has written of the current British administrative fashion as 'neo-Taylorism' – a revival of the scientific management set out by F.W. Taylor in *The Principles of Scientific Management* in 1911:

> The central thrust, endlessly reiterated in official documents, is to set clear targets, to develop performance indicators to measure the achievement of those targets, and to single out, by means of merit awards, promotion or other records, those individuals who get 'results'.
>
> (Pollitt 1990: 56)

Of course, as discussed in Chapter 3, 'Taylorism' has been subject to criticism and rejection by succeeding waves of organisational theory. That it has been resurrected in the 1980s and 1990s is not surprising given the cyclical nature of the social sciences; that no attempt is made to anticipate the objections that have been raised to the original version is more surprising. Pollitt (1990: 58) has noted that in most of their public statements Conservative Ministers have simply ignored the wealth of literature – now nearly three-quarters of a century's work, on both sides of the Atlantic – warning that such a hygienic dichotomy (between policy and execution) is unattainable.

In short, the question of being in favour or opposed to Next Steps moves has effectively been 'sold' as being for or against reform, improvement and efficiency. To argue against is to be in favour of the sin of inefficiency. There seems no room for doubt about the methods as opposed to the intention and goal. A better case for the changes might relate to human resource management, cultural change and quality management. Hoggett (1991) notes that 'devolved service units' are a feature of both the private and pubic sector. Featherstone (1991: 45) has argued that there are pressures for self-actualisation for managers. Agency-type structures might encourage this.

MARKET TESTING: IS IT COMPATIBLE WITH NEXT STEPS?

The Office of Public Service and Science created in 1992 has three small sub-units that relate to this general area. There is the Citizen's Charter Unit, the Next Steps Project Team and the Efficiency Unit. The last named is currently pushing through the ideas of market testing that were outlined in the *Citizen's Charter First Report* (Cm 2101, 1992). Picking up the idea of competitive tendering that had earlier been imposed on local government the Report indicated that nearly £1.5bn worth of central Government activity (affecting 44,000 jobs) would be market tested by September 1993. This involved,

> identification of promising areas for external competition, eg professional and specialist services, executive and clerical operations, IT services and project management.

In fact by September 1993 provisional figures reported that less than half the volume of review had been completed on schedule. By December 1993, however, more than two-thirds of this first major market testing round where completed – albeit late. But as we shall see below this increased rate of completion perhaps signalled the erosion rather than the success of market testing.

In many ways market testing is different, and far more radical, than Next Steps agencies. It starts from the premise that the real motor force to drive down costs is competition. In the Next Steps system the targets were negotiated beteen the departments and their satellites: this could lead to the setting of targets that were too soft.

If Next Steps policy suffered some problems in that there was a reluctance in some quarters to see the fragmentation of the traditional civil service, it now faces a challenge from a different direction – those who see Next Steps change as too cautious. Market testing differs slightly from the other option of *contracting out*. In the latter case Government decides that the activity should be provided on behalf of Government by a commercial organisation. In market testing the end result may be contracting out, but it is more likely that the work will be given to an in-house team – who may well have had to promise to change the means of service delivery to keep the activity in the public sector.

By 1994 market testing was certainly the politically 'sexy' approach to the introduction of efficiency and it cannot be disguised that this blew a major hole in the autonomy of the Agency Chief Executives. Though 'out sourcing' might be a strategy that some autonomous managers might have introduced themselves, it is quite against the devolved philosophy of Next Steps to force the agencies through this sort of centralist route. Having been subject to the upheaval of agency creation, the staff affected are now to be subject to the unsettling process of competing for their own jobs. For the management the process is costly (in supporting in-house bids and constructing bidding procedures) and disruptive (in taking attention off the other priorities that the Chief Executive wished to tackle).

Moreover, the market testing has the same improvised feel that characterised the Next Steps process. Does the saving that is expected allow for the fact that redundancy payment might be needed? Does the Government's statement that in-house bids should be supported mean that there is not a level playing field? If in-house bids are expected who in the department has the expertise to fix the tender specifications and evaluate bids? Can we believe that Chinese Walls will work between the evaluation team and the in-house? What is the motivation for the in-house team if any changes will attack standard pay and conditions? If a tender goes out of the civil service, how can a realistic in-house bid be made on the second round. What is to stop the in-house bid from being unrealistic? What penalties will there be for non-compliance?

Above all, the market testing programme is proceeding under the shadow of the Transfer of Undertakings (Protection of Employment) Regulations, 1981. In 1992 it was realised that many of the tenders that had been awarded in local government might have been contrary to a regulation that stated that if an undertaking passed into new ownership then the jobs, and conditions of the workforce were protected. There has to be legal debate as to whether any transfer falls within the scope of the policy. The most clear-cut case would be where outside managers took over the same accommodation and equipment of the authority, but many less clear-cut instances could be relevant. Even though TUPE preserves the jobs the first time the contract is let it seems (even) less clear what happens to staff when the contract is relet if the first contract holder is not successful.

In the light of this uncertainty all the Efficiency Unit can propose is that this is a 'grey area', and that once more cases have been through the courts matters might be clearer. Rather than suggest a pause until matters are resolved they suggest that bidders might be invited to submit alternative bids, the appropriate one to apply once the implications of TU(PE) are resolved. They assert that contractors will not be put off by such uncertainty. It is true that as the market-testing programme begins to affect more white-collar jobs (IT, specialist administration, etc.) compared with the competitive tendering in local government (which has mainly affected the low paid) then TUP(E) might be less of a problem. If the 'going pay rate' for such jobs is higher in the private sector then it will be easier for private sector employers to absorb staff from the public sector.

As to what particular matters might be subject to market testing the formula is the same as for Next Steps – along the lines of 'There are no hard and fast rules. It is up to the department to decide.' Departments are requested, not required, to contribute to the overall programe.

The new emphasis on market testing raises the issue of the relationship between that approach and the idea of agencies. Ministers tend to speak as if they are fully complementary, but controversy about this may have been the area that prompted the remarkable removal of the high-profile, Sir Peter Kemp from his position as Project Manager in the Cabinet Office in 1992. Are agency Chief Executives really autonomous (as Kemp advocated) or are they subject to centralist imposition of policies such as market testing?

The Market Testing Initiative came from the White Paper *Competing For Quality* in November 1991 (Cm 1730). This was produced within the Treasury and this source may be significant: there are at the very minimum some tensions between the market-testing approach and the Next Steps developments.

In the Preface to *Competing For Quality*, the then Chancellor, Norman Lamont, argued that the initiative stemmed from the Citizen's Charter, 'we aim to make public services respond better to the wishes of the users – above all by expanding choice and competition'. Though the connection between Next Steps and the Citizen's Charter were asserted, to those outside the centre of Government the links between Next Steps, the Charter approach and market testing are not clear below a very general level of assertion that they are designed to introduce efficiency. Do they support or contradict each other? They may all be aimed at improving the delivery of services, but it is less obvious that they dovetail together in a co-ordinated way.

As Sue Richards and Jeff Rodrigues (1993) point out, the hero of Next Steps (i.e. Sir Peter Kemp) was 'thrown out on his ear'. They asked, 'Why has there been such a sharp change in direction: the Agency initiative . . . seems in danger of being derailed by market testing, providing solutions from the private sector to achieve improvement.' They complain that there is no 'reasoned critique' that explains why the management reforms of the Next Steps agencies have been overtaken by the fundamentally different market-testing idea.

Though Ministers assert that all is coherence and complementary change, as Richards and Rodrigues say,

> Whitehall does not let ordinary citizens in on its family arguments, so we have to deduce what we can from the evidence available if we want to understand these events . . . in the absence of more open government the old art of Kremlinology comes in useful.
>
> (Richards and Rodrigues 1993: 33)

Does market testing give a better discipline than Next Steps targets?

As noted above it may be that market testing is the logical extension of the agency approach. The agency premise was that there should be a customer/client relationship between the department and the unit delivering the work. The market-testing idea is that the customer should 'shop around' among competing service delivery organisations. But, for better or worse, the original rationale for Next Steps agencies did not have these features.

In the agency model improvement was to come about by a planning approach of imposing on the agencies stiffer and stiffer targets, with a turnover of Chief Executives if performance was judged to be inadequate. In practice many targets are missed but Chief Executives remain in place. For example the *Next Steps Review*, 1993, shows that the NHS Pensions Agency was meant to clear pension age estimates within six weeks of request and 99 per cent within eight weeks of request, in fact the percentages attained were only 43.8 per cent and 83.4 per cent respectively. The Driver and Vehicle Testing Agency missed two targets by 1 per cent, and argued that this was near enough as there was sampling error to take into account. It argued that another target on driving test waiting lists was missed because there was a previous backlog of applications. Ironically the more and more detailed the targets an agency is set, the less control there is as missing one or two targets is seen as less important the more there are.

The 1993 *Review* says that in 1992 the Insolvency Service should

- hold first meetings of creditors within 12 weeks in at least 80 per cent of cases (75.9 per cent achieved);
- report to creditors within 9 weeks in at least 75 per cent of cases (72.1 per cent achieved);
- submit reports within 10 months in at least 80 per cent of possible prosecution cases (74.1 per cent of bankruptcy and 57.1 per cent of company liquidation reports achieved);
- submit reports within 15 months in 80 per cent of cases identified as requiring disqualification in the public interest (33.9 per cent achieved);
- complete the administration of 24,000 cases (21,236 achieved).

All these failures are perhaps explicable as the targets were based on 36,000 cases, but in fact the recession meant that there were over 42,500 cases to be dealt with. But the fact remains that the original Next Steps philosophy laid stress on changing Chief Executives. In evidence to the Treasury and Civil Service Committee in July 1990, Peter Kemp said,

> I think that if the agencies started going wrong in a broad way as opposed to one or two cases, the remedy should not be for the core departments to interfere. What should happen is fire the people in charge, change the people in charge.

The Insolvency Service experience shows the inadequacy of such a model of control.

CONCLUSIONS

In search of coherence

It may be necessary to emphasise that this chapter is not arguing that agencies should not be introduced or, if introduced, will fail. The complaint is that there is really no coherent justification. We have major innovation with very little explanation that makes sense in terms of the academic literature. We have change that is never convincingly related to what went before.

The non-practitioner's task is to ask questions about how the current model differs from its predecessors and fits into our conventional understanding. When Goldsworthy (1991: 35) comments on the short residential conferences held by the Next Steps Project Team, it is in terms of a put-down for academic critics: 'They are lively and productive occasions, with the emphasis on developing practical solutions rather than indulging in theorising.' 'Theorising' is clearly a pathological behaviour. If the agency advocates are determined to avoid a theoretical dimension, they should not then be sensitive to criticism of its absence.

But not all critics are outside the civil service. We have seen that the Lawson memoirs prove Treasury concern. And an interview with *The Independent* quoted Sir Peter Kemp – now an ex-civil servant – as arguing that change had been botched,

> unhappy, unsure of itself and becoming 'littered with policies that do not work.' The controversial market testing programme – the review process that can lead to contracting out – had, he claimed, 'gone hopelessly awry'.
>
> (*The Independent*, 15 November 1993)

The practical world can survive and thrive while out of step with the only available principles. As we shall see in connection with the doctrine of ministerial responsibility, it is practised (or rather not practised) in a way foreign to the old textbook ideas. The theoretical 'story' told about maintaining democratic control of administrative actions through the House of Commons holding a Minister personally responsible is 'not on'. The House of Commons political majority is almost always in the business of protecting their governmental colleague rather than embarrassing the party. Collective responsibility can be invoked to 'cloak' a departmental error.

Few of the current generation of academics have not followed the rise and fall of the Fulton Report and its reforms, Programme Analysis and Review (PAR), the Central Policy Review Staff (CPRS), and corporate management. On the other hand, the Next Steps protagonists seem to have little knowledge of the inheritance of failure – and to react to reminders of the track record in a self-justifying and defensive way. The academics see themselves as playing the part of 'institutional memory' (in Hood's phrase) which the service refuses to acknowledge.

More generally, the grudging (where not hostile) academic reception to administrative changes seems to be based on the weakness of the justification rather than the changes themselves. To date, we are asked to expect that change is much easier than our experience tells us is possible. The 'story' is that the old was bad and the new is good: that a simple change in structure will produce rapid and costless improvement. To date, the propaganda in favour of the changes appear to break the first rule of the New Right. The advocates seem to believe that, when it comes to organisational change, there is indeed a free lunch.

Simon James has described the critical (in two senses) role of civil servants in policy-making, and how this can be confused with obstruction,

> When Chancellor Dalton (Labour) fulminated against civil servants as 'congenital snag-hunters', he was right: it is their duty to hunt out the snags before the machine is set running. Ministers, who come and go are eager to make their mark, want to implement their ideas fast. Civil servants, who have to live with the consequences, need to ensure that the new policy will not stall or break down after a few months. When it comes to the crunch, ministers can and do overrule official fears, but at their own risk, as the implementation of the community charge (Poll Tax) showed.
>
> (James 1992: 35)

If we apply this ideal of the constructively sceptical civil service to the pattern of policy development on agencies and market testing it appears not to fit. As well as Ministers being short term and out to make a personal mark, we seem to have organised matters to have them advised by a succession of civil servants with the same priority. Civil servants are seconded into the centre to help implement a rolling programme: criticism seems to have been organised out of the process as staff wish to be seen as achievers. This means there has been too much emphasis on the pace of reform rather than on the quality.

This chapter has tried to record the poorly signposted slip in fashion from the target setting of Next Steps agencies to quite a different model of progress whereby competion from bidders (in market testing) was to be the engine of increased efficiency. As early as 1994 the market-testing model was itself under threat. Of the first £1.1bn worth of so-called market tests, as set out in the *Citizen's Charter First Report* in November 1992, only £200m worth was actually tested – the in-house teams winning two-thirds and the private sector being awarded about £70m. There was a limited amount of privatisation as an outcome of this review process, but by far the most prominent outcome of the market-testing exercise was the letting of over £700m worth of work by so-called 'strategic contracting out' in which the in-house teams were not allowed a bid. In the light of these decisions to pre-empt the market-testing opportunities, there appears to be the start of a post-market-testing terminology.

The fragmentation of the traditional departments of Government, plus the delivery of governmental services by non-governmental bodies that are the consequence of market testing, means that our image of Government has become even less distinct in a way that only reinforces the general argument in Chapter 1. As part of its inquiry into public spending in Scotland in August 1993 the Scottish Select Committee tried to list which Scottish administrative units were relevant. They immediately faced the terminological point that the Scottish Office is a department with other departments within it. They found:

- Departmental or Managerial Units within the Scottish Office (three: i.e., Scottish Office Home and Health Department, Scottish Office Industry Department, Central Services).
- Vote-financed Next Steps agencies within the Scottish Office (five: e.g., Scottish Prison Service).
- Departments or Managerial Units outside the Scottish Office but within the Secretary of State's responsibility (four, two of which are Vote-financed Next Steps agencies: e.g., Scottish Record Office).
- Department outside the Scottish Office and the Secretary of State's responsibilty but for which the Secretary of State is the Lead Minister (one: i.e. Forestry Commission).
- Nationalised industries or treated as such in the Public Expenditure Survey (five: e.g., Caledonian MacBrayne).
- Public corporations or treated as such in the PES (twenty controlled by External Finance Limits: e.g. Scottish Homes and seventeen NHS Trusts; and five Scottish New Towns).
- NHS Boards and other bodies (nineteen).
- Executive non-departmental public bodies not classified as public corporations. These divide as follows:

  Financed by Grant in Aid (eighteen: e.g., five Colleges of Education);
  Grant in Aid (without Accruals Accounts)(one: Scottish Legal Services Ombudsman);
  Grant with full accruals accounts (two: e.g., Edinburgh New Town Conservation Committee);
  Grant and subject to Companies Act or Friendly Society Regulations (five Agricultural Research Institutes);
  Costs borne on vote without separate accounts (five: e.g. Crofters Commission);

No Government funding and produce full accruals accounts (six: e.g., Scottish Examination Board);

No Government funding and produce no accounts (two: e.g. Police (Scotland) Examination Board);

Local authority contributions and do not produce full accruals accounts (seven River Purification Boards);

Private sector bodies (339, including 249 registered housing associations and twelve universities).

Such a list is of course impenetrably complex; that is its purpose. It is a sign of the organisational mess of British administration. In January 1994, John Garrett MP submitted a memorandum to the Public Accounts Committee that noted that the former thirty civil service departments were being transformed into thirty ministerial head-quarters, 150 agencies, hundreds of quangos and thousands of contracts with private contractors.

The fog is getting thicker.

Note: Material in this chapter updates and extends Working Paper No. 6, *Next Steps Agencies: from Managing By Command to Managing by Contract?*, Aberdeen Papers in Accountancy, Finance and Management, 1992. Next Steps agencies will be discussed in more detail in O'Toole and Jordan (eds) 1994.

Chapter 6

Public and private
Boxes or mirrors?

The fact that there is a breakdown in the certainties of the structure of central Government (and they were perhaps always suspect), with a proliferation of agencies, trusts, quangos, contractual arangements, aggravates the problem of deciding where the public sector ends and the private begins. There is, surprisingly, difficulty in deciding which parts of the administrative map are clearly 'Government' and which are not; which institutions are departments of Government, even who are civil servants. Moreover, as we saw in Chapter 1, bodies beyond the mainstream centre are often lumped together under the rather debased label 'quango' or its more precise term 'non-departmental public body'. The fact that there is doubt over 'Government' is the starting point for a discussion of the complexities in the relations between Government and the private sector business. If we cannot define Government we have difficulty in recognising its boundaries.

Traditionally the distinction between public and private sectors has been seen as a useful commonplace – that there were two discrete boxes into which specific examples could be fitted. Now the useful metaphor may be very different. It may be a 'hall of mirrors' in which the public sector operates through contracts with the private sector, and the private sector exists on public contacts and is controlled by governmental regulation. Each category is so involved with the other that boundaries are again – as in Chapter 1 – lost.

It is common to define the 'state' along the lines of that institution possessing a monopoly of the capacity for the legitimate use of violence within a society. However, if the focus is moved from state to Government and from law and order to the realm of economic activity, then the outstanding characteristic is the *lack of monopoly* by Government in pursuing governmental ends. In seeking to attain economic objectives the Government has to manipulate, compromise, or 'ear stroke' not command or dictate. Although the rhetoric in Britain is often that of *laissez-faire*, the experience is often of governmental intervention – even during the Thatcher period of violently anti-interventionist rhetoric. This may be unwilling intervention, but domestic companies are competing with foreign industries which are themselves subsidised. The 'level playing field' argument pushes Government into emulating competitor arrangements. Foreign aid linked to trade can be transmuted into aid for domestic companies. Governments are often 'bankers of last resort'. The nationalisation programme of the post-war Labour Governments was perhaps more to bail out industries than to grasp the 'commanding heights of the economy'. The Heath Government of 1970–4 had to disregard its own rhetoric and, in a mood of political pragmatism, take both Rolls-Royce and Upper Clyde Shipbuilders into public ownership. Paradoxically the recent Conservative Governments' wish to 'get out of industry' has coincided with a mushrooming of political consultancies that only exist because of the importance of Government in the operations of the private sector.

Governments are increasingly held responsible by the electorate for the fate of industry and the economy. The electorate also demand the regulation of industries in terms of price or environmental effects. As Thomas (1981) shows in *The Government of Business,* fears for public health forced *laissez-faire* Governments to intervene in the nineteenth century. Governments also intervene in pursuit of 'winners'. Privatisation has meant re-regulation, not deregulation. Some industries, such as the water industry, are (arguably) more heavily regulated in the 'private' sector than they were in the 'public'.

The drift to Government intervention is not simply under the push of the electorate but also due to the pull of industry. When industry is not wanting Government 'off its back' it wants it 'on its side'. Industry often prefers the safer waters of Government control and assistance. As Wyn Grant says,

> the question remains whether what British business needs is not so much freedom from the shackles of the state but a mutually supportive relationship with government.

> (Grant 1987: 9)

In the concluding section of this chapter we see that Michael Heseltine claims that even Conservative Governments must, in practice, intervene.

One problem in this discussion is the complication introduced by the fact that Government is multi-faceted. In their study of the electronics industry – *Hostile Brothers* – Cawson, Morgan, Webber, Holmes and

Stevens (1990: 359) distinguish between 'Government as customer', 'Government as financier', 'Government as producer', 'Government as researcher', and 'Government as regulator'. Though the term 'Government' popularly refers to the party political elite, in fact the relations of industry to Government are generally with the bureaucracy. A two-box system of classification into 'Government' and 'industry' is unrealistic in that necessarily there is an important zone where there are ambiguous species. Even nominally free-standing industry is often heavily constrained, if not controlled, by Government. As noted in Chapter 1, books on British administration seem inevitably to resort to images of chaos. Johnson (1982: 209) discusses 'pragmatism run wild', and Hood (1982: 44) complains of the difficulty in 'gaining any intellectual bearings on this vast and apparently formless mass of organisations'.

This pessimism has not infected everyone who has written on this subject. In *Understanding Big Government*, Richard Rose found the boundaries comparatively clear cut. He claimed that the existence of Government implies the presence of private sector organisations that are not a part of Government. He says,

> the fact that government organizations, profit-making corporations, trade unions and non-profit-making bodies such as universities are all part of the same society does not mean that they are interchangeable . . . The existence of relations between public and private sector organizations no more abolishes the differences between them than does the existence of diplomatic relations between America and Russia. . . A government organization is no less a part of government if it influences the private sector, nor does a private sector organization lose this status if it lobbies government.
>
> (Rose 1984: 13–14)

Later in the same book he argued,

> The political system can be conceived of as a set of organizations, but there are very sharp distinctions between government organizations (for example, the Ministry of Defence or the Office of the Prime Minister) and extra-governmental organizations (for example, a pressure group promoting nuclear disarmament, or a party organization) . . . government differs from market organizations . . . because of what Lindblom (1965, p. 12) has described as 'the troublesome concept' of sovereignty. In bargaining between a government organization and a private sector organization, the government can invoke its sovereign authority to change the rules by which the

disagreements are settled and in the extreme case, to abolish an organization.

(Rose 1984: 154)

The sovereignty point is important. When the Conservative Government had its differences with the Greater London Council in the 1980s the Government could (and did) as a last resort dismember the GLC. It could (and did) ban trade unions within the GCHQ. Yet, at the same time, in the world of practice this is normally too drastic a power to have much credibility. Conceding Rose's theoretical distinction does not remove the boundary problems with which we are concerned. Rose himself goes on to make many qualifications to the clear-cut picture presented above. He accepted (1984: 163) that the lack of a European-style public law framework had augmented the confusion. Rose also noted that,

> Government is a plurality of organizations, they are so numerous that neither social scientists nor politicians can easily count how many organizations constitute a government. For example, a survey by President Carter's Reorganization Project (1977) required 45 pages to catalogue one-line descriptions of organizations in the executive branch of the United States federal government.
>
> (Rose 1984: 151)

He cites (1984, p. 155) a study published by Goodsell in 1983 which claimed that the twenty major federal agencies in the US consisted of 14,818 separately identifiable units. Government and business is thus not easily distinguished one from the other as, instead of a homogeneous 'G', there is a multiplicity of sub-organisations with their own goals – often shared with non-governmental actors. This complexity is reinforced by the New Public Management (Hood 1990) that has stressed the business-like expectations for sub-governmental units. To what extent is there a fundamental difference between a part of Government that has competed for its own work in a 'market testing' situation from a private sector organisation that might do the same task for a fee?

Matching the proposition that Government is less easily distinguished from business as it is becoming more business-like is Murray's convergence thesis (1975) that sees the breakdown of a public/private divide through the transformation of business. Gunn summarises this argument as follows:

> He proposes a continuum of types of organisation rather than a simple polarisation of public versus private. Business firms can no

longer think in terms of profits as their single, simple objective and conversely, public organisations have increasingly to justify the resources they expend.

(Gunn 1987: 11)

Such characteristics of modern government make it likely that there will be boundary problems within Government and between Government agencies and other parts of society, and the practice that parts of Government identify with client groups suggests that the most useful analytical division might not pay overmuch attention to constitutional categories. This point was better made as long ago as 1939 in E. S. Griffith's, *The Impasse of Democracy*:

It is in my opinion that ordinarily the relationship among . . . legislators, administrators, lobbyists, scholars – who are interested in a special problem is a much more real relationship than the relationship between Congressmen generally or between administrators generally. In other words he who would understand the prevailing pattern of our present governmental behaviour, instead of studying the formal institutions . . . may possibly obtain a better picture of the way things really happen if he would study these 'whirlpools' of special social interests and problems.

(Griffith 1939: 182)

The rest of this chapter develops the notion that the whirlpool or the hall of mirrors are better metaphors for the subject than the discrete boxes or Russian dolls approach.

Though there are differences between 'G' and 'non G' these differences are certainly much less than political rhetoric allows. From the point of view of Government they may be able to obtain their goals through taxation, regulation and investment as much as ownership. Rose (1984) spells out what he considers to be the five categories which account for an overwhelming number of Government organisations. These are, he suggests,

1 Organisations headed by elected officials, state-owned and principally funded by tax revenues (e.g. local government and central Government mainstream departments).
2 Organisations headed by appointed officials and state-owned but not primarily financed by public funds (e.g. nationalised industries).
3 Organisations headed by appointed officials, and owned and financed by Government funds (e.g. the BBC, a national broadcasting authority dependent on a compulsory user licence).

4 Organisations principally financed or owned by Government, but headed by officials appointed independently of Government (e.g. universities).
5 Fringe organisations (what we might loosely call quangos).

Problems exist for all five of these manifestations of Government in terms of their distinctiveness from the private sector. For example, in connection with type 4 are universities Government organisations (Rose 1984: 13)? Though in a formal sense they are not (the staff are not civil servants), the degree of financial control might give a different *de facto* status. In allowing as 'Government' concerns which are 'principally financed . . . by government' then Rose is allowing a category which could be perhaps even stretched to include a Government-contract-based company such as parts of GEC. These boundaries are at best debatable.

D.L. Thompson (1985) notes that the private sector is a potential alternative to the public sector in virtually every activity of Government. In areas such as hospitals, education, roads, similar functions are provided by different types of organisation. Ownership apart, there are important senses in which private bodies can still be providing public functions. Thompson (1985: 3–7) considers a range of reasons why it should be preferable in particular circumstances to develop indirect administration and implementation of governmental goals.

1 It allows choice, which is itself valued as a good thing.
2 The public might prefer not to deal with 'Big Government'.
3 Possibly there is more creativity in smaller bodies and the provision of multiple means of service delivery allows innovation, learning and reliability.
4 The Government has the appearance of something smaller.
5 Public sector might not want to handle some problems; the problems can be offloaded. Constraints within the public sector can be by-passed.
6 The public sector might lack experience or expertise in an area.
7 The private provision might be cheaper (the privatisation rationale).
8 The service might be more 'cuttable' if Government does not deliver it itself.
9 Alternatively, the private provision builds up a constituency in favour of an activity.

There are thus a large number of reasons why Government should wish to use the private sector for service delivery, but these activities remain public in the sense that the Government is ultimately determining policies and providing resources.

An even more radical argument is pursued in Barry Bozeman's *All Organizations are Public* (1987). His opening remark is that, 'Some organizations are governmental, but all organizations are public.' In other words he argues that though not all bodies are governmental, all are affected by political authority. This rejects the idea that there is a self-contained private sector and replaces it with an image that sees all organizations as public to a greater or lesser degree (and usually greater). As part of the broad (and unresolved) debate as to whether management is a generic activity with similarities in public and private sectors, he says,

> Many familiar and even time-honoured managerial assumptions are beginning to creak with old age. In an environment in which some business organizations receive the majority of their funds from government and quake at the prospect of entering unsheltered markets, old-style 'bottom-line management' has less meaning. In an environment in which government organizations seek profits and hire marketing and advertising personnel to boost their public image traditional public administration nostrums have less relevance.
>
> (Bozeman 1987: xv)

Bozeman confirms the refrain we have already identified.

> In many ways, the problem of conceptual ambiguity is a symptom of another problem; the blurring of sectors, government and business organizations are becoming more and more similar in respect of their functions, management approaches, and public visibility. . . Private organizations are increasingly being penetrated by government policy, and public organizations are increasingly becoming attracted to quasi-market approaches.
>
> (Bozeman 1987)

Bozeman thus suggests that all organisations should be examined in terms of two dimensions – economic authority and political authority. He argues,

1 public pertains to the effects of political authority;
2 organizations can be more public in respect to some activities and less public in respect to others;
3 all organizations are public, but some are more public than others.

> (Bozeman 1987)

When he looks at the US aerospace industry he is able to distinguish different degrees of 'publicness' – from General Dynamics which sold 99 per cent of its production to the US Government (or sanctioned sales to other customers) and Boeing where the percentage was only eighteen.

The industry relied on Government on ways other than sales. Profits were controlled by the laws which allow Government to review levels of profitability on contracts. Government funded research by grants or by tax credits. Government supported the construction of facilities and even leased sites to the companies. Bozeman demonstrates a life cycle in the industry, with Government acting when firms have been in danger of folding. Government was also important in aiding the development of the industry.

He shows how the industry was affected as Government contracting moved from 'cost plus per cent profits' to 'cost plus fixed fee', to 'total package procurement'. He shows how the industry can be affected by regulation – though not necessarily to their disadvantage. New emission and noise controls led to a new generation of aircraft – with an ordering boom. He raises the question that the aircraft industry might be an exception but he does point out that there are plenty of obvious candidates for the exception label. What about universities, private hospitals, the motor industry, the oil industry, agriculture? As Bozeman says, 'At some point, "special cases" begin to add up to generalizations.'

Colebatch's study (1991) of the narrow topic of the motor vehicle repair industry in New South Wales is based on an importantly broad reformulation of the links between 'politics' and 'business' that rejects the notion that these are distinct and separated patterns of social life. He argues that the discovery that this separation cannot be maintained has been a problem for both practitioners and academics. He extends the argument from Jackson and Van Schendelen (1987: 1) about the 'increasing degrees of independence or interpenetration' between Government and business. Colebatch queries whether it is still fruitful to present the relationship as between two discrete sectors:

> The empirical studies have tended to find that both governmental and non-governmental participants are involved in the action, and to describe this as the involvement of the public sector in the private sector. . . But the question which needs to be asked . . . is whether the conceptual framework is still appropriate for the empirical material.
>
> (Colebatch 1991: 4)

Table 6.1 Coalitions supporting and opposing actions

Supported by	Opposed by
Department of Industry (and its Minister)	Treasury (and its Minister)
Manufacturers	Importers
Unions	Farmers
Left-wing Government MPs	Right-wing Government MPs

This is precisely the theme of this chapter. Have political scientists failed to follow their material and accepted for too long a self-serving distinction made by politicians?

Colebatch is uneasy with the assumption that Government 'intervenes' in the economy – as if the economy exists and operates independent of the Government. He notes that the coalitions in support of action are likely to cross boundaries: thus a particular course of action is likely to be supported and opposed as indicated in Table 6.1. He asks whether it is meaningful to ask if the resulting action is the work of 'Government' (1991: 6).

PARA-GOVERNMENT ORGANISATIONS

Another source that rejects the two-box idea is *Delivering Public Services in Western Europe* (1988) edited by Chris Hood and Gunnar Fole Schuppert. This draws attention to the international trend towards 'para government organisations' (PGOs). They say PGOs may be common enough but they challenge conventional, bred-in-the-bone ways of thinking about public services (1988: 2).

They show that the core public bureaucracy (i.e. the mainstream civil service) is only one means of delivering public services. They also discuss the independent public enterprise and private or independent enterprise (1988). The first category is the 'public corporation' type. Hood says it is public but has a legal personality distinct from that of central administration. The independent enterprise is a body which is seen to be delivering public services not created by special statute. Examples given are firms providing public services on contract, charities providing services by agreement with public authorities, trade associations operating voluntary regulation schemes negotiated with public authorities and so on. Clearly, it can be argued that privatisation has often produced such PGOs rather than 'pure' private sector bodies. Hood discusses the

'myth' of the private sector (in Hood and Schuppert 1988: 79) in which
the use of organisations such as private companies, charities and associations as instruments of Government, offends against commonly held
views of what the institutional world ought to look like.

With regard to this fictional account of how the public sector is
controlled by the accountability of directly elected politicians, Hood
quotes Fuller (1967) who argued that it did not matter if what was
assumed was patently false as a statement of fact, so long as it has
convenient consequences.

Hood, in a way that is germane to Part II of this book, notes that
(1988: 83) the development of PGOs can be interpreted as a way of
keeping alive certain 'dignified' myths of British Government by 'efficient' mechanisms which in practice go clean counter to these myths but
keep up appearances by unobtrusively papering over the cracks of the
conventional doctrines. He notes Johnson's explanation for the development of such a trend towards para-Government which was simply
'opportunistic pragmatism' and a complete absence of any coherent
doctrines of administrative design (Johnson 1979, quoted in Hood and
Schuppert 1988, p. 83).

THE NEW POLITICAL ECONOMY?

The iron grid image that separates out the Government and private
worlds can be contrasted with the position adopted in Bruce Smith's *The
New Political Economy* (1975). Smith's argument is in line with Bozeman –
that all significant economic activity is so heavily influenced by Government that it is illusory to suggest that Government and non-Government
are discrete. In the preface Smith claims,

> the public business that is conducted outside the regular departments
> and ministries of government. The economy and large parts of the
> private sector engaged in non-economic activity, have become drawn
> into the orbit of government influence to an unparalleled degree. So
> great is the interpenetration between the 'public' and the 'private'
> sectors that this basic distinction – on which the political rhetoric and
> dialogue of modern times has rested has ceased to be an operational
> way of understanding reality.
>
> (Smith 1975)

The notion of a growing public sector can be expressed conveniently
by the ratio between public expenditure and GDP. There are surprising
difficulties however in measuring these basic statistics. In Britain in the

1970s we agonised at the prospect of a public expenditure consuming more than 60 per cent of GDP. Roy Jenkins (from within a Labour Cabinet) argued in a speech in Llangefni,

I do not think that you can push public expenditure significantly above 60% and maintain the values of a plural society with adequate freedom of choice.

(Cited in Heald 1983: 13)

Now, over a decade later after ten years of so-called Thatcherism, the figure is still above those inherited from Labour – but the hysteria has abated. The fact was that when the British definitional practices were re-examined we no longer seemed to be far out of line with other countries (see Heald 1983: 31).

In his introductory chapter to the *New Political Economy*, Smith suggests,

The sharing of authority with private and quasi-private institutions is a central feature of modern government. . . The usual Weberian notions of bureaucracy (and other older organization theories) as a hierarchy of fixed offices performing standardized tasks are clearly inadequate as a description of the new public sector in the United States. The reality in fact, is that modern government is much more loose-jointed with a permeable outer skin, and shot through with confusing arrangements when looked at from the traditional perspective.

(Smith 1975)

Smith (1975: 4) argues that even in the (nominally) *laissez-faire* system of the nineteenth century there was a greater role for Government than theory perhaps allowed. In practice the infrastructure that permitted private enterprise to flourish was provided by Government. Smith thus argues that even in the *laissez-faire* epoch the lines between 'private' and 'public' were blurred. He comments that, 'the smooth continuum of history provides few tidy lines of demarcation for the scholar's convenience'. None the less, he breaks out three main historically based types of political economy. Selected features from Smith's typology are set out in Table 6.2. While this typology is introduced here as appearing to be a rough aid to the description of modern economies, it must be acknowledged that it has had a negligible impact on public administration or public policy, or on the language and activities of public administrators. Indeed, taken at face value, the Thatcher Administrations acted in direct contradiction to the features of the *New Political Economy* but the thesis of this chapter is the superficial appearance was misleading.

Table 6.2 Historical pattern of political economies

Early industrialisation	Managed economy	New Political Economy
Early and mid nineteenth century US and UK	Late nineteenth and early twentieth century	Post-World War II
Government intervention in the provision of social overhead capital	*Laissez-faire* gradually replaced by regulation	Massive governmental intervention in all phases of social and economic life; private/public more blurred

Source: Condensed from Smith 1975, Fig. 1.

In the 1980s in Britain (and elsewhere) there has been the major phenomenon of privatisation. The rhetoric of that tide of activity seemed to rest heavily on the simple two-box idea of clear-cut 'public' and 'private'. It assumed that something vital happened when an activity moved from the 'Government box' to the 'market box'. While conceding that the Smith idea has not been 'in good currency', it should not be assumed that it is thereby deficient. It can be argued that we have clung on to that terminology for reasons as weak as those that have accounted for the retention in Britain of academic notions such as ministerial responsibility – a mixture of unthinking acceptance and a reluctance to accept the consequences of its rejection in terms of a need for a new language of discussion.

CORPORATISM

Smith's approach connects with that of Pahl and Winkler who (writing in a very different tradition) in *New Society* on election day in October 1974 predicted 'the Coming Corporatism'. A summary of their article claimed that, 'Whichever way today's voting goes, many underlying trends will not change.' A major one they identified was increased state control of the economy – but not traditional nationalisation.

Although 'corporatism' has been an academic fashion in the 1980s, and although Pahl and Winkler were the British pioneers, it has not been their version of the label that has been popularised. Their version was essentially about, 'a comprehensive economic system under which the state intensively channels predominantly privately-owned business towards four goals. . . '

Later in the article Pahl and Winkler note

The essence of corporatism as an economic system is *private* owner-ship and *state* control. It contrasts with Soviet socialism's state own-ership and state control, and pure capitalism's private ownership and private control. . . Going beyond Keynesian aggregate demand management and counter-cyclical intervention ('fine tuning'), corpor-atism attempts detailed control of economic activity and conscious direction of resources.

(Pahl and Winkler 1974)

In their support they cite the well-regarded work by Andrew Shonfield (1965) in which he had pointed out that, 'the economic order under which we live and the social structure that goes with it, are so different from what preceded them that it is misleading to use the word "capit-alism" to describe them' (cited in Pahl and Winkler 1974: 74). Their own classification of the major types of economic system is shown in Table 6.3.

It might appear perverse – and it is certainly a matter of dispute – as to whether such a notion as corporatism can have any relevance after successive terms of Mrs Thatcher's Government with their well-advertised claims of deregulation of business. But arguably the substance of Government influence is difficult to dissolve. Corporatism, they suggest, can be seen as more than a journalistic expression about policy-making over beer and sandwiches and be seen as a distinct type of economy in which private industry is regulated in the public interest.

Pahl and Winkler's conclusions about the economic order were (unusually) based on empirical work. This seemed to suggest that some kind of state control was acceptable to those actually in business. Pahl and Winkler wrote,

Will business leaders tolerate state controls on their decision-making freedom . . . the directors we studied had no objection to a type of state control which they thought they could control – the government shielding them from the vicissitudes of competition and the trade cycle, but leaving them managerial discretion . . . What the directors

Table 6.3 Pahl and Winkler's types of economic system

| | | Ownership | |
		Private	Public
Control	Private	CAPITALISM	SYNDICALISM
	Public	CORPORATISM	SOCIALISM

Source: Pahl and Winkler 1974, p. 74.

of large companies do not want is laissez-faire competition. What they do want is capitalism without competition, a combination of state support and private control.

(Pahl and Winkler 1974: 74)

The range of controls, incentives and influences held by Government is so extensive that what the current pattern has to be distinguished from is traditional capitalism.

A study of regulation in Europe edited by Leigh Hancher and Michael Moran, *Capitalism, Culture and Economic Regulation* (1989), concluded that,

> The most striking feature of economic regulation to emerge from the preceding chapters is that it is dominated by relations between large, sophisticated and administratively complex organizations . . . Such bodies obviously include the various agencies of the state-government departments, quangos and specialized regulatory bodies – but they also encompass organized interest groups, trade unions and firms. The importance of the large firm in the regulatory process is particularly notable. Indeed an important theme . . . is the importance of the large, often multinationally organized, enterprise as a locus of power, a reservoir of expertise, a bearer of economic change, and an agent of enforcement in the implementation process. Understanding economic regulation, then, means *understanding a process of intermediation and bargaining between large and powerful organizations spanning what are conventionally termed the public and private domains of decision-making.*
>
> (Hancher and Moran 1989, emphasis added)

As central Government creates more departmental agencies as executive arms are these units still Government? If the work of Government is privatised is it then non-governmental? – when, for example, the funds are still from Government (such as cleaning services) or where there is governmental control of the industry as per the English water authorities. What about controls on profits as on the gas industry? What about Golden Shares as a means to control privatised concerns? What about the Government massaging debts to put the privatised entities in a favourable light?

In *Public Money*, Gretton and Harrison (with Beeton) claimed,

> it is likely there are now more public servants charged with monitoring the performance of British Telecom and British Gas than there ever were in the relevant departments before privatisation.
>
> (Gretton *et al.* 1987: 25)

THE BLURRING OF PUBLIC AND PRIVATE

There are six main planks to the case that the public/private divide is more than a matter of an imprecise boundary and involves a scale of problems that throw the categories into doubt:

1 One line of argument is that the governmental category (and the wider public category) is itself so incoherent that the boundary is a significantly broad zone. Moreover as new administrative forms are devised within Government with the purpose of making administration more efficient and businesslike – departmental agencies, trading funds, and so on – the problem grows. The introduction of these different administrative forms has meant changes that are either purely superficial or changes which detract from the distinctiveness of the private sector.

2 Second, there is the area of the 'contract state': Government-sponsored or Government-controlled industry. Where a company becomes oriented to Government as a customer it is reasonable to assume that the status is not the same as when the customer is non-governmental. An article in *The Independent* on 1 December 1989 argued that British Aerospace could be regarded as a wholly owned subsidiary of the British Government. It claimed that over 80 per cent of turnover was heavily influenced by the Government as a customer or as an influence on foreign governments. The Government retains a director on the board.

3 Third, there is the capacity of Government to determine by its actions or inactions the prosperity or otherwise of whole industries or classes of activity. For example, the state of health of something like milk or beef production is effectively Government-determined. Activities like raspberry production or sheep production which seem far removed from the effects of Government depend on Government response to the flooding of markets by East European pulp or the EEC sheepmeat negotiations.

4 Fourth, there is the 'favourite son' style of special policies introduced to aid, or ensure the viability of, particular products or companies. For example in the 1981 Finance Act a clause was introduced to provide a tax concession for Shell and Esso to build a petrochemical plant at Mossmorran. The plant already attracted the usual array of governmental incentives, but because of the possibility of a glut of such products, Shell and Esso were threatening to pull out unless further inducements were forthcoming. Accordingly the Scottish Office as 'sponsor' department persuaded the Treasury to make further

assistance available – to the dismay of their competitors in the market, BP and Shell (Bruce-Gardyne 1986: 4).

5 There are Government policies which affect geographically restricted numbers of companies. There is still a regional policy scheme which essentially gives incentives to 'steer' investment to areas of highest unemployment. A related example of selective assistance by area – but which became a means to channel advantage – is the Enterprise Zone idea which began as a sort of experiment in the total withdrawal of Government influence. According to an early version of the idea (from Sir Keith Joseph in 1977) a new Conservative Government would set up a series of 'demonstration zones' within the most depressed parts of the nation's cities in which Government would be virtually dismantled in order to see just what the unfettered market could achieve. In practice the Government backed-off from interfering with low-wage controls, employment protection legislation, health and safety requirements and many planning controls. At the same time many positive Government-funded benefits were introduced. The EZ idea became very like the sort of selective regional assistance programme it was meant to replace (see Jordan 1984). Other disguised or indirect regional aid has been identified as being channelled through the local 'rates' system. The Uniform Business Rate shifted costs from the North to the South. Thus without the Government necessarily thinking about the consequences for individual companies, whole classes of company in terms of area were helped or handicapped.

6 Finally, there are governmental policies which are neutral to particular industries or industrial locations but affect all industry. There are, for example, the investment allowances which can be claimed by all industry. These are less conspicuous than grants handed out by Government but it is money which is forgone by the Treasury. Similarly, Government policy on matters such as the exchange rate and interest rate have repercussions for the breadth of industry. Thus in 1980 when the British Government allowed the pound to exceed £2. 40, exporting was made difficult. Grant (1982, p. 2) has claimed that decisions on the exchange rate, taxation, money supply, interest rates, and public expenditure often have more far-reaching consequences than the succession of *ad hoc* and small-scale palliatives that often are held to constitute industrial policy.

Grant (1982: 14) distinguished between the social market and the selective intervention approaches to industrial policy. The former (once again fashionable) term – in pure terms – is characterised by economic and fiscal controls which, combined with legal regulation, are neutral between firms and industries. The selective intervention approach, as defined by Grant, is less *laissez-faire* and views as likely and desirable microeconomic attempts to influence particular firms within broad industries. While the first instincts of British Governments need not always have been in favour of selective intervention, the electoral costs of appearing indifferent to key industries has often been of irresistible force. Moreover, as Grant has pointed out,

> it is difficult for a nation state to refrain from subsidising their industries
> . . . the Federal Republic of Germany, the supposed bastion of social
> market capitalism, provides extensive aid to a range of industries. Failure
> to provide at least matching assistance to British industries would leave
> them competing internationally on unequal terms.
>
> (Grant 1982: 17)

Steel in a broad-ranging survey of the literature in Britain on Government/industry relations has pointed out that,

> Government has not just one but literally hundreds of relationships
> with industry. The functions of the Department of Industry constitute
> only a relatively small part of the whole picture. Firstly, there are a
> number of departments such as Employment, Energy, Trade and
> Transport, whose work is mainly concerned with industry. Secondly,
> the Treasury's macro-economic policies have a major impact upon
> industrial decisions . . . the work of almost every other domestic
> department impinges upon industry.
>
> (Steel 1982: 449)

Indeed, Steel goes on to show how regional Ministries and a whole range of quasi-governmental bodies and local authorities are relevant for industrial policy. Unqualified assertions about the Thatcher Government and its dismantling of controls cannot hope to catch the complex detail of practice.

WHY INTERVENE OR REGULATE?

In essence the claim is that the private sector in the UK as in most other countries is firmly embedded in a context that is shaped by political decisions. The argument is thus explicitly against any notion that we can compartmentalise discussions into public and private; the private sector is inevitably Government influenced. To date the links that have been (lightly) sketched have been primarily financial but regulatory control affects companies in further ways. As Wyn Grant argues (1987: 1–2), even if one believes that markets are the best way to respond to the preference of consumers it is inevitable that market-oriented Governments will themselves be involved in market activity.

First, there are areas of activity in which markets fail or where the short-run benefits of competition are outweighed by longer-run costs. Grant's example here is agricultural markets where it is difficult to obtain an equilibrium between supply and demand. An example of market failure might be the privately rented housing market whose deficiencies lead to council housing, but it can be argued that it was the restriction on economic returns on rents that lead to a limited number of rented units and poorer facilities. At one time we would confidently have said that coal was an example of market failure and that the investment need for a modern coal industry was such as to force it into single ownership. Education could be provided entirely by markets but Government has political reasons in stepping back from such an arrangement.

Second, he says, there is involvement where the Government intervenes to evolve a legal framework of regulations within which markets can operate smoothly and efficiently. Here there is legislation to prevent behaviour that would itself discredit the market idea. If misleading advertising were allowed this would be bad for the cheated consumer. It would be bad for the more ethical company which would be robbed of custom, and it would be bad for the market system if it brought it into poor regard. It would also be unwelcome for the Government as the public seem to hold the Government responsible for all activity – whether it genuinely has much to do with Government or not.

There is an obvious argument for the Government to prevent monopoly which market theory tells us is bad for the consumer and efficiency, but to protect that aspect of the market one might have to restrict the actions and desires of companies in the market – telling one company it would be a bad idea if it pursued its market freedom to take over another. Alternatively the Government might allow a near-monopoly as with telephones or gas supply but attempt to regulate that 'near-monopoly' with special regulatory rules.

Third, the Government feels a need to intervene to prevent harmful social consequences that could result from the unrestrained action of the market. This is regulation to deal with the 'externalities' of company activity. These are restrictions on the right of companies to pass on business costs of their activities to other firms or concerns. For example, the individual firm might see planning restrictions as an interference on their freedom, but without restrictions neighbouring companies might see the behaviour of that firm as intrusions. In enterprise zones, for example, there is much more control than was first anticipated as it is necessary to control the 'bad neighbour' effect. After all why should I put a major investment into my high status corporate headquarters if you develop your scrapyard or waste incinerator next door? Some sectors seek governmental regulation. Regulation is often a protective measure in favour of sectors who want to limit price competition or control access to their markets. This in turn leads on to the notion of regulatory capture that supposes that the body doing the regulation is often the instrument for the interests that they are supposed to control. The agency becomes dependent on the industry for information and over time adopts the industry's own definition of the situation. Industries which oppose regulation often quickly become supporters once introduced. At a simple level, if one has developed a properly safe and hygienic chip shop one is keen on regulations that will stop some 'cheap start' operation from undercutting it. If one is in the tobacco industry then regulations on advertising make it more difficult for competitors to squeeze successful brands. One might not oppose some kinds of restriction because they would preserve advantages.

The argument that there is an inevitably close relationship between (even) a Conservative Government and industry is supported in a book published in 1987 by Michael Heseltine. He claimed,

> The Department of Trade and Industry will deny that there is, or should be, any view from the centre of how British industry might develop and prosper . . . That is not how government is behaving. The truth is the present Government, like all its predecessors for at least the last 50 years, is up to its neck in the business life of this country, stimulating enterprise, stifling another and interfering at every turn . . . Commercial judgements are constantly being made across the whole range of government in every hour of every working day . . . The debate should be concerned . . . not with whether a British Government should have a strategic approach to industry but what that approach should be . . . Governments everywhere acknowledge responsibility for creating a favourable climate for industry . . . The most serious industrial managers are now increasingly and articulately dismissive of a 'hands-off' relationship between government and industry.
>
> (Heseltine 1987: 7–11)

Dunsire, Hartley and Parker (1991: 21) examined the empirical evidence available on the issue of whether a change in organisational status (within the public sector, or between the public and private sectors) affected performance. They show that, 'Much current public policy has been based on the belief that resources are more efficiently used in the private sector, or under public sector emulations such as the trading fund.' They note three mechanisms that are held to bring about this improvement:

> (a) the policing role of the capital market;
> and/or (b) an increase in competition;
> and/or (c) a change in managerial incentives.

They further note however that (b) and (c) can be implemented without a change of ownership and that a change of ownership does necessarily entail them. They cite Forsyth (1984), 'Selling a Government firm makes no difference to the competitive environment in which it operates; ownership and competitive structure are separate issues.' After reviewing the record of ten organisations in the UK which had altered their formal status in the 1970s and 1980s they concluded that in most cases there was no support for the thesis that change in ownership improves enterprise performance.

Other empirical work by economists has reached mixed conclusions but much has confirmed that it is not ownership that is the significant factor but competition. This line of evidence would be particularly sceptical of the privatisation of near-monopolies (Borcherding, Pommerehne and Scheider 1982, cited in Bos 1991). Millward and Parker (1983) concluded that:

> there is no systematic evidence that public enterprises are less cost effective than private firms. The poorer performance, in this respect, exhibited in the studies of refuse collection and water supply. . . has to be balanced against the absence of any significant difference in Canadian railways and Australian airlines and the superior performance in US electric power.

> (quoted in Bos 1991)

In brief conclusion we can accept that the public/private divide is convenient, widely accepted and easy to understand. It is, however, also a blunt and ideological division that has petrified thought on the actual relations between the two categories. In practice the private sector is heavily influenced by the Government and there are pressures on parts of the bureaucracy to be more businesslike.

Part II

Accountability without certainty

Chapter 7

Collective ministerial responsibility
A prime ministerial strength?

It is widely agreed that the principle of collective ministerial responsibility is central to British constitutional discussion, yet most academic accounts have of necessity the tone employed by parents who after spending five years persuading small children that fairies exist have then to take some trouble to explain that they don't.

It is worth establishing as a starting point that the British Constitution is not a firm, clear or certain guide to political practice. If it is argued that it is these qualities that distinguish a constitution and that a constitution circumscribes action, then we must consider seriously the proposition that in Britain we have no constitution. Peter Hennessy (in Marshall 1989: 80) quotes John Griffith's comment prompted by the circumstances of the Westland affair in 1986, 'the Constitution is what happens'.

Hood and Jackson (1991: 163) cite a long-established Japanese practice of accepting explanations or descriptions of phenomenon which no one actually believes for a moment but are convenient to adopt for public utterance. Ministerial responsibility is a convenient British fiction because it is inconvenient or impossible to agree on an alternative: so we must pretend.

This discussion essentially argues that the account that we received from Dicey (*Introduction to the Study of the Law and the Constitution*, 1885) has become overtaken by,

- the existence of more interventionist Governments;
- the increased reliability of party control of Parliament by the pro-Government majority part;
- the emergence of a class of professional politicians who cannot afford, or choose, to leave public life.

But no replacement formula has emerged. We have discourse in a language that is inappropriate. Principles once touted as absolute are revealed to be obsolete.

The concept of ministerial responsibility is usually seen as a great principle fallen on hard times. It might be better put that it is a pair of principles which have fallen. There are two concepts of responsibility: the first collective (or joint responsibility) attempts to ensure that the process of governing is carried on by an administration compatible with parliamentary (and hence public) wishes. The second (individual ministerial responsibility) – which is considered in the next chapter – is that Parliament scrutinises the work of the separate departments, confirming (or refusing to confirm) the relevant Secretary of State in Office. These notions are central to the conventional image of Britain as a democratic polity; they are central to most descriptions of democratic practice. Hence it is disturbing to find them subject to such a welter of contradictions, qualifications and interpretations. If these ideas are in question then so must be the conventional account of our democratic system.

In one sense this discussion of ministerial responsibility is rather 'old hat': the discipline (changing metaphors) has been chasing other hares. But, arguably, there is a void in more fashionable topics such as New Public Management. What sorts of accountability are implied in these discussions?

Each of the two initial principles in fact conveys several different meanings. Thus the discussion of ministerial responsibility involves a number of very different propositions.

COLLECTIVE RESPONSIBILITY AS RESPONSIBLE GOVERNMENT

The first principle – collective ministerial responsibility – holds that the members of the Government are collectively responsible to Parliament. Marshall (1989: 1) makes the point that this system of Government is a contrast with the separation of powers model of the US. In the separation of powers model the executive and the legislature are autonomous and separately elected with no power to dismiss the other.

The collective responsibility notion holds that the Government continues in place at the discretion of the legislature; that a dissatisfied Parliament can remove the offending Government. Birch terms this the idea of 'responsible Government' and cites the Durham Report of 1839 as follows,

When a ministry ceases to command a majority in Parliament on great questions of policy, its doom is immediately sealed; and it would appear to us as strange to attempt for any time, to carry on a government by means of ministers perpetually in a minority, as it would be to pass laws with a majority of votes against them . . . it has been the habit of ministers rather to anticipate the occurrence of an absolutely hostile vote, and to retire, when supported only by a bare and uncertain majority.

(Birch 1964: 132)

Birch argues that this principle was altogether more novel than Durham implied when he set it out, but certainly by the end of the century it would have appeared uncontroversial. The major issue remaining relates to Durham's 'great matters of policy'. The original formulation covered only matters of some substance.

We need therefore to distinguish between a specific defeat and a generally untenable position for a Government. Though the Durham Report does imply that defeat on a major policy implies resignation, it did also, rather inconsistently, advance the other idea of 'perpetually in a minority'. This latter prerequisite for resignation is very different from the single defeat idea, but somehow both of the qualifications ('great matters of policy' and 'perpetually') were lost and collective responsibility came to mean that Government was supposed to resign if it lost a single vote even on a minor matter, or if it lost on a specific vote with no hint that generally the Government was unacceptable. At first sight this evolution of the principle appears to show an increased vigilance in Parliament and constitutes a more vigorous scrutiny of Government: Government appears at risk on even minor or one-off issues. Yet, of course, these changes were advanced by the Government, not its critics. This paradox was prompted by the fact that the Government had most to gain by apparently broadening the ground rules for control. It was the Government who could then say to critics in Parliament that *any* defeat, on *any* issue was of such gravity that Government would fall. It left Parliament with only such a massive sanction that, dominated by Government supporters, it was unlikely to use it. The image implicitly put forward by Government Whips was of a supermarket display of baked beans: to move one can might bring down the whole. As recently as 1964 Graeme Moodie in *The Government of Great Britain* was setting out that,

it is now assumed as a matter of course that any defeat in the House
of Commons must be reversed or else lead to the Government's
resigning or dissolving Parliament.

(Quoted in Marshall 1989: 33)

So the first line of Government defence against scrutiny was essentially a
bluff – that any attempt to change Government action on particular
policies ran the risk of Government resignation and (probably) an
election which would threaten the Government's own (majority) supporters. But, particularly in the time of the very narrow Labour majorities in the 1960s and 1970s, it was convenient for the Government to let
this bluff be seen for what it was: because the Government might lose a
particular issue it backed off from the threat that Government itself
would fall over a minor defeat. A new principle was conveniently
discovered to the effect that even if the Government loses an unambiguously vital part of its programme it would not now feel obliged to resign
until and unless this was confirmed in a general vote of confidence.

Marshall notes that the confidence principle (as he labels it) needs
careful stating and is now generally phrased more narrowly than it
would have been even in the 1970s,

Possibly as a result of smaller parliamentary majorities and distur-
bances in internal party discipline, defeats, even serious defeats, in the
House of Commons are not now thought to entail the constitutional
consequences that were once thought inevitable. Only defeats on
specific motions of no confidence are thought to compel governments to resign or advise dissolution.

(Marshall 1989: 3)

This is a two-step procedure – defeat on legislation, followed by con-
firmatory defeat in a vote of confidence. (The two could be combined in
a single stage by making a matter a vote of confidence.) This two-step
process does not stop the party Whips from talking as if there would be
some instant disaster if the Government loses any important part of its
legislation. They would, wouldn't they. Nor does it stop the Opposition
talking as if resignation were an instant penalty for loss of a major vote.
In 1976 Mrs Thatcher claimed that defeat on the Labour Government's
Expenditure White Paper was such a case:

When there is a defeat on a matter of major economic strategy, a
matter central to the historic nature of the power of the House of
Commons over the Executive, that is a resigning matter.

(Quoted in Marshall 1986: 56)

However, in practice Governments now survive defeats on single items of policy. Marshall (1986: 56) shows that this refinement of the principle to demand a double defeat was still controversial in 1977 when there was strong reaction to *The Times* when it put forward the view that,

> there is no constitutional principle that requires a government to regard any specific policy defeat as evidence that it no longer possesses the necessary confidence of the House of Commons.

The rediscovery of what was no doubt true – that there was no strong convention of resignation over a specific matter – conveniently emerged to assist Government once it discovered that the threat against its back-benchers was no longer effective. If the Government's bluff against defeat was not to work, then it had to disown the catastrophic consequences it once said were inevitable. Marshall contrasts different editions of the major law textbook by Hood Phillips: *Constitutional and Administrative Law.* The 1962 edition said a Government was bound to resign or advise the Queen to dissolve Parliament after defeat on a major issue. The 1978 edition referred only to defeat on a motion of confidence or no confidence.

In 1992 in discussion over a parliamentary vote on a 'paving' procedure leading to the reintroduction of the 'Maastricht Bill' to the House of Commons found 'Downing Street sources' trying to get back to the notion that on 'matters of great substance' a Government would resign if defeated and seek a General Election. As we have seen this was once an interpretation that was widely accepted, but it was a view that had been superseded by the two-step (defeat, then vote of confidence) version. This leaked view was, of course, an attempt to force Conservative Party Eurosceptic rebels back into line. They were being told that they could not expect to wreck the Government's European policy and then later vote in support of a vote of confidence.

However, this line that the Government's future was inextricably linked to the fate of one vote on one bill was very much a matter of tactics by sources 'close to the Prime Minister'. In July 1993, when the Government was defeated on the Social Chapter aspect of the bill, several options appeared possible including a suddenly discovered process whereby the Maastricht Treaty could have been signed in spite of Parliament. In fact the Government chose to make this a 'matter of confidence' and twenty-nine Conservative rebels then chose to support the PM and Cabinet. Had that vote been lost the PM seemed inclined to seek an election but, alternatively, he could have been ousted from office and replaced by a new Conservative PM – who might, or might not, then have sought an election.

Norton (in Marshall 1989) demonstrates that in fact in the nineteenth and twentieth centuries there were hundreds of defeats for the Government on matters of sufficient party importance to see the imposition of a 'whip'. He says that between February 1905 and February 1978 (inclusive) there were at least eighty-four Government defeats on whipped votes (fifty after April 1972). He says that only in a minority of cases did the Government seek to reverse the defeat, seek a vote of confidence, or resign. He says that only in two cases did it resign – in both cases after defeats on declared votes of confidence in 1924, and on only three occasions were defeats followed by confidence motions. Norton concludes,

> The popular views of the Government's required response to defeats in the lobbies rest upon no continuous basis of practice, and hence, in this sense, may be described as myths.
>
> (Quoted in Marshall 1989: 35)

One could equally well conclude that the convention that *called for* resignation upon defeat was part of our ritualistic Constitution. Like most of the rest of the Constitution it was an understanding to ease the lot of the Government: it protected the Government from back-bench rebellions. In Britain the Constitution is a set of arrangements facilitating governance. This unrealistic notion of the seismic consequences of minor action presented some self-image as a democratic society and protected the Government from scrutiny.

However, even if the idea that defeat on a major bill or other proposal has been refined to mean that this must be confirmed by defeat on a specific vote of 'no confidence', there is retained an insistence that Government requires that there is no withdrawal of approval by the House of Commons. There is still a notion that government in general must proceed with the consent of the legislature. Durham's idea of the unacceptability of a Government 'perpetually in a minority' still holds. Even if there has been a current relaxation of the convention – in its interpretation that any defeat equalled resignation – this does not seriously infringe the idea of democratic accountability that underlies the core version. While the convention may have been subtly altered in this regard, this is not one of the fundamental alterations in the play of the game. The underlying notion is still that a Government must be acceptable to the public as reflected in the composition of the House of Commons. (Though the House of Commons in the 1980s and 1990s reflected the views of the public less proportionately than it did when two main parties dominated the electoral process.)

Geoffrey Marshall warns that it is possible to imagine PMs who felt it their duty to soldier on in the general interest even after a vote of no confidence. In such a scenario the speech writers would say things such as,

> In view of the importance of (defeating the IRA/defeating specula-tion on the pound/defeating foreign dictators) it is not the time to subject the country to the uncertainty of an election. When the crisis is over the public will be invited to make their decision on the firm and resolute actions of the Government. Until then an election could only damage the likelihood of a satisfactory outcome.
>
> (Marshall 1986: 56)

At that point we should stop pretending that the issue of collective responsibility as a democratic check has any value whatsoever. Even the elastic Constitution must have a breaking point. The example might be improbable. A less unlikely scenario would be where a minority Government is in power, which believes that a small potential coalition partner could be ignored because it would have too much to fear in a General Election and thus would be relied upon to sustain the Govern-ment in Office. On a vote of confidence, however, the potential partner abstains and the Government is defeated. If the Government speedily concluded a new deal with that party, what would stop the new coalition from asking for another confidence vote?

The principal erosion of the working of the convention that meant that the Government was answerable to the House was the development of party cohesion. This has frustrated the idea that Government is at risk through parliamentary scrutiny. Party cohesion means that the real accountability to the House of Commons is a one-off post-election matter. Once the Government is safely in Office it need not worry over-much at the prospect of being forced out. The party majority that determined which party took office will sustain it in Office. The majority of the members of the House of Commons see their task as supporting the Government. Moreover, if the Government is dismissed their own electoral futures could be damaged.

The impact of the collective ministerial responsibility convention has obviously been altered more significantly by the development of a usually reliable party majority within Parliament (existing to sustain and protect the Government of the day) than the later change in the convention to mean that defeat on a specific vote can be reconciled with continuing in Office. Birch (1964: 135) points out that between 1832 and 1867 no fewer than ten Governments were brought down by adverse votes in the Commons; that Lord John Russell who had questioned this meaning of the collective responsibility principle in 1839 accepted it and resigned immediately his Governments were defeated in 1852 and 1866. Birch points out that in the 1832 to 1867 period no Government survived a full term of Parliament, whereas since 1868 most changes of Government have been brought about not by a parliamentary reversal but by an adverse result in a general election. He argues that since elections take place infrequently the idea that a Government is held continuously responsible through the possible withdrawal of parliamentary support has been frustrated. Modern Governments attempt to submit themselves for election when things are going well – and they have every chance of being successful – not when mistakes have occurred.

COLLECTIVE MINISTERIAL RESPONSIBILITY AS UNITY OF OPINION

While the term was losing its importance in the sense of controlling and even changing Government, a different idea began cohabiting under the same label. In current use the revised convention concerns the homogeneity of views of Government members and limits their freedom to express dissent from both general and particular governmental policy. Each Minister must (in public) defend the record and proposals of the Government. (Or at least must express dissent with sufficient skill to avoid too blatant a contradiction of the 'rule'.) If Ministers fail to be seen to be supportive the sanction will be in the hands of the Prime Minister (i.e. their demotion or dismissal) rather than in the hands of Parliament. The classic expression of this version of the convention was Melbourne's remark to his Cabinet colleagues that it did not matter what was decided as long as they all told the same story (Gilmour, 1969: 214). This is the 'hang together or hang separately' proposition. Lord Salisbury argued in the House in 1878,

> For all that passes in Cabinet every member of it who does not resign is absolutely and irretrievably responsible and has no right afterwards to say that he agreed in one case to a compromise, while in another he was persuaded by his colleagues . . . It is . . . only on the principle that absolute responsibility is undertaken by every member of a Cabinet, who, after a decision is arrived at, remains a member of

it, that the joint responsibility, of Ministers to Parliament can be upheld, and one of the most essential principles of Parliamentary responsibility established.

(*Hansard*, Vol. 239, cols. 833–4)

The notion that Administrations should not be drawn from opposed groups, which Birch (1964: 133) sees as appearing to be the rule about 1815, has come to mean that there should be no variation of views from within the single governing group. The reason for the development of this interpretation can be related to the original version of collective responsibility only by the most ingenious. It can be argued that if Ministers were found saying different things then the idea of clear-cut electoral choice – for or against the Government – would be lost and it would be difficult to hold the Government 'responsible'. But it is not impossible to imagine the operation of the Mark I responsibility (democratic acceptability) without the requirement for Cabinet solidarity (Mark II). If (say) the Government arrived at the House of Commons with a proposal for a poll tax, the House could – were it so inclined – support the proposal whether or not it was recommended by the whole Government or only by a dominant faction of that Government.

What makes the above example so improbable that even consideration is difficult, is the disposition of political power in Government rather than any constitutional factors. A PM, under these circumstances, would find less troublesome colleagues. Opposition parties have also adopted this 'united we stand, divided we fall' principle even though there has been no theory of an Opposition responsible to the public. In fact the solidarity principle follows from the political costs to the governing party in being seen to be factious. The Mark II idea of collective responsibility as concerning a single governmental view on policies thus stems from the fact that a divided party is likely to be an electorally unsuccessful party – and the fact that promotions within the Government are likely to go to those who do not 'rock the boat'. A single view emerges because dissent is disadvantageous both for the party and for the dissidents. In this sense of collective responsibility *the Cabinet is united against the scrutiny of the House of Commons*. It is not a contribution to accountability but to its avoidance. It allows the PM, not the House of Commons, to control the Government. The rationale lies in the easier making of policy. The guide to business provided by the civil service for new Government members, *Questions of Procedure for Ministers* (May 1982), states that

Decisions reached by the Cabinet or Ministerial Committees are binding on all members of the Government. They are, however, normally announced and explained as the decision of the Minister concerned . . . Collective responsibility requires that Ministers should be able to express their views frankly in the expectation that they can argue freely in private while maintaining a united front when decisions have been reached.

The then Cabinet Secretary argued against the publication of the memoirs of Richard Crossman on the grounds that,

Ministers will not feel free frankly to discuss and surrender their personal and departmental preference to the achievement of a common view, nor can they be expected to abide by a common decision, if they know that the stand that they have taken and the points that they have surrendered will sooner rather than later become public knowledge.

(in Marshall, 1989: 48).

This solidarity is not for Constitutional but political reasons. It seeks to prevent Ministers playing for popularity in the party and the public by getting their opposition to unpopular (and perhaps necessary) policies. A Minister with an eye to the future might, for example, oppose public expenditure cuts on specific items as such opposition wins friends.

Sir Ian Gilmour, who was later to be a conspicuously tentative supporter of Mrs Thatcher while in her Cabinet, has argued that, apart from considerations of security, the point of secrecy in any gathering is to prevent people competing for power or popularity outside the gathering by what they say or do inside it: 'The spectacle of ministers currying favour in their own party by dissenting from unpopular decisions would be more than their colleagues could bear' (1969: 214).

The leak and the coded signal as practised by some of Mrs Thatcher's critics have been tolerated by Prime Ministers – though for some such as Sir Ian Gilmour himself, John Biffen and Jim Prior, the provocation to the Prime Minister has not been indefinitely resisted. The leak has however been defended by Patrick Gordon Walker. He argued that the requirement of secrecy was intolerable in that as political animals Ministers sometimes had to break the norm,

In every Cabinet the leak will be deplored and condemned; but it is paradoxically necessary to the preservation of the doctrine of collective responsibility. It is the mechanism by which the doctrine of collective responsibility is reconciled with political reality.

(Walker 1972: 33–4)

It can also be noted that – from the Prime Minister's perspective – the Press Secretary exists as a licensed leaker. Leaking by Cabinet Ministers is often to challenge an account that has been given to the press that better suits the PM than other Cabinet members in its thrust.

Though leaking exists in practice it seems that an extension of the argument of the need for solidarity is being constructed. This justifies not consulting the Cabinet at all on the grounds of the need to avoid leaks. To ensure collective responsibility members of the Cabinet are not informed.

It is, of course, also the case that the unanimity was against the Crown – to prevent the monarch from dispensing with the services of individual Ministers – but generally, arguments that relate to the Crown should be dismissed. Mention of the 'Crown' (or the Royal Prerogative) is almost invariably an authoritative and impressive sounding legitimation for something that has no sounder rationale.

Prime Ministers can dispense with the services of Ministers on a specific issue, or with the services of those who are seen as unenthusiastic about the general policy preferences of his or her colleagues. There are few examples that can be cited of Ministers voluntarily resigning because they cannot accept the collective (which almost invariably means prime ministerial) view. There are few resignations on general grounds – though when Ministers do finally go they tend to ask 'for other past offences to be considered'. Suddenly, after the loss of office, the unacceptability of broad Government policy is much clearer.

George Brown's resignation as Deputy Prime Minister was accepted in 1968 after he was not consulted on the Government's decision to close the banks for a day to suit the American authorities in their attempts to control a chaotic gold market. However, the particular incident was claimed by Brown to be symptomatic of a general approach by the PM. His resignation letter stated,

> The events of last night and the long hours of this morning have brought to a head a really serious issue which has . . . been troubling me for some time. It (the problem) is, in short, the way this Government is run . . . I regard this general issue as much more fundamental than any particular item of policy.

WESTLAND AND COLLECTIVE RESPONSIBILITY.

When he resigned from the Conservative Government in 1986 Michael Heseltine said he did so on the grounds that no opportunity was being permitted by the PM for his Cabinet colleagues to come to a collective decision on the relative merits of two ways of dealing with the crisis at the small helicopter manufacturers, Westland. There was a European consortium solution advanced by his own department (Ministry of Defence) and there was an American option preferred by the Department of Trade and Industry and its Secretary of State, Leon Brittan. Heseltine felt that the PM was preventing the Cabinet from hearing his arguments as a means of denying the Cabinet the opportunity to back his 'European' solution. In the Thatcher leadership election crisis of 1990 Heseltine said that in the Westland episode he had given the Prime Minister five weeks' notice that he would resign if she refused to allow Cabinet discussion of his views. He said,

> I can remember very clearly the Cabinet at which she decided the matter had to be ended. It's the only time I remember the Prime Minister reading out conclusions of a meeting . . . which didn't take place.

The Westland events confirm the proposition in Chapter 4 that much Government business is done in Cabinet committee rather than the full Cabinet – and in informal non-Cabinet committees rather than the official system. The series of ministerial accounts of these events show that the expectation was that such matters were dealt with in committee. In Mrs Thatcher's own account (1993: 425) she records how she held a series of meetings around June 1985 with Michael Heseltine, Norman Tebbitt, Nigel Lawson and others. As the matter moved further into crisis she records holding two meetings (5 and 6 December) with Michael Heseltine, Leon Brittan, Willie Whitelaw, Norman Tebbitt and Nigel Lawson. At the second meeting she claimed there was a clear preference for Leon Brittan's position that a deal between Westland and the American firm Sikorsky was best. However, as Geoffrey Howe, Norman Tebbit and Michael Heseltine strongly dissented Mrs Thatcher then decided to put the matter to a formal Cabinet committee. This was E(A) which was the principal sub-committee of the Economic Committee.

This raises two important points. First, a considerable amount of business was conducted outside the formal system. Second, she recorded that E(A) was 'enlarged as appropriate': the forum is not neutral when the selection of committee and its composition is determined by the PM.

Mrs Thatcher concedes that their meeting on 9 December had assumed that a subsequent meeting would take place, but she argues that it was not so much cancelled as simply not needed when it was realised that Westland was not interested in the European solution that Michael Heseltine was keeping in play. Heseltine tried to raise the matter at a full Cabinet on 12 December but he was told that it was not on the agenda and no papers had been pre-circulated. It was on the agenda on 9 January, but Heseltine found that it was introduced in a way that focused discussion on the need to ensure that Ministers agreed in public. All Ministers were asked to clear answers to questions via the Cabinet Office. At this point Heseltine claimed there had been no collective Cabinet discussion and that there had been a breakdown in Cabinet Government. He left the Cabinet and the Government.

Though the resignation stemmed from the specific circumstances of Westland, Heseltine, like George Brown (see p. 201), none the less presented his resignation as being about the general way in which the Cabinet proceeded rather than simply a difference over Westland.

The Heseltine resignation was a very different category of business from the slightly later resignation of his colleague Leon Brittan – to be discussed as a (possible) example of individual ministerial responsibility (see p. 209).

Nigel Lawson also presented his resignation as Chancellor on the grounds that collective deliberation of policy was being prevented by the PM:

> For our system of Cabinet Government to work effectively the PM . . . must appoint Ministers . . . then leave them to carry out the policy. When differences of view emerge . . . they should be resolved privately and, where appropriately, collectively.

The famous failure to consult the full Cabinet about the deflationary budget in 1981 was no doubt to avoid protests from the 'wetter' elements. But this means that in practice collective responsibility is determined by the PM.

Any decision to resign at a particular point carries the probability of the action seeming out of proportion. When the main issue on the political agenda at the time of the Brown and Heseltine resignations was the state of the British economy it could be argued that they would have done more to advance their views by remaining to fight their corners in the Whitehall system rather than by 'opting out'. Resignation also raises the tricky matter of timing – the 'dirty hands' argument. If a Minister is so concerned at the general way in which things are handled why did he not resign at some earlier point. George Brown (1971) conceded in his memoirs that,

Looking back, I am sure that it would have been better for me politically to have resigned before I did . . . There was the occasion . . . when the Prime Minister decided . . . not to devalue the pound in 1966 . . . Or on South Africa; or on health charges; or on education . . .

(Brown 1971)

In his resignation speech in the Commons in 1990, Sir Geoffrey Howe hinted at this difficulty when he admitted that he might have 'wrestled too long' with his conflicting loyalties.

Criticism of the way things are done in Government by those who have lost Office is often explained away as the expression of some personal disappointment, thus when in 1987 the former Leader of House of Commons in Mrs Thatcher's second administration, John Biffen, complained of her 'Stalinist' regime, he was criticised for making remarks moved by 'nothing more than pique' (*Sunday Times*, 5 July 1987). One of his critics observed that he had been in – and gone along with – the system about which he was now complaining. Sir Geoffrey also had to bear criticism that his claims about policy differences were merely means to get back at the PM for removing him from any powerful office in the Government and giving him his token status as Deputy Prime Minister.

The Biffen example also raises the point that 'resignation' is often a diplomatic cover for a dismissal. Biffen was reportedly reluctant to write the ritual resignation letter since there was no way in which his was a case of voluntary resignation. His letter avoided the usual cliches concerning the privilege and pleasure of serving the PM.

A complication of the principle that everyone who was party to a debate on policy should keep quiet on the occasions on which they are in a minority (the good loser version) sounds less reasonable when it is realised that the PM can (according to Michael Heseltine) ignore decisions that go against her/him; can 'drop' those who disagree; and junior members of the Government who have no real opportunity to influence these decisions are none the less bound by Cabinet decisions – or even prime ministerial pronouncements such as granting the Americans the use of British bases to bomb Libya. (Even the Secretary of State for Defence – far less the full Cabinet – was not consulted.)

In October 1992 it was widely reported in the press (after leaks from disgruntled Ministers) that the proposal to close thirty-one coal mines was not discussed at full Cabinet. It was taken by 'a small committee of about half a dozen Ministers, headed by Mr. Heseltine, President of the

Board of Trade, working with the PM' (*Daily Telegraph*, 16 October 1992). Even Ministers who were represented on the Committee complained that they were unaware of details affecting their departments. Apparently the first that most Ministers heard of matters was a statement by Michael Heseltine (President of the Board of Trade) at the end of a Cabinet committee on Europe. As recently as Marshall and Moodie's (1971) of *Some Problems of the Constitution* there was a quite lengthy discussion as to whether or not collective responsibility applied to those who were not party to the decision. By now it is uncontroversial.

In 1986 during the Westland episode, Mrs Thatcher could assert without fear of contradiction (even outside the Cabinet) that, 'Decisions reached by the Cabinet or Cabinet committee are binding on all members of the Government.'

As noted above, the Opposition has also followed this line on the need for no conflict in public – though there is no 'constitutional' argument involved. The only area of doubt perhaps relates to Parliamentary Private Secretaries who are unpaid assistants to Ministers but despite being unpaid are considered in the Government and bound by collective responsibility. There were instances of Parliamentary Private Secretaries surviving in post despite voting against the Wilson Governments, but Mr Callaghan and Mrs Thatcher 'firmed up' on this. What counts is the political weight of the offenders. Wilson was able to sack Brian Sedgemore while he was PPS to Tony Benn over the disclosure of a Treasury document but he did not sack nine PPSs who rebelled jointly in December 1974. They were simply too numerous.

In principle the unanimity rule suggests that members of the Cabinet must support the collective line or else. If we look back at Salisbury's argument that a member of the Cabinet is inside and jointly responsible or must resign, the wording seems to imply that he was prescribing an ideal that all-too human Ministers might not be inclined to follow. If he did not see this as a problem his phrase 'absolutely and irretrievably responsible' would not have been necessary. He seems to be (vainly) trying to invent a form of words that will not allow exceptions – and presumably he did this precisely because he anticipated ministerial behaviour.

The cases of officially sanctioned non-observance of the revised (unanimity) principle are few and celebrated. Each is so clearly related to the difficulties within the governing party that the exceptional non-enforcement of custom need not destroy the expectations about the custom. The first of the suspensions of the principle was in 1932 when Snowden, Samuel, Sinclair and Maclean, after offering their resignations, remained in Ramsay MacDonald's National Government on the under-standing that they had 'permission to disagree' with the Cabinet's abandonment of free trade. On the matter of the EEC referendum Mr Wilson allowed seven members of his Cabinet to campaign against the recommendation of the Government that there should be a vote in favour of continuing British membership. (They were not allowed to speak against the Government in Parliament and Eric Heffer was sacked from his junior post in the Government as a result of ignoring this restriction.) Marshall notes (1986: 57) that the 1932 dispensation was under the unusual circumstances of a Government coalition. Thus the 1975 decision was an even bigger break from convention. There was a similar dispensation in 1977 over the European Assembly Elections Bill.

These cases are officially sanctioned (by the PM) occasions for Government members to disassociate themselves from the Cabinet line. Other cases are where individuals are tolerated, no doubt because in the judgement of the PM it causes less political difficulties to live with – more or less – discreet signals of dissent. Thus Jim Callaghan was demoted in Cabinet status in 1969 but allowed to remain a Cabinet member when he had sided against the PM and the 'In Place of Strife' (trades union reform) proposals at a joint meeting of the Cabinet and the NEC of the Labour Party. Ellis (1980: 370) notes that in June 1973 some Labour Ministers joined in a vote in the National Executive Committee of the Labour Party against nuclear testing because the matter had not been considered in full Cabinet. In 1974 Tony Benn and two non-Cabinet Ministers (Hart and Lestor) survived in Government after voting in the NEC against a joint British/South African naval exer-cise. Again the outcome is a result of political choice by the PM (Ellis, 1980: 381).

After a decision in 1977 to enter the 'Lib–Lab' pact to keep the Labour Government in Office, the PM revealed (to the briefed press) that the vote was 20:4 in favour. The four Ministers (named) who voted against (Benn, Orme, Shore and Millan) were in effect warned that they had to support the Government or leave it (Ellis 1980: 378).

It might be argued that to suspend collective responsibility (in the sense of solidarity) is a breach of a constitutional convention. But to breach this new version of the principle is a far less serious matter (for democratic norms) than to breach the original version of responsible Government which holds that Government can persist only with the support of the House. The breach of the unanimity rule is the erosion of a working practice, but for a Government to stay in Office without parliamentary support would infringe a basic notion of democracy: it would be tantamount to a coup. When the Labour Government lost a vote of confidence in 1979 there was no question but that it had to leave Office – but when it earlier lost a motion that the salary of the Secretary of State for Industry should have his salary cut in 1976 this was acceptable to political opinion when it took the opportunity to have the decision reversed a few days later. Likewise, defeats on public expenditure in 1976 and on sanctions against companies breaching pay guidelines were restored by explicit votes of confidence (Turpin 1985: 68).

We have then seen that one sense of collective responsibility has disappeared. The mechanical resignation if defeated in the House of Commons is no more (and it always was less than the textbooks suggested). The importance of identifying the different senses of collective ministerial responsibility is shown when we note that the failure of collective responsibility as meaning that the Government is united is a very different matter from the failure of collective responsibility as parliamentary accountability. The failure of collective responsibility in the sense of all Ministers singing the song prescribed by the PM would not in any very direct way threaten our democratic system: maybe even the reverse.

Crossman explicitly argued that collective responsibility had been transformed from its original sense '*and it enormously increases Prime Ministerial power*' (1972: 64 emphasis added). The dominance of the PM is not a Thatcherite or even novel phenomenon. In his introduction to his 1914 edition of *The Governance of England*, Sidney Low observed:

> The Prime Minister's influence and importance are growing. He is acquiring now and again enlarged attributes, beyond those he possesses as chairman of the executive board, and chief of the dominant party . . . The increasing size of Cabinets has caused the figure of the Prime Minister to stand out more prominently above the ranks of his colleagues . . It follows that the Premier is acquiring the attributes of an Imperial Chancellor, and that he is performing certain duties to which the 'collective responsibility' of the Cabinet cannot easily be applied.
>
> (Low 1914: xx–xxii)

We tend to have a confused discussion of the important matter of the accountability of Government because very different propositions exist under the label of collective responsibility. What is often welcomed as a restraint on the power of Government is transmuted into the baser meaning of conformity with prime ministerial leadership.

COLLECTIVE RESPONSIBILITY AND THE FALL OF MRS THATCHER

Looking back at the circumstances that led to a change of Prime Minister in 1990 it is clear that it had something to do with collective responsibility. The precise relationship is complex and possibly unique. Sir Geoffrey Howe clearly disagreed with the policy of the Prime Minister over Europe and therefore resigned. However, a series of Cabinet colleagues argued that the resignation speech did not set out differences from Cabinet (as opposed to prime ministerial) policy. This shows that the logical force of the Howe resignation was that the PM was in breach of collective responsibility. Howe was resigning because she was out of step.

There is an old Aberdeen story about a proud mother watching her son parade up Union Street with the local regiment who observed, 'They are a' oot o' step except my Jimmy.' With regard to collective responsibility on Europe the senior figures in the Cabinet were all out of step except Mrs Thatcher.

When Douglas Hurd was interviewed by Brian Walden on the issue he repeatedly drew attention to what he very precisely entitled the Thatcher/Major plan for the hard ECU (European currency unit). He was saying that the PM was intimately associated with the plan that was the policy collectively subscribed to by the senior members of the Cabinet. Interviewed on *Newsnight*, Kenneth Clarke argued that there was a policy which 'Euro enthusiasts' such as himself could back. He repeated the claim that Cabinet policy was agreed. 'The fact is that we have agreed upon a policy which makes us a European party which defends British interests . . . The fact is within the Cabinet we have agreed policies that unite us.'

In other words both Ministers were reminding the PM of the collective policy she was obliged to defend. The trouble for the collective Cabinet was that the PM was too ready to break cover as a reluctant European. Although the Government's policy was negotiation with European partners, as Sir Geoffrey pointed out in his resignation speech, the Prime Minister seemed all too suspicious of the enterprise. He referred to her nightmare image as she looked out on the Continent to find it positively teeming with ill-intentioned people scheming 'to extinguish democracy', 'to dissolve our national identities', to lead us 'through the back door into a federal Europe'. He quoted a correspondent who had noted that, 'People throughout Europe see our Prime Minister's finger wagging and hear her passionate no, no, no, much more clearly than the content of the carefully worded texts.' Sir Geoffrey argued that the PM was undermining the efforts of others in the pursuit of governmental policy, 'How on earth can the Chancellor and the Governor of the Bank of England, . . . be taken as serious participants in the debate against that kind of background noise?' He noted that each step forward risked being subverted by some casual comment or impulsive answer. When Sir Geoffrey revealed that the commitment to join the Exchange Rate Mechanism was made only under the threat of resignation from the Chancellor and the Foreign Secretary then the tentative nature of prime ministerial enthusiasm was plain. Michael Heseltine expressly argued in his first round campaign for the leadership.

> That is why Sir Geoffrey Howe resigned. That is why Nigel Lawson resigned. That is why I resigned because the Prime Minister feels so strongly on these matters that collective Cabinet responsibility is not acceptable to her.

The last thing that fragile Cabinet unity required was Mrs Thatcher's off-the-cuff advocacy of a referendum two days before the first round leadership vote. Cecil Parkinson, Douglas Hurd and John Major all signalled that this was 'not on'. Her behaviour confirmed her defiance of *collective* responsibility.

Therefore it appears that Sir Geoffrey represents a very special case of collective responsibility resignation. He resigned in support of Cabinet policy. His problem was he was out of step with the PM who could neither change the agreed policy – nor stomach it. Sir Geoffrey was the man who resigned because his Prime Minister would not be bound by collective responsibility. Margaret Thatcher was the PM who both stretched the power of the PM to dominate the Cabinet and found there were limits yet.

Chapter 8

Individual ministerial responsibility
Qualified to death?

BACK TO BASICS?

The basic idea of *individual* ministerial responsibility is that it is a means of ensuring parliamentary control over individual Ministers and departments. If any department is found wanting in terms of important matters of policy or administration, then the Minister (i.e., Secretary of State) should be held responsible to Parliament – to the extent of losing his or her office if the matter is serious enough. In the 1990s there were calls for resignation under this heading that included the Home Secretary (Brixton prison/IRA escapes), the Transport Minister (suppression of a report critical of DOT role in navigation safety), Home Secretary (immigration case), the PM (*re* his position in relation to the BCCI banking debacle). The main reason these calls were fruitless was that this principle – like that of collective responsibility – immediately runs into the party political factor that it would be politically embarrassing for the pro-Government majority party in the Commons openly to criticise its own leading members. None the less the term is still a common component of our currency of constitutional debate – without any serious attempt to reconcile it with party political realities. The principle is described in *The British Constitution* by Jennings:

> If the minister chooses. . . to leave the decisions to civil servants, then he must take the political consequences of any defect of administration, any injustice to an individual, or any policy disapproved by the House of Commons. He cannot defend himself by blaming the civil servant.
>
> (Jennings 1966: 149)

The Select Committee on the Treasury and Civil Service in 1986 described this *traditional* version of IMR as follows,

The traditional view, exemplified in the famous Crichel Down case, is that Ministers are responsible and accountable to Parliament for all that occurs within their departments. It follows that if a significant mistake is made by the department, *the Minister should resign. . .* [emphasis added].

There is no doubt that it is individual ministerial responsibility (IMR) rather than collective responsibility that has generated the greater academic and journalistic attention in the twentieth century. This appears to be the case for varied reasons: the number of cases of its potential application are greater (departmental errors presumably occur more often than Governments lose the confidence of the House); because often some scandal is involved, and because there is even more scope for argument over exactly what the convention means.

It is quite possible that the constitutional symmetry of the two legs of the Constitution – collective and individual ministerial responsibility – is a piece of over-simplification. In fact it is frustratingly difficult to find a pre-twentieth-century source that gives the two principles some kind of equality. Dicey, for example, claims,

> a Minister or Ministry must resign if the House passes a vote of a want of confidence.
>
> (Dicey 1962: 457)

> a Minister who cannot retain the confidence of the House of Commons, shall give up his place, and no Premier even dreams of disappointing these expectations. . .
>
> (Dicey 1962: 444)

> ministerial responsibility means two utterly different things, the responsibility of Ministers to Parliament, or, the liability of Ministers to lose their offices if they cannot retain the confidence of the House of Commons
>
> (Dicey 1962: 325)

It is quite possible to read into these sentences a concern about the responsibility of Ministers (individually) but in fact Dicey was principally concerned with the sense of Ministers (collectively). He discusses at length and in several places, the consequences of a Government attempting to ignore the convention that,

> government must be carried on in accordance with the will of the House of Commons, and ultimately with the will of the nation as expressed through that House.
>
> (Dicey 1962: 442)

Dicey (1962: 26) presents as one of his conventions of the Constitution 'Ministers resign office when they have ceased to command the confidence of the House of Commons.' As noted above, this kind of remark can be easily read as meaning that individual Ministers resign office when they have personally lost the confidence of the House, though he could conceivably have meant that Ministers (i.e., the Government) resign. Another ambiguity in his sentence concerns the status of the 'convention'. This term apparently was to cover maxims that were 'universally admitted to be inviolable' and others have, 'nothing but a slight amount of custom in their favour'.

He wrote at length of how other processes to drive unpopular Governments out of Office had fallen into disuse because they had come to recognise a convention not to overstay their parliamentary support. Dicey's argument seems wholly artificial. He advanced the view that the power of the conventions was because to breach them would be to indirectly 'bring the offender into conflict with the Courts and the law of the land' (1962: 446). He argued that a lack of a majority would mean that the Government would be unable to pass The Army (Annual) Act (the Mutiny Act). This would make military discipline impossible:

> every person, from the Commander-in-Chief downwards . . . would find not a day passed without his committing . . . acts that would render him liable to stand as a criminal in the dock.
>
> (Dicey 1962: 447)

He argues that Ministers (perhaps by the 1990s now atrophied) resign by convention because there was an understanding that if the House of Commons insisted on withdrawing support from the general business of the Government there was a constitutional black hole into which Government would in any case fall. In his view a convention arose to short-circuit other action that the House could take to remove Ministers. But his is an explanation of the emergence of the convention. By the 1990s we need an explanation for the demise in so far as it relates to individual ministerial responsibility. Such a strict convention runs into problems in implementation. In dealing with the problems the convention has been subject to so many qualifications that the proposition that it now exists in the original sense is difficult to sustain.

Jennings does present individual ministerial responsibility in a clearer manner,

Each minister is responsible to Parliament for the conduct of his

Department. The act of every civil servant is by convention regarded as the act of his minister.

(Jennings 1946: 184)

But even the first edition of *The Law and the Constitution* was 1933: this is a late enunciation of 'Victorian' principle.

The matter of why conventions are followed or not has been a separate and substantial debate. Marshall (1986: 5) points out that Dicey contradicts himself when he distinguishes between conventions as rules that bring their violators into conflict with the law of the land and rules that 'may be violated without any consequence than that of exposing the Minister or any other person by whom they were broken to blame or unpopularity'. As Marshall says, this seems to concede that the threat of the courts in the background is not always the basis of a convention. Marshall cites Jennings's argument that conventions are obeyed, 'because of the *political difficulties* that would follow if they are not' (emphasis added). This distinction is important in that in the latter interpretation suggests (realistically) a far less certain application of the principles.

It can be argued that if the cases of ministerial responsibility are so keenly debated we cannot be in the area of 'convention'. As Dicey presented the conventions they operated with mechanical thoroughness; the error was directly linked to the consequence. The issue here is whether IMR in operation is still a working belief of politicians and influences their actions or whether it is simply a form of words. This chapter concludes that when politicians express views on the meaning of individual ministerial responsibility they tend to express a series of clichéd phrases about 'the right thing'. They do not have a well-developed and coherent version – far less do they have a sophisticated theory that would take account of the complicated legal arguments.

One suspects that, ironically, the notion of a responsibility of individual ministers for the activities of their civil servants has been articulated in the textbooks more clearly as the power of the civil servants has grown in the twentieth century. In other words the principle has been clarified as it has become less practical. Robert Peel as Home Secretary in 1822 had a staff of fourteen clerks, a précis writer, a librarian and various porters and domestic officials. The Foreign Office employed twenty persons in 1821. The volume of legislation has increased from around 47 pages in 1901 to 222 by 1991 (from *Hansard Society* 1993, p. 399). Whereas once it was not absurd to assume that the Secretary of State knew of all the business of his department, is this still a reasonable starting point for a discussion of responsibility?

The basic version of individual ministerial responsibility involves the political head of a department accepting a personal culpability (and sanction) for the mistakes made in his name. This definition can be used to exclude many ministerial resignations such as when a Lambton, Profumo, Ridley, Jellicoe or Mellor resigns because of some *personal* action unrelated to their ministerial life – or if the issue is the Minister's own error, as when Dalton resigned in 1947 after he briefed a journalist with budget details early enough in the afternoon to allow the newspaper to anticipate his speech. Although Marshall (1986) sees cases such as Cecil Parkinson's resignation over personal difficulties in 1985 as individual ministerial responsibility it can be argued that the distinctive quality of IMR is when the Minister carries the can for a member of the department, not for some conduct of his own that did not affect his discharge of departmental duties. When David Mellor resigned in 1992 it was over the political embarrassment caused by his extra-marital adventures and the acceptance of a holiday at a Marbella villa from the daughter of a sometime member of the Palestine Liberation Organisation in apparent breach of governmental rules about hospitality. Such matters did not involve departmental responsibility.

Even when sticking to individual ministerial responsibility as a means of ensuring control of departments we can distinguish two quite different propositions: (a) IMR as enforced democratic accountability, and (b) IMR as anticipatory personal behaviour. With the former version the Minister is *driven* from Office by a vote in a hostile Parliament; in the latter the Minister can be expected to *stand down* even if he is not voted out.

This second idea of Ministers acting on their own initiative is not to be confused with their acting in response to personal misjudgement of the Profumo/Dalton/Parkinson/Mellor/Mates type, but to say that there seems to be a school of belief that Ministers act in a spirit of self-sacrifice. The 'buck stops here' idea seems to suggest that when something goes wrong in the department the Minister *offers* his resignation. In this sense the then Home Secretary, Kenneth Baker, was quite correct to contemplate resignation over the escape of two IRA suspects from Brixton prison in 1991. There was a departmental error and he headed the department. Had he actually followed through and resigned there might have been more life in the convention. The second sense of individual ministerial responsibility implies self-dismissal. The Minister resigns not because there is a hostile majority in the House of Commons but in anticipation of the disapproval of his social equals.

This idea of 'correct behaviour' by a Minister can be put in a context of the elaborate codes of conduct that had multiplied in Victorian and Edwardian Britain. These rules of etiquette existed for matters such as the protocol of visiting, of marriage, of the behaviour of weekend guests. Ministers whose departments had erred would, in this environment, feel under a real obligation to demit Office. It is commonplace to apply the phrase 'the rules of the game' to political behaviour. This has perhaps become such a cliché that we have lost sight of the fact that the remark implies that in the second connotation of IMR there are similar expectations about 'proper' behaviour in the good (amateur) sportsmen and the Victorian gentleman politician. The likelihood of Ministers conforming to an idea of self-imposed punishment fits in with the belief that correct behaviour was to be equated with sporting codes.

Dicey cites with approval Freeman's remark,

> We now have a whole system of political morality, a whole code of precepts for the guidance of public men, which will not be found in any page of either the statute or common law, but which are in practice held hardly less sacred. . . by the side of our written Law, there has grown up an unwritten or conventional Constitution.
>
> (Dicey 1962: 419)

The ethic of politics as sport suggested that one 'walked' and did not wait to be adjudicated 'out'. It is no doubt possible to argue that such codes of behaviour were massively ignored. The conventions in sport and politics were what was 'done' by the gentleman existed irrespective of what gentlemen actually did. In Brian Dobbs's book *Edwardians at Play* he documents the transfer of sporting ethics into wider society. He points out there is nothing so effective as a private income in enabling one to take a moral stance (1973: 32).

But the two senses of individual ministerial responsibility are connected. Just in case the idea of self-sacrifice did not come to mind, there was, as noted above, a willingness to vote a member out of Office. In the mid-nineteenth century, the so-called 'Golden Age of Parliament', the possibility existed of back-benchers feeling they had a prior duty to scrutinise rather than defend Government. But to vote a Minister out was a sanction for which they had no need if the 'walking' expectations of the convention were met. Ministers who did not 'volunteer' would find that the House was prepared selectively to dismiss Ministers who had not satisfactorily administered their departments. But this idea of eviction from Office is different from the self-sacrifice version of the term.

We have established the core of the traditional meaning, but a further distinction can be made between cases where the Minister resigns because there has been some error or unsuccessful policy in which he and his political colleagues in the department had a role, and the cases where the flaws emerged in spite of – or at least without the active participation of – the Minister. There are problems with both variants. With the former there is the immediate conflict with collective responsibility. Are there any activities which are not covered by the collective version?

The latter interpretation can appear unfair in implementation if it involves the Minister resigning over something in which, by definition, he had little participation. This may be a harsh doctrine but it does seem to be at the heart of the folk memory of the political community. In the traditional formulation the Minister was expected to accept blame for the misdemeanours of his staff. As George Brown argues in his memoirs about the resignation of Sir Thomas Dugdale in 1954. He (Dugdale),

> was in no way personally responsible for the decisions . . . I am sure that [resignation] is the right doctrine, and that we ought all to defend it. Ideally, a Minister ought to be so good that he can't be misled by his officials. If he is misled, well, it may not be personally his fault, but he has got to carry the can.
>
> (Brown 1971)

The argument here appears to be that – like Low's case of the butler and the spoons (see p. 218) – the Minister is deficient in letting others do wrong in his department. *He is resigning not because of his involvement in error but because of his error in not being involved.* In 1991 Kenneth Baker argued that he did not resign because the escape of the Brixton prisoners was not a policy matter but an operational matter. It can to the contrary be argued that the holding of prisoners in such a gaol under the conditions that lead to an escape was a policy matter (especially if the security forces had prior knowledge of a plan), but even without that argument the traditional doctrine would have expected a resignation.

It is reasonable to say that the traditional doctrine is unfair and unworkable but that means that some of the 'moral high ground' about 'carrying the can' has to be abandoned. Moreover, it means that we need to develop a theory of accountability that does not rest on ministerial responsibility.

THE INCOMPATIBILITY OF COLLECTIVE AND MINISTERIAL RESPONSIBILITY

If it is to be assumed that the control of administration in Britain is to be effected through the devices of collective and individual ministerial responsibility a large difficulty exists. Sidney Low, with his first edition as early as 1904, pointed out how the two ideas of collective and individual MR could not really stand together. His starting point was that,

> The accountability of ministers to Parliament, and through Parliament to the nation, is the theoretical basis of our modern English Constitution.
>
> (Low 1914: 135)

He continues,

> ministers, in the fullness of their powers, are at any moment to be arraigned, not merely for their own acts, but for the acts of their subordinates, before the Assembly [i.e., House of Commons],which is again itself responsible to the sovereign People. This is the doctrine of ministerial responsibility, which is by many regarded as the main shaft and supporting pillar of the political edifice.
>
> (Low 1914: 138)

Further, he says,

> It has been said that the essence of good government is the power to find the proper man to hang if things go wrong. We like to think that we have satisfactorily provided for that. We can always 'hang a minister', we murmur to ourselves . . . we can without violence or disturbance of the normal machinery of government, maintain a constant control over all the departments of the executive. We have always before our eyes the minister, and that minister is responsible to us; and if, through negligence or incompetence, he does not do his work properly, we know how to deal with him.
>
> (Low 1914: 138)

But all this is to set the theory up to be knocked over. Low shows that in practice,

> the way to punish a minister, . . . is by an adverse vote in the House of Commons on a question that would involve the defeat of himself *and his colleagues* . . . He himself will lose his large salary and his fine position; he will have the mortification of dragging down his colleagues . . .
>
> (Low 1914: 140; emphasis added)

Low is thus drawing attention to the fact that the responsibility of Ministers is *collective*, that – in Morley's words in his biography of

Walpole – the Cabinet is marked by united and indivisible responsibility. Low says that if the Minister does not take a line of policy independent from his Cabinet colleagues, he is sheltered behind the shield of joint responsibility:

> This means that he carries on his departmental duties under the protection of the entire Cabinet and that the whole force of the party machine will be brought to his assistance when required.
>
> (Low 1914: 14)

He points out that the delinquent Minister is able to thereby escape individual ministerial responsibility by sheltering under the probability that the House cannot selectively punish him on an individual basis and so the sort of punishment for laxity or incompetence that operates in private life and most pursuits and avocations does not pertain: 'If a butler, after being told that he is responsible for the plate chest, carelessly allows the spoons to be stolen, he may be dismissed without a character, and may never again get a good place' (Low 1914: 149).

In the realm of individual ministerial responsibility there was no corresponding certainty of retribution for offending Ministers; IMR just does not operate in the mechanical manner of the basic theory. As Low states,

> It is practically impossible to bring a minister to book unless the House is prepared to sacrifice the whole Cabinet to punish him . . . The party machine always does intervene, if the occasion is sufficiently serious, to protect the departmental chief. . .
>
> (Low 1914: 148–9)

Moreover, even in the unlikely event of a Minister being 'detected and punished' by the House of Commons, Low was not impressed by the severity of the sanction: 'the distinguished amateur is bowled out rather sooner than expected, and has had a shorter innings than he desired'.

Low legitimately links the triviality of the loss of Office in the Victorian political world to the social status of Ministers. Unlike the position of American Cabinet officers who tended to exchange a residence in cosmopolitan Washington for a law office in a remote western town, the loss of office in Britain was, for Low, hardly catastrophic,

> But the pavilion is not a bad place from which to watch the game for a time, especially if it happens to be a pavilion well kept and well

furnished . . . Our ministers do not break their hearts when they lose office. They are rich . . . and distinguished persons, occupying a fine position in the most agreeable society in the world . . . The worst punishment parliament or the electorate inflicts upon the minister who has forfeited its confidence (beyond the loss of a salary which he is often too wealthy to miss), is that of sending him back to his friends, his estates, his sports, his studies, and his recreations. . . so long as the leading performers are a group of men for whom politics is only one of the occupations or the amusements of an extremely comfortable existence.

(Low 1914: 152–4)

We can extend the metaphor of the sporting ethic to say that self-imposed resignations are less likely to be found among today's full-time and professional politicians than in the amateur days of Low. For them the consequences of resignation are much more severe. However, it is possible that the attractions of well-paid City posts and newspaper columns may encourage politicians to resign more freely – they offer the comfortable existence outside politics once available to those of private means.

So individual ministerial responsibility in the self-sacrifice sense might be more appealing as the degree of sacrifice is conspicuously reduced. Crossman (1972: 58–9) argues against the punitive version that the House of Commons could demand the dismissal of the Minister. He counters, 'Every Minister is covered by full collective Cabinet responsibility.' In his mischievous style Crossman proposes,

But now, very often, the worse a Minister manages his Ministry, the more difficult it is to get him removed because it would be an injury to the prestige of the Government. So the more the House of Commons bellows against the Minister, the stronger usually is the Prime Minister's determination to protect him. . .

(Crossman 1972: 58–9)

IMR: DID IT EXIST?

Collective responsibility has been reinterpreted to be a club with which the PM can impose discipline, but the fate of IMR has been less straightforward. As early as the start of the century Low suggested that it is not simply the convention as recorded in some sources: that it simply did not operate as commonly assumed. This was confirmed by Professor S. E. Finer in his classic article (1956) which looked at historical examples. Finer began by citing definitions, including the following one from *The Economist* of 24 July 1954,

> [If Ministers] . . . fail to take early and effective action to counter potential miscarriages of justice within their departments they must expect to step down from office.

(Finer 1956: 377)

Finer sets out three propositions that follow from the conventional interpretation of the convention:

(a)   Ministers are expected to explain and defend the exercise of their powers and duties to Parliament;

(b)   Any Minister who has lost the confidence of the House can by vote of censure or other devices, be compelled to resign; and that

(c)   The second may occur as a consequence of the first.

(Finer 1956: 378)

Finer says that for a convention to exist proposition (b) should follow from proposition (a) – and that it should regularly do so. Finer was anticipating (and rejecting) later interpretations to the effect that responsibility simply means that the Minister discovers who was at fault and takes remedial action. Finer rejects the argument that responsibility merely means that the Minister answers for his civil servants in the sense that only the Minister can stand up in the House and explain what has happened – and, if necessary, relate what he has done to prevent the malpractice happening again. In such a view of the convention there is no obligation for resignation and, as Finer says, 'there is no correlated constitutional remedy for departmental mismanagement. . . '

If the convention merely means that the Minister answers *to* the House of Commons *about* anonymous civil servants then there is a lack of direct accountability – another sort of hole in the theory of democratic checks. Finer argues that the convention – as expressed in political tradition – was that responsibility in this context means the *liability to lose office*. He cites a convincing list of authorities – Bagehot, Low, Todd, Keith and Jennings to make the point that IMR involves, 'possible forfeiture of office in face of disapproval by the House'.

The core of Finer's important article was to show that there is in fact only a handful of cases where the Minister appears to have been punished by loss of Office for the misdeeds and neglect of his civil servants or for departmental policy error. Finer establishes a series of four factors that inhibit the operation of the so-called convention.

Removal and reappointment

Here Finer notes that the effect of resignation can be ameliorated by reappointment. An example might be the resignation of Richard Luce as a Foreign Office Minister in 1982 over the invasion of the Falklands and his reappearance as a Minister of State in 1983. Finer's argument is that such reappointments undermine the punitive side of the original resignation, and that might be the case with examples he gives such as the resignation of Sir Samuel Hoare from the Foreign Office in 1935 and his reappearance at the Admiralty (with a say in foreign policy) six months later. But the Luce case perhaps illustrates that there is a case where a comparatively minor (if any) error can be appropriately dealt with by a period in the 'sin bin' rather than *sine die* suspension. More disturbing for the punitive theory of the convention was the fact that Luce probably enhanced his reputation by the propriety of his resignation.

The case of the resignation of Sir Thomas Dugdale in 1954 is one which recurs frequently. After his resignation (see pp. 225–8) he did not reappear as a Cabinet Minister but he was elevated to the House of Lords. Lord Carrington, after his Falklands resignation, similarly was not reappointed to a British ministry but did get prime ministerial backing for the important appointment as Secretary-General of NATO.

Personal factors

Here Finer appears to have in mind the tendency of some Ministers to have a greater tenacity towards Office than others. The convention of resignation is weakened by an increased probability that Ministers will find justification for staying in Office in a way that eviscerates the spirit of individual ministerial responsibility. In 1992 the Chancellor of the Exchequer was obliged to remove the British currency from the Exchange Rate Mechanism. Such a major reversal of policy would, in the spirit of traditional IMR discussions, suggest that the Chancellor would have resigned. The fact the criticism subsequently revealed was that the timing of the withdrawal perhaps cost an avoidable £2bn is a further reason for those inclined to consider resignation. Finer gives the instances of three Victorian examples where Gladstone explained to the monarch that in times past the three would have been summarily dismissed, but he had to explain that all three, 'have shown a tenacity of attachment to office certainly greater than is usual'. Two points can be made by way of extensions to Finer's observations. The first is that this personal attachment to Office presumably only operates as a variable for the 'correct behaviour' version of the convention; the niceties of feeling of the individual have no effect where there is a decision by the House that Office should be lost. A second elaboration of the Finer category is to consider the attitude of the PM. In recent years the important factor has not been immovable Ministers sitting tight to the frustration of the PM, but rather where the PM has declined to accept the proffered resignation of the Minister – for example, Lord Carrington from his post as Parliamentary Secretary at the MAFF in the Crichel Down affair in 1954; John Nott from his position as Secretary of State for Defence in 1982 over the Falklands.

The acceptance of offers of resignation may not have to do with the circumstances that lead to the offer but to background factors. Thus it has been suggested that the offer by Dalton to resign – over what was a detail of timing in briefing a journalist – was accepted because the PM wanted rid of him for other reasons. A variation of the PM's importance in accepting a letter of resignation is where the PM insists on resignation: the form of words covers the different activity of a sacking.

Reshuffle

Finer observes that many Ministers are protected from any need for resignation by a reshuffle of offices by the PM. Two minor variations seem to exist. There is the pre-emptive reshuffle after the Minister is removed from the firing line and there is the delayed reshuffle where the immediate crisis is weathered – as with Strachey after the ground nuts scheme fiasco in the Attlee Government.

Collective solidarity

Like Low, Finer lays emphasis upon the collective responsibility argument to frustrate the operation of any idea of IMR. He points out that Shinwell was protected as Minister over an air fuel crisis in 1947 by the proposition that it was the Government collectively that should be censured. Similarly, in defending his Chancellor from attacks in 1978 the Prime Minister, Jim Callaghan, told the House of Commons that,

> The task of the Chancellor of the Exchequer is central to that of the whole Government's economic . . . policy . . . therefore . . . the House should make up its mind on the whole record of the Government and that, if the House cannot support us this evening, I would ask for a dissolution of Parliament and go to the country.

Collective MR was thus invoked to protect the individual Minister. When IMR operates some special factors must exist. Finer saw resignations as the 'haphazard consequence of a fortuitous concomitance of personal, party and political temper'.

FACTORS ACCOUNTING FOR RESIGNATION

For Finer the issue with IMR was to explain the *limited number* of (exceptional) occasions when these individual resignations do take place:

Lack of party majority

His first explanatory category is where there is no absolute party majority in the House. In these circumstances there can more easily be a majority prepared to oust a Minister. He found that five out of the twenty cases he uncovered (in the period 1855–1955) fitted this explanation.

Offend party colleagues

If we look at the major recent cases where IMR has been advanced as 'explaining' behaviour we find that Finer's second explanation of the occasional implementation of IMR is relevant. This was where, the 'Minister's act has not so much offended the opposition as alienated his own party, or a substantial element of it'. This second factor seems relevant for certain of the more contemporary possible examples of the resignation 'convention'.

Resignation as a consequence of ministerial values

Another reason for resignation along the lines of IMR is captured by the term 'punctilio'. This term indeed now seems to be used only in the circumstances of IMR resignations. The dictionary definition describes 'exact observance of forms' – a sort of scrupulous regard for the rules. There is something quaint and rather dated about both the word and the behaviour. Thus Ministers who do resign in accordance with the so-called convention of IMR are often believed to be applying rather higher standards to their conduct than those employed by others in public life. Therefore one factor in the application of the convention is the inverse of the 'personal factor' that Finer found sometimes obstructed its implementation as Ministers showed 'tenacity of office'. Some Ministers do take the convention more seriously than others and volunteer more readily. Lord Carrington, who as we shall see was one of the main recent examples of a 'resigner' (over the Falklands), in fact previously offered his resignation from the Ministry of Agriculture over the Crichel Down episode in 1954 and from the Admiralty over the Portland security issue in 1961.

In accepting the resignation of the Minister of Agriculture, Sir Thomas Dugdale, in connection with the Crichel Down affair (see pp. 225–8) the PM noted that,

> your decision to sacrifice your office will be regarded as chivalrous in a high degree.
>
> (Nicolson 1986: 193)

In discussing the Dugdale case in his 1971 memoirs, George Brown observed that Sir Thomas, 'took the traditional, old fashioned view . . . Tommy Dugdale's self sacrificing defence of the doctrine of ministerial responsibility was a noble one'. Lord Carrington was also praised in the Lords *precisely because his resignation appeared so unfair and unnecessary.* Lord Windlesham claimed 'it is by acts of selflessness of this sort that the British parliamentary system maintains its honour'. Lord Shackleton, in a House of Lords debate, similarly observed,

> the fact that he has followed the great British tradition . . . that, feeling he was the responsible minister, whoever else may have been to blame . . . he must go.

Such actions may have been motivated by the highest intentions, but as Finer has demonstrated there is no tradition, in practice, for Carrington *et al.* to follow such self-inflicted justice. Ministers both within and outside the FCO were intimately involved. It is yet again worth distinguishing between the 'punctilio' that would encourage the belief that a Minister should offer his resignation because he was ultimately culpable for departmental difficulties (the traditional view) from a more modern version where the Minister 'does the right thing' because it is more convenient for his party and Cabinet colleagues.

With a handful of exceptions there is not much evidence of IMR as a matter of personal honour by which the Secretary of State will remove himself when something amiss has happened in his administrative territory through the activity of staff responsible to him. When this does happen there is little doubt that it is respected as behaviour that accords with the convention – though the real convention is to do precisely nothing and sit tight.

Though there is no conscious connection, the respect in Britain for this sacrifice by the innocent Minister for the errors of others probably taps the importance of this idea in the Christian tradition. There is something noble about the idea that Ministers should have this spirit of self-sacrifice. Without self-sacrifice there is the accusation that a breach of the rules is being condoned. In the debate in 1959 on brutality in the Hola Prison Camp in Kenya, Enoch Powell advised the Colonial Secretary, John Lennox-Boyd, to resign although he recognised 'his personal blamelessness'. Powell took the view that the resignation would be welcome and exemplary *precisely because* the Minister was not involved.

This role of 'taking the fire' rather than 'taking the blame' has been a feature of recent British resignations. Thus in resigning Carrington argued, 'the nation feels there has been a disgrace. Someone must have been to blame. The disgrace must be purged. The person to purge it should be the minister in charge.' He argued that this could 'stop the search for scapegoats'. Lord Whitelaw suggested that Carrington resigned less because he was responsible – as the FCO had been aware of the problem – than because of the need to satisfy the back-benchers 'they were out for blood' (1989: 266) and the hostility of the press.

There are thus a few Ministers such as Carrington who will resign because they or their department have been party to a policy disaster. There are many who will stay put in these circumstances. There are a further small group who will be told that while the PM is grateful for their efforts the whips advise that the party will not stand for it and they will have to 'offer' to go. Whether these are resignations forced by the party or by the PM for not defending the individuals more vigorously, or by their own punctilio, is difficult to disentangle.

Example 1: Crichel Down

The most celebrated of all the post-war cases of individual ministerial responsibility, the Crichel Down affair, has sustained the myth of departmental error redeemed by the ministerial sacrifice. As Nicolson's book (1986) about the case states in his first few sentences,

> This is the story of a great parliamentary and press controversy. . .
> that came close to splitting the Conservative government and party in
> the closing years of Winston Churchill's leadership. The uproar and
> crisis were resolved by the resignation of [then]. . . Minister of
> Agriculture, Sir Thomas Dugdale. He took much of the blame on
> his own shoulders. . .
>
> (Nicolson 1986: v)

It is the burden of Nicolson's book that such a familiar summary is misleading

The essence of the case involved 725 acres of land in Dorset. It was compulsorily acquired by the Air Ministry in 1937 as a bombing range and passed into the hands of the Ministry of Agriculture in 1949. (The Ministry of Agriculture could not themselves have acquired it by compulsion for their purposes.) Various farmers, including Lieutenant-Commander Martin, had been assured that they could bid for the land when it ceased to be used by the Air Ministry. Martin's complaint stimulated (eventually) an inquiry on the handling of the case on behalf of the Minister of Agriculture by Sir Andrew Clark QC – and (eventually) the resignation of the Minister, Sir Thomas Dugdale.

D.N. Chester argued,

> Sir Thomas Dugdale's decision to resign was a brave and welcome reinforcement of the doctrine of ministerial responsibility.
>
> (Chester 1954: 389)

John Griffith wrote of Dugdale that,

> His sanctification came about because within a short period after his political cruxification [the metaphor is worth noting] writers on the constitution and others, held him up as one who had died in a good cause; he had offered himself up as a living sacrifice on the altar of the doctrine of ministerial responsibility. Here was a man, they said, who was blameless, not knowing what his civil servants were up to (and they were up to no good) because they did not tell him, who nonetheless accepted that his position as political head of the department required him to resign.
>
> (Griffith 1987: 35)

Nicolson's book makes it plain that the conventional summary that the Minister resigned because of errors committed by his officials was seriously wrong. The Minister was informed about key decision and did not accept that his officials had failed. As a senior civil servant noted in a review of Nicolson's book in *Public Administration* in 1987, 'the authorized version of events, which has since been accepted as correct in countless academic and political writings, is little less than a travesty'.

In a letter to *The Independent* in 1986 Dugdale was reported as telling a colleague the exact opposite from the customary interpretation, 'No, I know that will be said, but I have no fault to find with my officers' (cited in Griffith 1987). He explicitly rejected the idea that he was resigning in terms of traditional IMR. Indeed his unpopularity with his Conservative colleagues appeared to be in large part because of his *reluctance* to be seen handing out punishment within the department (Nicolson 1986: 201). As Herbert Morrison said in the debate on 20th July 1954, 'This is a victory for the 1922 Committee. . . Now the 1922 Committee has the scalp of a Minister' (Griffith 1987: 40). This argument is that he was pushed by back-benchers and did not jump out of a sense of punctilio.

The events of 1954 failed to fit in with the requirements of simple IMR in that the ministerial resignation took place *after* the inquiry in public and report by Sir Andrew Clark. This report – now discredited by Nicolson – made public criticism of several civil servants. The ministerial resignation thus did not meet the traditional claim that anything done wrongly within a department was done by the Minister and that civil servants should retain their anonymity.

Though the events of the Crichel Down case in 1954 are sometimes taken to be textbook IMR, Nicolson's re-examination (1986) of the detail confirms the importance of the mood of back-bench colleagues in the resignation decision – and how the PM reacts to that expression of mood. Nicolson says,

> As a result of the party's agriculture committee meeting, there were. . . three meetings of the back bench 1922 committee. . . these meetings culminated in an 'angry' meeting on 15 July 1954, at which Maxwell Fyfe attempted to 'turn the tide' running against the government but failed.
>
> (Nicolson 1986: 192)

He quotes Douglas Brown's early account of the story which claimed that Ministers present at the meeting left it,

> with the knowledge that the government could not control its own supporters unless it made some further gesture . . . Four days after . . . Sir Winston Churchill discussed the situation with Sir Thomas Dugdale, at that meeting the scapegoat was selected.
>
> (Nicolson 1986: 192)

Churchill announced Dugdale's resignation to the Cabinet on 20th July 1954 as a *fait accompli*. He said Dugdale had decided to go, 'in view of the strong feelings aroused among Government supporters by the report of the Crichel Down Inquiry . . . that the only dignified course for him to follow was to resign his office. . . '

Dugdale went to placate his party colleagues rather than in pursuit of 'constitutional brownie points'. In his speech in the debate in which Dugdale resigned, the Labour spokesman, George Brown, complained that Dugdale had been 'hunted and harassed' from office by his own party. (Of course the tone of Brown's speech was determined by the fact that just before the debate started, Sir Thomas warned him that he was to use the occasion to resign; otherwise he would no doubt have engaged in a bit of his own hunting and harassing.)

Example 2: Westland

The best example of Finer's category of offending party colleagues may be that of Leon Brittan who resigned after the deliberate leaking of a letter from the Government's law officer with the intention of discrediting the stand taken by Michael Heseltine in the Westland dispute which divided Whitehall in 1986.

According to Robert Harris's account (1990: 131) the Department of Trade and Industry Chief Information Officer was anxious, in the wake of the prosecution of Clive Ponting, not to leak a classified letter, and had to be ordered to do so by No. 10. None the less the resignation was of the Secretary of State for Trade and Industry and not the PM. Mr Brittan's departure came after pressure from colleagues and a difficult meeting with the Conservative Backbench 1922 Committee. His resignation letter to Mrs Thatcher stated,

> it has become clear to me that I no longer command the full confidence of my colleagues. In these circumstances my continued membership of your Government would be a source of weakness rather than strength . . . and it is for this reason that I have tendered my resignation.

It is instructive to note that not only was the protective concept of collective responsibility not thrown around him, the contrary notion at the time seemed to be that the individual had to go to save the collectivity – the safety valve or scapegoat idea. Nigel Lawson says (1993: 679), 'had he made public all he knew, she could not have survived; but he chose not to do so. As it was, he meekly accepted the role of scapegoat.'

In the mood of the time something had to happen – and Mr Brittan did not perhaps have deep personal support in the House of Commons. Even Margaret Thatcher flatly says that the enforced resignation was under pressure from the back-benches, 'It was a meeting of the '22 committee, not any decision of mine, which sealed his fate . . . I tried to persuade him not to go (1993: 435). Nicholas Ridley (1992: 52) refers to the 1922 Committee 'baying for blood'. This is the reversal of the collective MR principle. Brittan will not serve as an example of IMR as he did not acknowledge that the department had erred. He was a victim of new IMR (Invalided by Mob Rule).

Example 3: Falklands

We can extend Finer's list of factors of why IMR is brought (occasionally) into play. The Foreign Office resignations in the Falklands case again performed the role of diminishing criticism of the Cabinet as a whole and the PM in particular. The FO Ministers did not resign because they felt that there had been some error to be expiated but because their going improved the political climate for those who remained. Moreover, the Carrington case does not really fit the category of vicarious error because there was no hint that any errors were made by civil servants without the thorough involvement of Ministers: as we note in detail below, Lord Carrington did not accept that the FO had been negligent. In an interview on BBC television he claimed that,

> much of the criticism is unfounded. But I have been responsible for the conduct of that policy and I think it is right that I should resign.

If Carrington was resigning for the errors of others the remarkable constitutional innovation was that it was for the errors of his ministerial colleagues rather than his civil servants. In various aspects – from advocating negotiation with the Argentinians, to suspicion of the with-drawal of HMS *Endurance* from the area on cost grounds – the Foreign Office was pressing what (with hindsight) was the correct line. It was the Home Office and not the FCO that failed to include the inhabitants of the Falklands in the definition of citizenship in the British Nationality Act.

The Franks Report on the Falklands records that the FCO was frustrated by collective decisions. For example the danger in removing the HMS *Endurance* was raised with Mr Nott (Secretary of State for Defence) as a consequence of the 1981 Defence Review. Lord Carrington's letter argued that, 'until the dispute with Argentina was settled, it was important to maintain the British Government's normal presence . . . any reduction would be interpreted by both the Islanders and Argentina as a reduction in Britain's commitment. . .' Lord Carrington wrote again in January 1982 stating that the withdrawal of the *Endurance* was being interpreted as a lack of commitment to Britain's sovereignty. Although Mrs Thatcher endorsed the decision to remove the *Endurance* in a parliamentary reply in February, Lord

Carrington yet again raised the issue later in the month. The FCO can thus be seen to have been unusually persistent on the issue.

In 1982 Lord Carrington sent a briefing paper to the PM and other members of the Defence Committee advising of the difficulties of the negotiations and that the matter would have to be considered in the Defence Committee in March. The PM's comment was that it had to be made clear to the Argentinians that the wishes of the Islanders were paramount. It could thus be argued that the PM made a Fortress Falklands policy necessary but failed to provide the resources. Were a resignation in order the most 'just' might have been that of the PM – as 'Minister for the Security Services' (see Hennessy 1989).

The Franks Report noted, however, that in the critical months the matter of the Falklands was not on the agenda of the full Cabinet or the Defence committee, 'it could have been advantageous . . . for ministers to have reviewed collectively. . . the current negotiating position' (para. 292). This was not a case where the Foreign Office was pursuing an unsuccessful policy independently of the rest of Whitehall.

Again back-bench worry seems to have played an important part in the Ministers' decision to go. Lord Carrington's resignation letter mentioned the strong criticism in Parliament and there was a Conservative Party meeting after the parliamentary debate on 3 April. Judge (1984: 42) suggests that a section of the Conservative parliamentary party awaited an opportunity to settle old scores with Carrington: retribution not only for the Falklands failure but also his handling of Zimbabwean independence, the pro-Palestine tilt of his Middle East policy and his attention to European duties at the very time of the Argentinian invasion. However, the back-bench view that 'someone was to blame' was in all probability not very precisely targeted and would have been just as well satisfied by a resignation from the Ministry of Defence. The Secretary of State for Defence, John Nott, did offer his resignation but this was turned down by the PM – again underlying the importance of the PM in this. The Falklands resignations do not fit the notion of retribution for a departmental error but they do fit the ideas of a back-bench unease and a resignation as a lightning conductor to deflect criticism from the Cabinet.

QUALIFIED TO DEATH

Finer suggests that no such working convention as IMR has really existed. In trying to 'square' the lack of examples with the continued advances of the convention, there has been a refining of the circumstances in which the convention should operate. Arguably, in being 'realistic' about when the convention is brought into life means qualifying it to death. During the debate in which Dugdale resigned the Home Secretary Maxwell Fyfe set out a set of categories which he claimed underlay the IMR convention.

These were,

1 Where a civil servant carries out an explicit order by a Minister, the Minister must protect the civil servant concerned.

2 Where a civil servant acts properly in accordance with the policy laid down by the Minister, the Minister must equally protect and defend him.

3 Where a civil servant makes a mistake or causes some delay, but not on an important issue of policy and not where a claim to individual rights is seriously involved, the Minister acknowledges the mistake and he accepts the responsibility, although he is not personally involved. He states that he will take corrective action in the Department.

4 . . . where action has been taken by a civil servant of which the Minister disapproves and has no prior knowledge, and the conduct of the official is reprehensible, then there is no obligation on the part of the Minister to endorse what he believes to be wrong, or to defend what are clearly shown to be errors of his officers. The Minister is not bound to approve of action of which he did not know, or of which he disapproves. But, of course, he remains constitutionally responsible to Parliament for the fact that something has gone wrong, and he alone can tell Parliament what has occurred and render an account of his stewardship.

(Cited in Chester 1954: 399)

In fact the new formulation did not resolve ambiguities. It did not say what the Minister was obliged to do in cases (1) and (2). Did he actually have to resign? Rule (3) implicitly says that on minor matters there should be no resignation, and rule (4) says that Ministers have no responsibility for matters in which civil servants have acted without their knowledge. This all has an air of reasonableness about it but it is a direct contradiction of that strain in the traditional interpretation that stated that the Minister was responsible for allowing things to go wrong – *even if he was not party to the actual errors.* If this is an authoritative statement of the doctrine of individual ministerial responsibility, it was a revised doctrine. There was no longer any demand for resignation and there was no sense of vicarious responsibility for the deeds of civil servants.

Marshall (1992: 11) says there is (now) a consensus that a Minister cannot be expected to resign where mistakes are made by civil servants that he could not have avoided by exercising reasonable care in his own role. In such a case, a Minister may apologise and state that failings in the department's procedures will be corrected. This is a succinct statement of the current convention but it is not the convention that once was held to operate (as opposed to 'operated'). This castrated version of the doctrine operated in succeeding cases. When Lennox Boyd offered his resignation as Colonial Secretary in 1959 after allegations of brutality in the Hola Prison camp in Kenya the idea was dismissed by the PM as 'ridiculous, pointless and unjustified'.

This can be labelled the argument of 'span or scale'. Clearly there is to be a limit as to what is practical for a Minister to supervise. As Home Secretary, Kenneth Baker was at one time faced by 6,000 applications for asylum from the citizens of Zaïre alone (see Marshall 1992: 11). Barbara Castle as Minister of Transport was correct to claim in 1973 over a rail crash that, 'I think the House of Commons will no longer insist that a Minister is held personally responsible for the minutiae of the department. . .'

After the collapse of the Vehicle and General Insurance Company in 1971 there was a tribunal which publicly criticised two Assistant Secretaries and found that the work of an Under-Secretary was, 'below the standard of competence which he ought to have displayed and constitutes negligence'. However, the Secretary of State, John Davies, did not think it would be appropriate, 'for ministers and senior officials . . . to assume a responsibility greater than allocated to them in the tribunal's conclusion'.

In defence of his colleague the then Home Secretary, Reginald Maudling, noted that in his own department, 'we get 1 and a half million letters a year, any one of which may lead to disaster. No Home Secretary could be expected to supervise all those one and a half million letters. It is no minimising of the responsibility of Ministers to Parliament to say that a Minister cannot be blamed for a mistake made, if he did not make it himself and if he has not failed to ensure that that sort of mistake ought not to be made' (*Hansard*, Vol. 836, col. 159). Sir John Hunt in his evidence to the Expenditure Committee in 1976/7 argued, 'the concept that because somebody whom the Minister has never heard of, has made a mistake, means that the minister should resign, is out of date, and rightly so' (Eleventh Report, HC, 535 II).

When there was a mass escape of prisoners from the Maze prison in Northern Ireland in September 1983, the Secretary of State, James Prior, informed the House of Commons that he did not intend to resign as there had been no failure of policy involved. Referring to the Crichel Down episode he claimed that,

> I do not believe that it is a precedent or that it establishes a firm convention. It is the only case of its sort in the past 50 years, and constitutional lawyers have concluded that the resignation was not required by convention and was exceptional.

The Hennessy Report on the breakout found that the 'Governor must be held responsible' for the failure of security at the prison and it was he who resigned. (Turpin 1985: 70). Similarly when another IRA breakout took place from Brixton prison in London, the Home Secretary, William Whitelaw, informed the House of Commons that, 'In the circumstances, the governor, Mr. Selby, must himself accept and very properly does accept the primary responsibility.' Officials also carried the can in 1991. This direct accountability by officials is 'sensible' but it leaves very little room for ministerial resignation.

A new factor perhaps needs to be fed into the discussion – the disavowable activity. About the Westland leak, the former Press Secretary, Bernard Ingham (1991: 335), suggests that his concern was to 'keep the Prime Minister above that sort of thing'. He would not have been prepared 'to put such an idea to her'. This leaves open the possibility that conduct can be for a Minister but without the endorsement of the Minister. Is there still responsibility? In the leaking of the Solicitor-General's letter which led up to the resignation of Leon Brittan, the No. 10 staff appear to have taken pains not to compromise the PM. The argument can be made that in such circumstances the Minister (or Prime Minister) involved is responsible in the sense that what is conducted is for their benefit even if outside their direct knowledge. But such arguments are more sophisticated than is perhaps necessary. The whole notion of IMR falls down on more elementary grounds such as the scale of work for which a Minister is expected to be responsible and the consequences of new organisational forms such as the departmental agency which is designed to put the operational work at some distance from the 'responsible' Minister.

The concept of resignation as an appropriate sanction is further undermined when on occasions it is impossible to hang the correct man as there has been a turnover of Ministers – even of Governments. The tribunal on the Vehicle and General Insurance affair discussed above found that six different Ministers had held the office in the time under discussion. The Minister most responsible in a real sense may no longer be in post. When Lord Carrington offered his resignation after the Romer Inquiry into security risks at the Underwater Detection Establishment in 1961, the PM declined to pass the resignation to the Queen on the grounds that, 'It would not be right to visit on the First Lord a general criticism of organisational methods. Every Board of Admiralty for several years had been dealing with. . . [the subject]'. Macmillan also advanced the 'span' argument that, 'the doctrine of ministerial responsibility is well known – it is the ultimate responsibility. But in modern conditions it must be recognised that the minister's duty is to carry out his task as efficiently as possible' (*Hansard*, Vol. 642, cols. 1687–8).

There were some half-hearted calls at the time of the abolition of the poll tax in 1991 to the effect that something had gone wrong, money had been wasted and that someone should take responsibility and resign. Vernon Bogdanor wrote in *The Independent* under the title 'They Erred and Now Must Pay'. He claimed,

> the constitution has a further way of enforcing accountability. In 1982, Lord Carrington and two junior Foreign Office ministers resigned over the Falklands invasion because they blamed themselves for a policy that led to national humiliation.

This puts a questionable construction on the Falklands episode: we have noted above that Carrington did not accept that departmental policy had been wrong, but we see what Bogdanor is getting at. There was a massive waste of public money. How do we obtain satisfaction?

However, when Bogdanor describes Ministers as 'men of honour' – and implies that they are less than that if they fail to resign – then he is inventing a new sub-principle and forgetting Low and Finer. He asked for the resignation of Waldegrave because he was in charge of the working party in 1985 that produced the poll tax proposal. Pure individual ministerial responsibility seems to have related only to the Secretary of State's position. (See Theakston 1987: 68, for a discussion of the constitutional norms.) Secondly, in asking for Kenneth Baker's resignation Bogdanor in this instance seemed arbitrary. Kenneth Baker was appointed to the post of Secretary of State for the Environment only in time to have the tax dumped on his lap. It was hardly his creation. In any case this was not really a departmental policy. It may not have been subject to genuine discussion at Cabinet level (because of prime ministerial domination) but almost the whole of the 1991 Cabinet had some fingerprints on the policy. Clearly IMR was not the appropriate charge. Collective responsibility may have been a better 'fit' but there was no parliamentary mood to enforce that doctrine.

We have seen that Kenneth Baker declined to resign over the escape of two IRA suspects from Brixton in July 1991 (although he seemed to have elicited some admiration by claiming that he had 'considered his position') on the grounds that the escape was due to 'operational' rather than 'policy' failures. However, it later emerged that the Home Office had received warning of the escape and had followed the prisoners. He likewise was unfortunate enough to be in charge of the Home Office when ninety Iraqis and Palestinians were interned during the Gulf War, although there was to be no substantiated evidence that those detained were connected to terrorist groups. In late 1991 he was the first Minister to be found in contempt of court when the Home Office refused a claim for political asylum by a citizen of Zaïre and ignored a request by a judge that his compulsory departure from the country be delayed.

Mr Baker (2 December 1991) accepted 'full responsibility for the actions taken in this case by officials of the Home Office and the Parliamentary Under Secretary who dealt with it. I was in fact involved in the case at a late stage . . . I do not shirk any responsibility for this matter, nor do I shirk any responsibility for the actions taken by my officials or the way the Parliamentary Under Secretary handled this case'. Thus in two separate variations the Home Secretary accepted responsibility – but no obligation to resign – by making it clear that it was officials and the parliamentary Under-Secretary that were directly to blame. Roy Hattersley asked, 'Are there no circumstances under which you would feel it right to take the honourable course and resign from the office which you discharge so inadequately?'

In 1992 the Head of the London Ambulance Service, John Wilby, resigned after the failure of a new control system for dispatch of ambulances to emergencies. Of course this was not an example of individual ministerial responsibility (indeed to the contrary as the Secretary of State was not moved to resign although potential dangers had been brought to her attention), but it did – to no effect – act as a reminder of the spirit that was held to be at its core.

TREASURY AND CIVIL SERVICE COMMITTEE, 1986

Ministerial responsibility, post-Westland and the Ponting affair, was discussed by the Treasury and Civil Service Committee in 1986 (Seventh Report, 1985–6). The Committee considered a memorandum that had been drawn up in 1985 by the Cabinet Secretary, Sir Robert Armstrong, entitled *The Duties and Responsibilities of Ministers and Civil Servants*. Armstrong's line was that of a traditionalist,

> it is the Minister who is responsible, and answerable to Parliament, for the conduct of the department's affairs and the management of its business . . . It is Ministers and not civil servants who bear responsibility
>
> (Cited in Marshall 1989: 140–4)

This document was the subject of a symposium of views in *Public Administration* in 1987. Ann Robinson recorded that the reaction by the former press secretary to Harold Wilson, Joe Haines, to the Armstrong doctrine was that this read like a plea for the retention of the amateur captain county cricket. It is romantic and unrealistic. It deals with a situation which no longer exists. Fred Ridley noted that the Armstrong memorandum was more impressive after superficial glance than after close reading: 'style carries much of the argument, covering disputable facts and shaky logic'. Ridley points out the Treasury and Civil Service Committee (TCSC), noting that Armstrong's memorandum states principles as if they were certain truths but adds, 'We are, however, living in times of flux for the civil service, not only as regards its organisation and practice but also as regards our thinking about its role and in the constitutional system.' For example Armstrong claimed, 'The civil service as such has no constitutional personality or responsibility separate from the duly elected Government of the day.' Ridley makes the persuasive point that civil servants do not show their Ministers the papers of previous administrations, but asks what would happen if the Minister ordered their production. If the Minister is indistinguishable from the Crown, then there would seem to be no choice for the civil servant.

The Armstrong version was of course designed to limit the right of a civil servant to 'blow the whistle' on Ministers who sought to be less than frank with Parliament. Just as collective responsibility is used to prevent criticism of individual Ministers by Parliament so IMR in its modern version becomes a tool to protect the Minister rather than a means to hold him to account.

Robinson divided the evidence to the Treasury and Civil Service Committee into that which was traditionalist and that which was realist. Traditionalists, like Sir Robert Armstrong, asserted that the Minister was the appropriate and accountable target for criticism. The realists recognised that the traditional model did not operate in practice. The traditionalists need to be further divided into the pure traditionalists who support the punitive version of IMR that requires resignation and the 'revisionist traditionalists' who want the Minister to be responsible yet find plenty of reasons for avoiding sanctions.

It would be unfair to the pure traditionalists to imply that they were fooled by the extent to which the doctrine operates – their position was that IMR operated imperfectly, but there was no alternative. It should be restored to working order. Robinson cites the former civil servant, Sir Leo Pliatzky, who said that he could see no practical way in which, under our system, civil servants can serve Parliament or have a responsibility to it otherwise than through or on behalf of their Minister.

George Jones argued that Ministers must be answerable and not that they must automatically and mechanically resign when things go wrong. He argues (1987: 88), 'Those who seek to weaken the concept in its traditional form are conniving at a diminution of democratic control.'

The TCSC report restated the issue rather than resolved it. It said,

> The issue of accountability is of crucial importance in considering the relationship between civil servants, ministers and Parliament. The traditional view, exemplified in the famous Crichel Down case, is that Ministers are responsible and accountable to Parliament for all that occurs within their departments. It followed from this that if a significant mistake were made by the department the Minister should resign. . . Recent events would seem to confirm what may well have been true for some 30 years, namely that ministers are accountable for the Government's policies and their own actions or those carried out by civil servants on their specific instruction but not for actions by officials of which they are unaware. If this is correct it raises most important questions which need to be carefully analysed and answered. . . If Crichel Down is dead and Ministers are not accountable to Parliament for some actions of their officials, then who is? Not to put too fine a point on it, who ought to resign or be penalised if mistakes are made? If it is not Ministers, it can only be officials.
>
> (TCSC, Vol. I, paras 3, 145, 17: cited in Robinson 1987, p. 63)

The Government's response to the TCSC report, the 1986 Command Paper 9841, did not take things any further. It said,

> It has never been the case that Ministers were required or expected to resign in respect of any and every mistake made by their departments, though they are clearly responsible to Parliament for ensuring

that action is taken to put matters right and prevent a recurrence. The principle is clear; Ministers are accountable to Parliament for the policies and actions of their departments. The implications of applying that principle can only be a matter of judgement in each case.

Despite the repeated assertion of clarity this does no more than say 'it depends'.

Ann Robinson drew particular attention to the problem of maintaining a sensible notion of IMR in a context of the Whitehall developments considered in Chapter 5. She noted that the TCSC recognised that the introduction of new management devices into Government, particularly devolved budgeting under the Financial Management Initiative (FMI), raised questions about answerability.

In 1991 the Cabinet Secretary, Sir Robin Butler, addressed the issue in a talk to the First Division Association. He argued that Ministers had to be 'challengeable' in Parliament,

> about any action of the Civil Service . . . because in a democracy the ultimate sanction on a government is that they are not reelected and ministers are the only people in government who are subject to that sanction. Apart from the courts there is no other protection for the citizen.
>
> (Butler 1991: 4)

But this reiteration of the familiar was a prelude to another qualification:

> That is, of course, a different thing from saying that ministers must take the blame for every wrong decision of their subordinates. They cannot and should not take the blame for decisions of which they know nothing or could be expected to know nothing.
>
> (Butler 1992: 4)

This was a reversion to Maxwell Fyfe's fourth principle: 'The Minister is not bound to approve of action of which he did not know, or of which he disapproves.'

Sir Robin went on to accept the corollary of the argument that the buck did not always stop with Ministers. He talked of 'rewards for success but penalties for failure' for civil servants because if, *'the Minister is not blamed for wrong decisions which he does not take, someone else must be'* (Butler 1991: 4; emphasis added). He prepared a 'deal' for Ministers, Parliament and the public since much executed responsibility for state services had been delegated to named civil servants in Next Steps agencies. He said,

Ministers and the public are more likely to accept the delegation of responsibility which seems to me an essential element in running public services today if the delegation is buttressed by a knowledge on the part of those to whom such responsibility is delegated that their personal success or failure is in a direct sense dependent on the way in which they exercise those responsibilities.

(Butler 1991: 5)

This statement was not explicit on whether the punishment would be self-inflicted. Would Chief Executives of agencies voluntarily resign if there was mismanagement or, say, activity that was *ultra vires*? Would there be provision for their removal? Could the Chief Executive argue that the particular matter was too far from his direct responsibility? Would the resigning Chief Executive be eligible for a 'golden goodbye' in the way of some private sector executives whose operations had been unsuccessful?

CONCLUSION

It now seems obvious that Ministers do not resign when the complaint concerns far-away departmental business of which they know little. Nor indeed do Ministers decline to blame their advisers when faulty advice has been tendered to them. Ministers still offer their resignations far more often than they are accepted. After Peter Brooke, the Secretary of State for Northern Ireland, sang on a Dublin television chat show some hours following an IRA atrocity in the North, he apparently offered to resign. He received support and encouragement in Parliament for conforming to the 'sound chap' school of political behaviour – but this mood was eroded by a suspicion that the offer and the PM's subsequent consideration of it was something of a false ritual. It appeared too like an exchange between the PM and the Secretary of State calculated to invoke support – with no real prospect of acceptance. Ministers resign when they offend their own party and when the PM declines to use his or her authority in their support.

Individual ministerial responsibility is untenable as a description of behaviour but as a statement of principle we seem to cling to it because we cannot bear any alternative that would admit the direct account-ability of civil servants. But the topic is important, as without these notions what other theory of democratic accountability is available? Though it is easy to show how imperfectly these ideas allow for control of central Government, how much worse is the position is in the new

Next Steps agencies – where organisations are set up to be more independent of Ministers and yet we have no new constitutional doctrine to reconcile freedom from ministerial control with the retention of ministerial accountability?

Chapter 9

Administration and the law
Tinkering or transformation?

THE GROWTH OF JUDICIAL REVIEW

Until the 1980s there was no pressing need for students of administration to pay much attention to the legal system in general and the concept of judicial review in particular. Schwartz and Wade (1972: 322) noted that, 'Many leading lawyers of the era of the Second World War could say little about administrative law except that they had a distant recollection of having been taught at the University that there was no such thing.'

The first section of this chapter tries to document that there now *is* a subject to be reviewed. By 1994 the courts were used as a political resource – as in the attempt to prevent the opening of the Thorp nuclear processing plant. The growth in significance of judicial review in the past couple of decades is perhaps signalled by the fact that by 1986 it is given ten lines in the index of Harden and Lewis's *The Noble Lie: The British Constitution and the Rule of Law*, but in 1966 it did not feature in the index of a major and thorough law text such as Wilson's *Cases and Materials on Constitutional and Administrative Law*.

Judicial review is not the single weapon in the struggle for the democratic control of administration, but the widely regarded weakness of traditional devices such as individual ministerial responsibility means there has been both great interest in the possibility of a role for judges in scrutinising the activities of public officials and a surprising optimism in recent years that in Britain we had successfully balanced many conflicting requirements. Judicial review is, as noted, one of many devices for this purpose. They do not all sit comfortably together. For example, the introduction of the Parliamentary Commissioner for Administration (the 'Ombudsman') and other comparable figures in other areas of the public sector are held by some to erode the individual responsibility of

Ministers. The more recent wave of 'charters' also tries to hold the public service to account with penalties for poor service. However, judicial review certainly was the growth area in terms in the 'market' for accountability in the early 1990s.

For decades the main item on the agenda for legal reform in this area was for some kind of system of administrative law. Wilson (1966) recorded that the Committee on Ministers' Powers of 1932 had rejected the advice from Professor Robson that there was a need for a special Administrative Court. He notes that they sided with Dicey's view that such a continental-style court would favour the executive rather than the individual. He also notes the similar rejection of the proposals for an administrative division of the High Court or a general administrative appeal tribunal by the Franks Committee on Tribunals in 1957. Wilson claimed courts were relevant in an unsystematic manner only. In particular they have insisted that in many cases where a statute has merely granted a power without saying anything about the way that it should be exercised, natural justice requires that a person affected by its exercise should be given an opportunity to put his case (Wilson 1966: 540).

S. A. de Smith also began his work, *Judicial Review of Administrative Action* (1980), with the clear warning that the subject was less than the centre of British administration. On the specific matter of control of the police he advised,

> Judicial Review of administrative action is inevitably sporadic and peripheral. The administrative process is not, and cannot be, a succession of justiciable controversies. Public authorities are set up to govern and administer, and if their every act or decision were to be reviewable on unrestricted grounds by an independent judicial body the business of administration could be brought to a standstill.
>
> (de Smith 1980)

The fact that judicial review had been such a minor feature of British legal experience (in both England and Wales, and Scotland) was ascribed to judicial self-restraint. In other words, even where there might have been a case for such scrutiny by the courts, the judges kept off areas that would inevitably bring them in conflict with politicians and civil servants. De Smith (1980: 32) says, 'In the 1950s judicial self-restraint appeared to have won a decisive victory over judicial activism in a field where the contest might well have been an even one.' Lord Parker, then Lord Chief Justice, was quoted as saying, 'in modern Britain, where no agreement exists on the ends of society and the means of achieving these ends, it would be disastrous if courts did not eschew the temptation to pass judgement on an issue of policy. Judicial self-preservation may alone dictate restraint.'

Political scientists tend to describe Britain as lacking separation of powers which uses a separation of judicial, legislative and executive authority to limit over-powerful Government (as in the United States). In Britain the politicians have a place in the judicial system through to the law officers of the Government. British lawyers, however, claim there is separation of powers through the independence of the courts. In *Dupont Steel* v. *Sirs*, Lord Diplock remarked,

> It cannot be too strongly emphasised that the British Constitution, though largely unwritten, is firmly based on the separation of powers: Parliament makes the laws, the judiciary interprets them.
>
> (Cited in Marston and Ward 1991: 22)

Judicial restraint confined the courts to the application of law: the courts did not seek to affect or influence the content of the law. Lord Scarman argued that judicial restraint in interfering with legislation was vital,

> the constitution's separation of powers, or more accurately functions, must be observed if judicial independence is not to be put at risk. For if people and Parliament come to think that judicial power is to be confined by nothing other than the judge's sense of what is right . . . confidence in the legal system will be replaced by fear of it.
>
> (Cited in Marston and Ward 1991: 22)

Gavin Drewry (1988) has pointed out that by the time of the 4th edition of de Smith's work in 1980 the subject was undergoing something of a metamorphosis, 'if not perhaps from caterpillar to butterfly, then at least from small caterpillar to larger'. Drewry pointed out that the editor of the 1980 edition had to note,

> there has been a striking increase both in the frequency with which judicial review has been invoked and in the readiness of courts to intervene.
>
> (Drewry 1988)

Such is the scale of change in this territory that Rawlings (1987: 110) notes that by 1985 earlier 'overviews of the topic (of redress) were virtual museum pieces'.

Lord Diplock summarised the new facilities, which stemmed from Order 53 of the Rules of the Supreme Court in 1977 for those dissatisfied by decisions, as follows:

So order 53 since 1977 has provided a procedure by which every type of remedy for infringement of the rights of individuals that are entitled to protection in public law, can be obtained in one and the same proceedings by way of an application for judicial review. . .'

(Cited in Boynton 1986: 148)

In the Scottish system, in *West* v. *Secretary of State for Scotland* (1992), it was set out that the Court of Session has the power to regulate the process by which a person or body takes a decision if they have been given power or authority to decide by statute, agreement or any other instrument. The court emphasised that judicial review was not a machinery of appeal but was about ensuring that the decision-maker did not abuse the powers allocated, 'It is not competent for the court to review the act or decision on its merits.'

Government is responding to the possibility that actions might now be reviewed in a way not probable before. An internal Government document in 1988, 'The Judge Over Your Shoulder', advised civil servants of an increased willingness on the part of the judiciary to intervene in the day-to-day business of government. 'The Judge Over Your Shoulder' documented that the 160 cases in judicial review in 1974 had grown to 1,230 by 1985. It noted an increased willingness on the part of the judiciary to intervene in the day-to-day business of government, coupled with a move towards an imaginative interpretation of statutes.

The phrase 'imaginative interpretation' was not entirely complimentary. Thus though there were cases of this type before the 1960s the prevailing spirit then seems to have been of judicial restraint: 'that the law is not and cannot be a substitute for politics' (Griffith 1979: 16, cited by Drewry 1988). The change in mood towards an activist judicial review was shown when Lord Diplock stated that, '[it is] progress towards a comprehensive system of administrative law that I regard as having been the greatest achievement of the English courts in my judicial lifetime' (cited in Rawlings 1986: 139). In his 1981 Frank Stacey Memorial Lecture, Louis Blom-Cooper similarly noted 'a profound change in an important procedural aspect of administrative law'. He went on,

By a happy alchemy of legal elements . . . the appointment of a new Lord Chief Justice, a reassignment of the work of the Divisional Court of the Queen's Bench Division, and a redeployment of higher judicial personnel, the judicial review of administrative action has imperceptibly taken on altogether an entirely new shape and meaning. Acting both as delegated legislators and as court administrators, the High Court judiciary. . . has established, in all but name, a court manned by specialist judges. . .

In the space of a decade or two the treatment of the concept of administrative law was thus transformed in British texts. Drewry says that the report of the Justice/All Souls review of administrative law in the UK *(Administrative Law: Some Necessary Reforms)* took it to be more or less self-evident that the increase in judicial review cases had made redundant the traditional agenda of legal reform that advocated the transfer to Britain of a specialised administrative court comparable to the French Conseil d'Etat. De Smith, writing in 1973 noted 'the unusual but indisputable fact that over the past few years the most creative developments in the judicial sector of administrative law has been taking place in this country' (cited in Blom-Cooper 1981: 4).

Lord Justice Woolf in his 1986 Harry Street lecture has also drawn attention to the increase in applications for judicial review from 533 in 1981 to 1,230 in 1985 (cited in Sunkin 1988: 3). Feldman (1988) also described judicial review as a growth area and pointed out how rate-payers, those aggrieved by housing decisions, immigrants, environmental groups and others were increasingly prone to use the device against Government agencies. Review was also a regular feature in the battle on spending between the Thatcher Governments and local government. There were important and newsworthy instances such as the battle over London Transport's fares policy, the DOE intervention over the sale of council houses and the level of tolls on the Severn Bridge. Feldman (1988) notes that in the unsuccessful fight to save the GLC, its leader Ken Livingstone claimed on television that the law had become such an important part of policy-making that one even consulted a lawyer before going to the toilet. Feldman noted that there seemed to be a belief in some quarters that in judicial review proceedings judges are coming to control Government, taking over a policy-deciding role rather than sticking to legal adjudication.

In short we have moved quickly and substantially from the time when judicial review was a topic of interest only to those interested in comparative administration (since it was more associated with continental systems) or those approaching administration from a law background.

DIPLOCK CATALOGUE

In the course of the Government Communications HQ (GCHQ) case in 1985 Lord Diplock responded to the increased number of cases by setting out in a more systematic fashion the 'Diplock catalogue' of the three grounds for review:

- illegality;
- irrationality;
- procedural impropriety.

These grounds were intended to encompass various other sorts of argument about valid review. The three headings summarise a much more disparate debate about the grounds, extent and utility of review.

Fair play, legitimate expectations or procedural impropriety

Judicial review is the expansion of some earlier precedents rather than a completely new doctrine. Wilson (1966) cites the case of *Cooper* v. *Wandsworth Board of Works* (1863) in which Cooper failed to give the Board seven days' notice of his intention to build a house. According to the regulations the Board had the right to demolish the house and they did so. The complainant argued that although the statute gave such a right to the authority, the statute carried with it an assumption that no man should be derived of his property unless he had the opportunity to be heard. The court decided that there were reasons such as ignorance or the failure to deliver the notice that meant that the demolition of a house could not be reasonable unless the owner had the opportunity of a hearing; that there was little inconvenience to the authority in providing a hearing and there was the prospect of considerable loss to the owner if the statute was taken literally.

It has been decided over time that laws such as the Municipal Corporations Act (1882) which did not lay down specific procedural requirements for public consultation and natural justice (or 'fair play in action') none the less were to be read as if they did. This notion insisted on an opportunity for affected persons to argue their case at the appropriate time. Thus the dismissal of a Chief Constable was declared to be void because he had not been given an opportunity to state his case (*Ridge* v. *Baldwin*, 1964). This is generally read to be an assertion by the courts that they would ensure that rules of natural justice were followed where a public law was involved even where there was no specific basis in statute. Where the field of public law ends is not always clear. This has been taken, for example, to mean that students cannot have their courses terminated for poor attendance without hearings that would meet the requirements of natural justice (*R.* v. *Aston University ex parte Roffey* (1969), *Glynn* v. *Keele University* (1971)). Such procedural form based on natural justice has also been required of hearings before a Board of Visitors on serious charges within prison (*R.* v. *Board of Visitors of Hull Prison, ex parte St Germain,* 1979). In *R.* v. *Barnsley MDC, ex parte Hook* (1976), a decision by the relevant Committee to withhold a licence from a stallholder was quashed because the only complainant against the stallholder was the market manager who initiated the disciplinary action and sat on the committee. His evidence was not given in front of the stallholder or his representatives.

There is thus now a doctrine of '*legitimate expectations*'. In the Government Communications HQ (GCHQ) case of 1985 in which the Government gave great publicity to the security services by removing the trade union rights from staff in an 'eavesdropping' facility, it was ruled that on the basis of past practice the unions had a 'legitimate expectation' to be consulted on the ban of trade union membership within GCHQ. Thus in the GCHQ case it seems that the unions did make their point that there was a legitimate expectation of consultation before the withdrawal of union recognition and rights. The Government won the case on the point that national security in the place of employment in question overcame the power of the expectation. The GCHQ also confirmed a technical expansion of judicial review powers in that the Civil Service Order through which unions were banned was an Order made by the Sovereign under the Royal Prerogative rather than through parliamentary legislation.

In a series of local government finance cases in the 1980s the Secretary of State for the Environment was held at fault in not hearing sufficient representations by local authorities affected by his decisions. Under sections 48 to 50 of the Local Government Planning and Land Act (1980) the Secretary of State for the Environment had the power to reduce the level of rate support grant payable to an authority. Before doing so he had to lay certain orders before Parliament. The Secretary of State issued his decisions before the orders were approved. He also declined to meet local authority associations, saying that such a meeting would have no effect.

The Court of Appeal set aside his decisions and said that fairness demanded that the Secretary of State consider the objections. The Queen's Bench Division argued,

> His attitude was in effect that the policy was settled . . . the Secretary of State clearly decided to turn a deaf ear to any and all representations to change the policy formulated by him before he obtained his statutory powers. (Jowell and Oliver 1988: 77)

The 'Judge Over Your Shoulder' points out that the verdict was in spite of the fact that the Secretary of State's policy had been fully discussed with the local authorities and debated in Parliament before the Act empowering the cuts was passed. Diplock's concept of 'procedural impropriety' was wider than the simple idea of natural justice as established in the early cases as it also included failures by administrative tribunals to observe the rules set down by statute or other legislative instrument – even where such failure does not involve any denial of natural justice (Boynton 1986). In *R.* v. *Liverpool Corporation, ex parte Liverpool Taxi Fleet Operators' Association* (1972), it was considered that as the city council had pursued a policy of limiting the number of licensed taxis to 300 and as they had assured the taxi owners that they would not increase this without consultation, they could not then breach that undertaking without such consultation.

Ultra vires or illegality

Other pre-modern cases gave rise to the doctrine of *ultra vires*. This concerned not only the processes by which public bodies exercised their statutory powers but also to ensure that the decisions were consistent with the statutory power. Wilson cites the case of *Westminster Corporation* v. *London and North Western Railway Co.* (1905). This concerned the not usually controversial issue of public conveniences. The Public Health (London) Act of 1891 provided that every sanitary authority might provide and maintain public lavatories. Westminster used this authority to build a subway containing conveniences under Parliament Street. The London and North Western Railway Corporation objected to the fact that the subway entrance was opposite the entrance to their offices, and they claimed that in building a subway the Corporation was outside the scope of the Public Health Act. The House of Lords reversed a verdict of the Court of Appeal which had accepted in effect that the construction of the convenience was a means merely to provide a subway and hence was *ultra vires*. The Lords accepted the statement on oath of the chairman of the Works Committee of the corporation that the primary object of the exercise was the provision of conveniences.

A case which looks more controversial to modern eyes was *Prescott* v. *Birmingham Corporation* (1955). The Corporation introduced a scheme to give free travel to certain classes of the elderly. A ratepayer complained to the court that such a scheme which required a subsidy of the transport budget from the general rate fund was an inappropriate and *ultra vires* use of rate funds. Another conservative judgement concerned *Roberts* v.

Hopgood (1925) in which Poplar Borough Council were surcharged by the District Auditor because they had paid wages to staff of £4 per week and had failed to reduce wages when the cost of living had fallen. The auditor argued that these sums were so excessive as to be illegal as they were gifts rather than wages (Wilson 1966: 559). The local authority won an appeal to the Divisional Court but lost at the stage of the House of Lords. Lord Atkinson argued that,

> This . . . might be admirably philanthropic, if the funds of the council at the time they were thus administered belonged to the existing members of that body. These members would be generous at their own expense . . . The indulgence of philanthropic enthusiasm at the expense of persons other than the philanthropists is an entirely different thing from the indulgence of it at the expense of the philanthropists themselves . . . A body charged with the administration for definite purposes of funds contributed in whole or in part by persons other than the members of that body, owes,, in my view, a duty to those latter persons to conduct that administration in a fairly businesslike manner with reasonable care, skill and caution . . .

In the *Attorney General* v. *Fulham Corporation* (1921) the courts decided that legislation which permitted local authorities to provide wash-houses was *ultra vires* in allowing the councils to trade for profit. The courts have therefore – like the even more spectacularly inconsistent US courts – not been unchanging in their views.

In *Congreve* v. *Home Office* (1976) the issue was the attempt to stop TV licence holders taking out new licences before the expiry of their old ones in order to 'beat' a price increase. The Home Secretary threatened to revoke these licences after eight months. The plaintiff argued that this was an abuse of power since the licences were purchased lawfully and the Minister's discretion to revoke the licences could not be used for such purposes.

Lord Denning argued that those who purchased the overlapping licences had paid the appropriate fee for a full twelve months. As the Minister did not have good reason to revoke the licence, the mere fact that he could revoke licences was not the important consideration,

> It would be a misuse of the power conferred on him by Parliament: and these courts have the authority – and, I would add, the duty, – to correct a misuse of power by a Minister or his department, no matter how much he may resent it or warn us of the consequences if we do.

Padfield v. *MAFF* [see below] is proof of what I say. It shows that when a Minister is given discretion and exercises it for reasons which are bad in law the courts can interfere so as to get him back on the right road. . . The Minister relies on the intention of Parliament. But it was not the policy of Parliament that he was seeking to enforce. It was his own policy . . . I say it was unlawful . . . the department did not like people taking out overlapping licences so as to save money. But there was nothing in the Regulations to stop it.

Feldman (1988) describes the traditional *ultra vires* cases where the executive body is misinterpreting or exceeding its statutory authority. He notes that the interpretation of the concept has seemingly expanded in recent times to include the legality of acting on the advice of circulars or on other advice from the Government.

In *Padfield* v. *Minister of Agriculture, Fisheries and Food* (1968) the court decided that the decision by the Minister not to utilise a complaints procedure under the Agricultural Marketing Act of 1958 was not based on good reasons in law. In other words, though the Act implied that the Minister had wide freedom ('if the Minister in any case so directs') he/ she could only use this discretion within the spirit of the Act.

Irrationality (unreasonableness)

Another of the early and minor sounding cases of importance, that of *Associated Provincial Picture Houses Ltd* v. *Wednesbury Corporation* (1948) gave rise to the so-called Wednesbury formula. The case concerned the Sunday Entertainments Act of 1932 under which the local authority could allow cinemas to open on Sundays 'subject to such conditions as the authority thinks fit to impose'. The Corporation imposed a condition that no child under the age of 15 could be admitted. The cinema chain complained that this was an unreasonable condition to impose and that in any case it was *ultra vires*. In the Court of Appeal it was set out by Lord Greene that,

> the decision of the local authority can be upset if it is proved to be unreasonable in the sense that the court considers it to be a decision that no reasonable body could have come to. It is not what the court considers unreasonable . . . Some courts might think that no children ought to be admitted on Sundays at all, some courts might think the reverse . . . The effect of the legislation is not to set up the court as an arbiter of the correctness of one view or another.

Though on the face of it the Wednesbury formula was a statement of non-interference by the courts in the particular case under discussion, the concept of 'reasonableness' allowed later courts to intervene precisely on the grounds that what had taken place was not reasonable. *Wheeler* v. *Leicester City Council* (1985), was a case where the Council was not allowed to prevent the use of a rugby park on the issue of contacts with South Africa. This was considered unreasonable – though many would conclude to the contrary.

In *Avon CC* v. *Burscott* (1988), where the Council tried to secure a possession order against trespassing gypsies, the Court of Appeal reckoned that the local .authority decision was unreasonable on the grounds that they had not themselves provided provision for gypsies as instructed by statute. Feldman (1988: 24) describes irrationality as difficult to present though it apparently included the sort of matters covered by the Wednesbury formula of 1948 – 'taking account of irrelevant considerations, failing to take account of relevant ones, using a power for an improper purpose, behaving wholly unreasonably or acting in bad faith'.

In *R.* v. *The Lord Chancellor, ex parte the Law Society* in June 1993, the Queen's Bench concluded that although the Lord Chancellor had failed to consult the Law Society before introducing regulations which reduced eligibility for legal aid the court would not declare the regulations invalid since additional consultation would not have led to a different result. Thus the court decided there was no procedural impropriety. Moreover, Lord Justice Neill concluded, 'I am completely unconvinced that the choice [by the Lord Chancellor] that was made, though clearly regrettable, could be stigmatised as irrational.' In the review of the actions of the Secretary of State, John Gummer, over his refusal to hold an inquiry over the Thorp nuclear reprocessing plant, Greenpeace and Lancashire County Council suggested that he had acted unreasonably and irrationally. The decision was that the Minister might have been sensible to hold an inquiry in the light of the public concern, but Parliament had passed the legislation to give the Secretary of State discretion and so he had not erred in law (*The Independent*, 5 March 1994).

Lord Brightman, in *R.* v. *Hillingdon London Borough Council, ex parte Puhlhofer* (1986) stressed that the courts would not intervene unless there had been bad faith, a mistake in construing the limits of a power, or unreasonableness verging on absurdity. In another housing case in 1987 Judge Stuart-Smith endorsed the refusal to house a family which had deliberately made itself homeless by leaving housing in Bangladesh to move to Tower Hamlets. He said that before the court could interfere a

decision had to be, 'so outrageous and in defiance of logic that any
sensible person would have laughed at it'. As Rawlings observes,

> an administrator may be said to have acted unreasonably if, in reach-
> ing his decision, he 'asked himself the wrong question' or 'took into
> account irrelevant considerations', but in many instances he will only
> know that the questions were wrong or the considerations irrelevant
> when the courts tell him so. . . . Again, no practical guidance is offered
> to the administrator by tests of this type . . . the principles of 'fairness'
> and 'reasonableness' by which the courts test the validity of adminis-
> trative discretionary decisions are far too open-ended to offer any
> guidance to an administrator as how to go about his duties.
>
> (Rawlings 1986: 142)

Rawlings argues,

> Yet it is very clear that administrative decisions have been struck
> down as unreasonable which by no stretch of the imagination could
> fall within the extremely narrow – drawn category envisaged by Lord
> Diplock: recent examples might include the Tameside case 1977 and
> the 'Fair Fares' case, *Bromley LBC* v. *Greater London Council*, 1983. . .
>
> (Rawlings 1986: 142)

Review about content

It is the category of reasonableness that most opens the door to the
controversial notion of courts deciding on the merits of a decision rather
than its legality. As Harlow and Rawlings (1984) argue, the judicial
review of discretionary administrative action is itself highly discretionary. So the fact is that an increased volume of judicial review has
not brought with it any new certainty on restrictions of the power of the
Government. In a 1986 case of *Nottingham County Council* v. *Secretary of State
for the Environment*, the court decided that it could not intervene when
grants were based on a formula that worked against the interests of a
class of authorities – even though the 1982 Local Government Finance
Act required that the settlement be made in accordance with principles
applicable to all local authorities. Lord Scarman, in a House of Lords
decision, said that the courts must be wary of interfering with the
legislative process. It was not for the courts to decide if legislative
activity was reasonable. He confirmed Lord Justice Lawton's Court of
Appeal view that the Secretary of State was given the required authority
by Parliament:

He has to make a political and economic judgement. He may make a
sound one or a bad one. This court might have been able to make a
better one than he made; but we must remind ourselves that Parliament, no doubt for good reason, has not entrusted guidance to us.

This principle seems not to have been consistently maintained. Feldman
says, 'In view of all that, it is not surprising that people do not know
where they are.' We merely have new areas of doubt. Feldman cites the
Tameside case of 1977 to show that the court did not think it unreasonable for a Conservative Council to follow their manifesto promise to
change the policy of their Labour predecessors by reinstating selective
education at the last moment. However, the court did decide that it was
unreasonable for the GLC to follow their manifesto policy of a large
subsidy to London Transport in pursuit of their 'Fair Fares' policy.
(*Bromley LBC* v. *Greater London Council*, 1983).

Thus while the core notion of judicial review is that the activities of
public bodies are subject to the control of the courts over the *manner of
their decision-making* in practice it is often *the merits* of the decision that are
being discussed (see Ganz 1987).

It is held as a principle of British politics that there is parliamentary
supremacy or sovereignty in the sense that, 'Parliament . . . has, under
the English constitution, the right to make or unmake any law whatsoever; and, further, a right to override or set aside the legislation of
Parliament' (Dicey 1962 edn: 40). Only Acts of Parliament have this
status however. Delegated legislation, resolutions and any other form of
activity may all be tested in the courts to ensure that the requirements of
the enabling Act, or of some common-law legal principle, have been
fulfilled (Marston and Ward 1991: 4).

The key controversy over judicial review is *discretion over policy*; the
literature is very cautious (not to say ambiguous) on this. In *Madzimba-
muto* v. *Lardner-Burke* (1969) it was suggested that the Southern Rhodesian
Act 1965 had been passed contrary to constitutional convention, and
hence was not valid. At that time, however, Lord Reid concluded that
even if most people concluded a particular policy was improper,

> that does not mean that it is beyond the power of the Parliament to
> do such things. If Parliament chose to do any of them the courts could
> not hold the Act of Parliament invalid.
>
> (Marston and Ward 1991: 49)

Marston and Ward conclude that parliamentary supremacy makes
any attempt to protect individual rights against the whim of the

legislative body or executive difficult, but the growth in judicial review can, arguably, be seen as a possible route to some incomplete and *ad hoc* means of protection. Marston and Ward (1991: 68) accept that *Stoke-on-Trent City Council* v. *B & Q* amounts to a limited degree of judicial review of legislation. Thus in *Stoke-on-Trent City Council* v. *B & Q*, Justice Hoffman said,

> The power to review Acts of Parliament (on the grounds of proportionality) is new to the courts of this country. . . In some cases it will be apparent to the court that the legislative power has been used for an ulterior and impermissible purpose. In others exercise of the power will be clearly invalidated by some basic error of reasoning. But in cases in which different views were reasonably tenable, the courts have not attempted to usurp the functions of the legislative.
>
> (Marston and Ward 1991: 50)

In *R.* v. *IRC, ex parte Preston*, Lord Templeman declared the principle of law to be that the courts may intervene to review a power conferred by statute on the grounds of unfairness, only if the unfairness in the exercise of the power was such as to amount to an abuse of power (from Lord Scarman's judgment in *Nottinghamshire CC* v. *Secretary of State for the Environment*, 1980).

However, in *Hammersmith and Fulham London BC* v. *Secretary of State for the Environment* a similar case over the power of the DOE with regard to 'charge capping' the tax-raising powers of a local authority arose. Lord Bridge stated that if the Secretary of State's actions were within the terms of the Act they could be challenged only on the grounds of irrationality short of the extremes of bad faith, improper motive or manifest absurdity. He said the merits of the policy underlying the decisions are not susceptible to review by the courts and the courts would be exceeding their proper function if they presumed to condemn the policy as unreasonable.

This does, however, allow the courts the right to find that there was bad faith, improper motive or manifest absurdity. As Marston and Ward (1991: 177) argue, the notion of judgment based on the notion of absurdity, 'brings the courts to the very limits of proper judicial interference with executive action, and raises questions as to the separation of powers'.

Lord Chief Justice Glidewell noted in 1988 (Glidewell 1989) that the apparently limited task of judicial review as construed before the Second World War has been overtaken by the inventiveness of the courts and, 'it is this inventiveness which has given us the greater part of our modern administrative law'. He continued,

The rediscovery by Lord Goddard and Lord Denning that the courts have the power to quash for error on the face of the record has banished into limbo the sterile question whether a decision maker's error was within its jurisdiction, and so not capable of challenge, or a trespass over the jurisdictional boundary, when it might be.

(Glidewell 1989)

He gives an example of where in the past the courts showed a marked reluctance to interfere with, or even to get involved in, any matter that was thought to be properly within the sphere of central or local government. He said that one part of the explanation of such deference was concerns regarding the safety of the nation in wartime. He said, 'Certainly this is the only respectable explanation for the decision of the House of Lords in *Liversidge* v. *Anderson* (1942)'. He notes that in 1948 there was a process which allowed objections to Compulsory Purchase Orders in connection with the construction of Stevenage New Town. Before that process was complete the Minister made a speech showing that his mind was made up before receiving all these objections. In *Franklin* v. *Minister of Town and Country Planning* (1948) the court said that the Minister did not fetter his discretion or show bias by that speech. Glidewell (1987) notes, 'In effect the Minister was held to be immune from judicial control. He would not be so fortunate today.'

Thus in 1992 it was unexceptional when the NUM quickly and successfully challenged in the courts the proposed closure of thirty-one mines. The court concluded that the pre-closure process was mishandled – but that argument could have been a surrogate for expressing policy preferences. The courts, however, appear to be reluctant to intervene where policy is overwhelmingly a matter of value judgement.

The 'inventiveness' of the courts has meant that they have interpreted their jurisdiction as extending to the Criminal Injuries Board, the City Panel on Takeovers and Mergers, the Advertising Standards Authority, and the Code of Practice Committee of the British Pharmaceutical Industry, but not to decisions of the Jockey Club, the Chief Rabbi or the Football Association (Pannick 1992: 2).

Proportionality

Review of content has been further advanced by the inching towards a doctrine labelled 'proportionality'. In the GCHQ case Lord Diplock had suggested that his three main categories might be extended as a consequence of membership of the European Community. Proportionality states that a decision can be faulty if it is excessive in its impact in light of the original problem. In *R.* v. *Secretary of State for the Home department, ex parte Brind* (1990), Sir John Donaldson said that if the argument about proportionality was accepted (i.e. that the court should consider whether decisions were disproportionate to the needs of the decision) then the courts could soon substitute their view of what was appropriate. But none the less – despite such regular reminders to each other about the consequences – judges have been deciding cases on less restricted grounds.

Jowell and Lester remark, in 'Beyond Wednesbury: Substantive Principles of Administrative Law' (1988), that every now and again judges claim that juducial review is concerned not with the decision but with the process. They argue that it is better to recognise that the courts have and should have been implying principles allowing substantive review of administration. They say the (subterranean) categories have been:

- rejecting irrationality – decisions displaying no intelligible reason, arbitrary or perhaps 'consulting an astrologer or spinning a coin';
- the prohibition of decisions that violate accepted standards of administrative probity (such as fraud or bad faith);
- overturning decisions that unjustifiably violate fundamental rights and freedoms.

They see the European principle of proportionality as a part of the attack on decisions on administrative good practice and the protection of fundamental rights and freedoms. Decision-makers must use reasonable means to attain ends. The argument that started out in the Wednesbury decision to the effect that discrimination against a teacher on the grounds that she had red hair – presented by Lord Greene as an example of unreasonableness – seems to being teased out to be a general protection for rights against abuse.

How much judicial review?

Despite the new conventional wisdom of the importance of administrative law – and judicial review in particular – there is a convincing contrary view to suggest that we have not transformed the relations between the courts and the administative system.

Sunkin, Bridges and Meszaros (1993) show that between 1981 and 1991 the number of judicial review applications 'exploded' fourfold (4,740 cases in 1987–9 and the first quarter of 1991). However, these have been concentrated in two main fields: immigration and home-lessness. Out of 2,600 cases current in 1993, immigration and the homeless accounted for 500–600 cases each. They note that for a wide range of Government activity the potential remains undeveloped, 'There were, for example, relatively few applications relating to the millions of decisions taken each year on social welfare benefits and areas such as health, environmental protection, children's rights, social care and housing (other than homeless persons) remain largely un-touched by judicial review' (Sunkin *et al.* 1993: 19). They suggest that access to review might be more difficult than is generally supposed. Surprisingly their report, *Judicial Review in Perspective* (June, 1993), con-cluded that judicial review was used, 'more often as a weapon to limit . . . local government than as a constraint on the central state': Central Government was the subject of only 25% of all judicial review applica-tions they studied (and the Home Office was the subject of three-quarters of these). Only a third or so of all applications reach a trial hearing and only one in six of these result in a ruling against the public body challenged.

The impact of judicial review may, of course, not rest on the cases settled in the courts but on the cases which do not reach the court – because the behaviour of the officials is affected by expectations that the court could be involved (the anticipated reactions argument). Drewry notes that the (unjustified) impression of an avalanche of cases has caused some judges to try to choke off the growth by restricting the scope for review.

Does 'more' equal 'better'?

Undoubtedly the notion of judicial review is a fashionable idea and, in so far as it could be a curb on oppressive Government, more review is commonly seen as a measure of progress. But the data on the scale of review really indicates that it is easy to exaggerate review as a tool for that purpose. Feldman, however, argues against judicial review to establish unreasonableness as follows:

1. the values needed for the review have to be drawn, at least partly, from non statutory sources by non elected judges, leading to problems of accountability;
2. the values chosen by judges may conflict with other values relevant to good administration, which may not be in the judges' minds when making the decision;

3. the judges' values may conflict with political values and objectives adopted by administrators according to a plan approved by an electorate;
4. the uncertainty of review for some types of irrationality may impose a social cost by throwing a settled, and apparently effective, policy into confusion.

(Feldman 1988: 25)

Feldman sees less problems in the courts seeking to maintain that administration avoids irrelevant matters. He sees this as less uncontroversial than the attempt to judge reasonableness. Thus not all commentators are impressed by the number or significance of cases. As we have seen, Sunkin's evidence leads him to the conclusion that judicial review is 'sporadic and peripheral' and that 'it appears to have played a minimal role in the redress of grievances and have provided the community with a very partial and limited check against government illegality' (1987: 465).

In a House of Lords appeal on judicial review it transpired that when a solicitor had been consulted on a potential judicial review case, the lawyer 'frankly admitted that he knew nothing about judicial review'. David Pannick has commented (1992: 1) 'On the fundamental question of who is subject to judicial review and in respect of what, such is the state of uncertainty and confusion that even if that solicitor had made a detailed study of judicial decisions, he would have remained unenlightened.'

In July 1990, in *R. v. Secretary of State for Social Services and another, ex parte Stitt*, it was decided that the court could not intervene in a matter arising under the 1986 Social Security Act because Parliament had unambiguously given the Social Security Ministers the sole right to make decisions about categories of need which qualified for payment out of the social fund. The QC for the DSS, Michael Beloff, was unable to cite any other Act which gave such 'wholesale, unregulated and unsupervised powers'. The court ruled that although it might be undesirable for such legislation to be passed, it restrained itself from interfering – but there is no certainty that it exercises such restraint with consistency (see Law Report, *The Independent*, 6 July 1990).

Judicial review is not an unlimited safety net to allow dissatisfied customers of Government an avenue of complaint. Rawlings argues (1986: 137) that the existence of the new emphasis on administrative law has not controlled Government but legimated the growth of a more powerful state. The control is limited but the fact that there is an apparent control allows Government to extend its powers into what would be even more controversial new areas. He cites the White Paper on the *Review of Public Order Law* (Cmnd 9510) which argues that extended police powers over public processions are defensible precisely because there is a possibility of judicial review which gives 'an effective means of challenging any decision by the police to impose conditions . . .' As the courts have been reluctant to query police discretion the gain in powers is being traded against a hypothetical kind of limit.

Rawlings also notes that the Government, through its control of the legislature, can bypass the control of the courts by relegislating to avoid a particular judgment. There, judicial review can be bypassed by fresh and more explicit legislation. Rawlings (1986: 137) cites Prosser, who argued, 'any judicial decision producing change which causes administrative difficulty or increased expense is likely to face legislative nullification'. (See Zellick 1985.) Rawlings (1987) cites the case of Atkinson in which the courts found that the Supplementary Benefits Commission could not make certain kinds of deductions from the supplementary benefit of students during the vacation. The Secretary of State for Health and Social Security responded to this by not only changing the law but doing so retrospectively back to 1966 when the scheme had been introduced.

Sunkin (1988: 5) notes that the Social Security Act of 1986 was drawn up to avoid difficulties found by the DHSS in cases such as *R. v. Secretary of State for Social Services, ex parte Cotton* (1985). Cotton was refused benefit and succeeded in a case which showed that the Secretary of State had failed adequately to consult in determining regulations and that the regulations were *ultra vires*. The same Act, he says, expressly allowed the Government not to consult when making regulations in situations of urgency because of the *ultra vires* decision in which the case of *R. v. Secretary of State for Social Services, ex parte Association of Metropolitan Authorities* (1986), had found that the AMA were given insufficient opportunity to participate in consultation over Housing Benefit regulations.

Sunkin (1988) also instances the case of *Khawaja v. The Home Department* (1983). The House of Lords decided that the Immigration Service must have sufficient evidence to decide that a person is an illegal entrant. They cannot use the fact that an applicant has shown a lack of candour as the evidence of illegality. However, the change is not necessarily to the benefit of potential entrants. Sunkin shows that the Home Office switched to treating cases as being about illegal entry rather than overstaying visas. This was a procedure with reduced remedies through appeal on the merits of the case but only a judicial review of the procedures used.

He says that to avoid administrative disruption a judge can choose to recognise that an action was *ultra vires* but not strike down the offending regulations. He says of the decision in the AMA case above that it illustrated, 'how pliant judicial discretion can be in the face of administrative expediency'.

Thus the important case of the potential control of administrative decision and action by the courts falls into the British syndrome of retrospective justification for ill-considered empirical developments. That is not to say that developments may or may not have been desirable but to stress that theory consists of a form of words to sustain disparate practice.

Bibliography

Albrow, M. (1970) *Bureaucracy*, Basingstoke: Macmillan.

Allison, G. (1971) *Essence of Decision*, Boston: Little, Brown.

Amery, L. (1935) *The Forward View*, London: Bles.

Bacharach, S.B. and Lawler, E.J. (1980) *Bargaining*. San Francisco: Jossey-Bass.

Bagehot, W. (1963)*The English Constitution*, London: Fontana.

Baker, R.J.S. (1972) *Administrative Theory and Public Administration*, London: Hutchinson.

Barker, A. (1982) *Quangos in Britain*, Basingstoke: Macmillan.

Barnard, C.J. (1938) *The Functions of the Executive*, Cambridge, Mass.: Harvard University Press.

Bealey, F. (1988) *Democracy in the Contemporary State*, Oxford: Clarendon.

Berrill, K. (1981) *Strength At The Centre: The Case for a PM's Department*, London: University of London.

Birch, A.H. (1964) *Representative and Responsible Government*, London: Allen & Unwin.

Birkenshaw, P., Harden, I. and Lewis, N. (1990) *Government by Moonlight*, London: Unwin Hyman.

Blackstone, T. and Plowden, W. (1988) *Inside the Think Tank*, London: Heinemann.

Blau, P. ([1955] 1963) *The Dynamics of Bureaucracy*, Chicago.

Blom-Cooper, L. (1981) 'The Old Order Changeth', *Public Administration Bulletin*, No. 37, 2–13.

Blom-Cooper, L. (1982) , 'The New Face of Judicial Review', *Public Law*, 250–61.

Bos, D. (1991) *Privatization: A Theoretical Treatment*, Oxford: Clarendon.

Boston, J., Martin, J., Pallot, J. and Walsh, P. (1991) *Reshaping the State*, Auckland: Oxford University Press.

Bowen, G. (1978) *Survey of Fringe Bodies*, Civil Service Department.

Boyd-Carpenter, J. (1980) *Way of Life*, London: Sidgwick & Jackson.

Boynton, J. (1986) 'Judicial Review of Administrative Decisions', *Public Administration*, Vol. 64, 147–61.

Bozeman, B. (1987) *All Organizations are Public*, Jossey-Bass.

Bridges, E. (1950) *Portrait of a Profession*, London: Cambridge University Press.

Brown, G. (1971) *In My Way: The Political Memoirs of Lord George Brown*, London: Gollancz.

Bruce-Gardyne, J. (1986) *Ministers and Mandarins*, London: Sidgwick & Jackson.

Burns, T. and Stalker, G.H. (1961) *The Management of Innovation*, London: Tavistock.

Butler, D. and Halsey, A.H. (1978) *Policy and Politics*, London: Macmillan.

Butler, Sir R., (1990) Redcliffe-Maud Memorial Lecture, 'New Challenges or Familiar Prescriptions', *Public Administration*, Vol. 69, No. 3, 363–72.

Butler, Sir R. (1991) *FDA News, Vol. 11, No. 12, 3-4*.

Butler, Sir R. (1992) 'The Future of the Civil Service', *Public Policy and Administration*, Vol. 7, No. 2, 1–10.

Cabinet Office (1991) *Improving Management in Government: The Next Steps Agencies* (Review 1991), Cm 1760, London: HMSO.

Callaghan, J. (1987) *Time and Chance*, London: Collins/Fontana.

Campbell, C. (1983) *Governments Under Stress*, Toronto: Toronto University Press.

Campbell, C. (1993) 'The Aptitude of Whitehall for Coherence and Consistency: A Paragon Lost?', Paper to American Political Science Association, Washington, DC, 2–5 September.

Campion, G.F.M. (1950) *British Government Since 1918*, London: Allen & Unwin.

Carey, A. (1967) 'The Hawthorne Studies: A Radical Criticism', *American Sociological Review*, Vol. 32, No.3.

Castle, B. (1984) *The Castle Diaries*, London: Weidenfeld & Nicolson.

Cawson, A. (1986) *Corporatism and Political Theory*, Oxford: Blackwell.

Cawson, A., Morgan, K., Webber, D., Holmes, P. and Stevens, A. (1990) *Hostile Brothers*, Oxford: Clarendon.

Chester, D.N. (1954) 'The Crichel Down Case', *Public Administration*, Vol. XXXII, 389–401.

Chester, D.N. (1979) 'Fringe Bodies, Quangos and All That', *Public Administration*, Vol. 57, Spring, 51–4.

Chester, D.N. and Willson, F.M.G. (1968) *The Organization of British Central Government*, London: Allen & Unwin.

Cockerell, M., Hennessy, P. and Walker, D. (1984) *Sources Close To the PM*, London: Macmillan.

Colebatch, H.K. (1991) 'Getting our Act Together', XVth World Congress of the International Political Science Association.

Cooper, F. (1986) 'Changing the Establishment', Typescript.

Cooper, P. (1990) 'Public Law and Public Administration' in N. Lynn and A. Wildavsky, *Public Administration*, New Jersey: Chattam House.

Crosland, A. (1971) in M. Kogan, *The Politics of Education*, Penguin Education Special.

Crossman, R. (1963) 'Introduction' to Bagehot, *The English Constitution*, London: Collins.

Crossman, R. (1972) *Inside View*, London, Jonathan Cape.

Crossman, R. (1975–7) *Diaries of A Cabinet Minister*, London: Hamilton & Cape (Vols 1–3).

Cuckney, J.G. (1972) 'The Commercial Approach to Government Operations', *Management Services in Government*.

Davies, A. and Willman, J. (1991) *What Next/Agencies, Departments and the Civil Service*, London: Institute of Policy Research.

Delafons, J. (1982) 'Working in Whitehall: Changes in Public Administration 1952–1982', *Public Administration*, Vol. 60, No. 3, 253–72.

Dell, E. (1980) 'Collective Responsibility: fact, fiction, or facade?' in *Policy and Practice*, London: Royal Institution for Public Administration.

Dexter, L.A. (1990) 'Intra-Agency Politics', *Journal of Theoretical Politics*, Vol. 2, No. 2, 151–72.

Dicey, A.V. ([1885] 1962) *Introduction to the Study of the Law and the Constitution*, London: Macmillan.

Dobbs, B. (1973) *Edwardians at Play*, Pelham Books.

Dobson, S. and Stewart, R. (1990) 'Public and Private Sector Management', *Public Money and Management*, Vol. 10, No. 1, 37–40.

DOE (1986) *Enterprise Zone Information*, London: HMSO.

Doherty, M. (1988) 'Prime Ministerial Power and Ministerial Responsibility In the Thatcher Era', *Parliamentary Affairs*, Vol. 41, No. 1, 49–67.

Donoughue, B. (1987) *Prime Minister*, London: Cape.

Dopson, S. (1993) 'Are Agencies an Act of Faith?', *Public Money and Management*, Vol. 13, No. 2.

Drewry, G. (1988) 'Judicial Review – Quite Enough of a Fairly Good Thing?' PAC Conference, University of York.

Drewry, G. and Butcher, T. (1988) *The Civil Service*, Oxford: Blackwell.

Dunleavy, P. (1989) 'The Architecture of the British Central State, Part I: Framework for Analysis', *Public Administration, Autumn*, Vol. 67, No. 3, 249–75.

Dunleavy, P. (1991) *Bureaucracy and Public Choice*, Hemel Hempstead: Harvester/ Wheatsheaf.

Dunsire, A. (1973) *Administration: the Word and the Science*, Oxford: Martin Robertson.

Dunsire, A., Hartley, K. and Parker, D. (1991) 'Organisational Status and Performance', *Public Administration*, Vol. 69, No. 1, 21–40.

Elcock, H. (1991) *Change and Decay*, Harlow, Essex: Longmans.

Elder, N. (1970) *Government in Sweden*, Oxford; Pergamon Press.

Ellis, D.L. (1980) 'Collective Ministerial Responsibility and Collective Solidarity', *Public Law*, Winter, 367–96

Expenditure Committee (1977) Eleventh Report from the Expenditure Committee, 1976–7, *The Civil Service*, HC 535, London: HMSO.

Featherstone, M. (1991) *Consumer Culture and Post Modernism*, London: Sage.

Feldman, D. (1988) 'Judicial Review: A Way of Controlling Government', *Public Administration*, Vol. 66, No. 1, 21–34.

Finer, S.E. (1956) 'The Individual Responsibility of Ministers', *Public Administration*, Vol. 34, 377–95.

Flynn, A., Gray A. and Jenkins, W. (1990) 'Taking the Next Steps and the Management of Government', *Parliamentary Affairs*, Vol. 43, No. 2, 159–78.

Flynn, A., Gray, A., Jenkins, W., and Rutherford, B. (1988) 'Implementing the Next Steps', *Public Administration*, Vol. 66, 439–45.

Forsyth, P. (1984) 'Airlines and Airports: Privatisation, Competition and Regulation', *Fiscal Studies*, Vol. 5, No. 1, 61–5.

Franks Report (1983) Cmnd 8787, London: HMSO.

Fry, G. (1988) 'Outlining the Next Steps', *Public Administration*, Vol. 66, 429–38.

Fudge, C. and Gustafsson, L. (1989) 'Administrative Reform and Public Management in Sweden and the United Kingdom', *Public Money and Management*, Vol. 9, No. 2, 29–34.

Fulton Committee Report, (1968) Vol. 5, Cmnd 3638, London: HMSO.

Gaitskell, H. and Williams, P.M. (1983) *The Diary of Hugh Gaitskell 1945-1956*, London: Cape.

Ganz, G. (1987) *Understanding Public Law*, London: Fontana.

Gerth, H.C. and Mills, C. Wright (1948) *From Max Weber*, London: Routledge.

Gilmour, I. (1969) *The Body Politic*, London: Hutchinson.

Gilmour, I. (1993) *Dancing with Dogma*, London: Pocket Books, Simon & Schuster.

Glidewell, Lord Justice (1989) 'The Individual and the State,' in *Public Policy and Administration*, Vol. 4, No. 1.

Grant, W. (1982) *The Political Economy of Industrial Policy*, London: Butterworth.

Grant, W., with Sargent, J. (1987) *Business and Politics in Britain*, Basingstoke: Macmillan Education.

Gray, A. (1991) 'Review of *Administrative Argument*', Public Administration, Vol. 69, No. 4, 533–4.

Goldsworthy, D. (1991) *Setting Up Next Steps*, London: HMSO.

Gouldner, A. (1954) *Patterns of Industrial Bureaucracy*, New York: Free Press.

Gretton, J., Harrison, A. and Beeton, D. (1987) 'How Far Have the Frontiers of the State been rolled back between 1979 and 1987?', *Public Money*, Vol. 7, No. 3, 17–25.

Griffith, E.S. (1939) *The Impasse of Democracy*, New York: Harrison-Hilton.

Griffith, J. (1987) 'Crichel Down', *Contemporary Record*, Spring, 35–40.

Gulick, L. (1937) 'Notes On the Theory of Organization', in L. Gulick and L. Urwick (eds), *Papers on the Science of Administration*, New York: Institute of Public Administration, Columbia University.

Gulick, L. and Urwick, L. (eds) (1937) *Papers on the Science of Administration*, New York: Institute of Public Administration, Columbia University.

Gunn, L. (1987) 'Perspectives on Public Management', Paper to Public Administration Committee Conference, York

Hague, D., Mackenzie, W. and Barker, A. (1975) *Public Policy and Private Interests*, London: Macmillan.

Hailsham, Lord (1978) *The Dilemma of Democracy*, London: Collins.

Hailsham, Lord (1987) interviewed by A. Seldon, *Contemporary Record*, Autumn

Haldane Report (1918) Cd 9230.

Hammond, T. (1990) 'In Defence of Luther Gulick's "Notes on the Theory of Organizations"', *Public Administration*, Vol. 68, No. 2, 143–73.

Hancher L. and Moran, M. (1989) *Capitalism, Culture and Economic Regulation*, Oxford: Clarendon.

Hansard Society (1993) *Making the Law: Report of Hansard Society Commission*, London: Hansard Society

Harden, I. and Lewis, N. (1986) *The Noble Lie: The British Constitution and the Role of Law*, London: Hutchinson.

Harlow, C. (1983) *Commercial Interdependence*, London: Policy Studies Institute.

Harlow, C. and Rawlings, R.W. (1984) *Law and Administration*, London: Weidenfeld & Nicolson.

Harris, R. (1990) *Good and Faithful Servant*, London, Faber & Faber.

Haynes, R.J. ([1980]1985) *Organisation Theory and Local Government*, London: Allen & Unwin

Headey, B. (1974) *British Cabinet Ministers*, London: Allen & Unwin.

Heald, D. (1983) *Public Expenditure*, Oxford: Basil Blackwell.

Healey, D. (1990) *The Time of My Life*, London: Michael Joseph.

Heclo, H. (1977) *A Government of Strangers*, London: Macmillan.

Heclo, H. and Wildavsky, A. (1974) *The Private Government of Public Money*, London: Macmillan.

Henderson, Sir N. (1984) *The Private Office*, London: Weidenfeld & Nicolson.

Hennessy, P. (1986) *Cabinet*, Oxford: Blackwell.

Hennessy, P. (1989) *Whitehall*, London: Secker & Warburg.

Henry, L. (1990) 'Root and Branch' in N. Lynn and A. Wildavsky, *Public Administration*, New Jersey: Chatham House.

Herman, V. and Alt, J.E. (1975) *Cabinet Studies: A Reader*, London: Macmillan.

Heseltine, M. (1987) *Where There's a Will*, London: Hutchinson.

Hicks, H. and Gullet, R. (1975) *Organisations: Theory and Behaviour*, London: McGraw-Hill.

Hoggett, P. (1990) 'Modernisation, Political Strategy and the Welfare State', *Studies in Decentralisation and Quasi-Markets*, Vol. 2, SNUS, Bristol.

Hoggett, P. (1991) 'A New Management in the Public Sector', *Policy and Politics*, Vol. 19, No. 4, 243–56.

Hogwood, B. (1979) *Government and Shipbuilding*, Farnborough, Hants: Saxon House.

Hogwood, B. (1993) 'Much Exaggerated: Death and Survival in British Quangos', PSA Conference, Leicester.

Hood, C.C. (1978) 'Keeping the Centre Small: Explanation of Agency Type', Political Studies, Vol. 26, 30–46.

Hood, C.C. (1979) 'The Machinery of Government Problem', *CSSP Studies in Public Policy*, Vol. 28.

Hood, C.C. (1982) 'Governmental Bodies and Government Growth', in A. Barker, *Quangos in Britain*, Basingstoke: Macmillan.

Hood, C.C. (1990) 'Beyond the Public Bureaucracy State? Public Administration in the 1990s', Inaugural Lecture, LSE.

Hood, C.C. and Dunsire, A. (1981) *Bureaumetrics*, Farnborough: Gower.

Hood, C.C., Dunsire, A. and Thompson, S. (1978) 'So You Think you know What Government Departments Are . . .?', *Public Administration Bulletin*, Vol. 27, 20–32.

Hood, C.C. and Jackson, M.W. (1991) *Administrative Argument*, Aldershot: Dartmouth.

Hood, C.C. and Schuppert, G.F. (eds) (1988) *Delivering Public Services in Western Europe*, London: Sage.

Hood Phillips, O. (1962) *Constitutional And Administrative Law*, London: Sweet & Maxwell.

Huczynski, A. and Buchanan, D.A. (1991) *Organisational Behaviour*, Englewood Cliffs: Prentice-Hall.

Ibbs Report (see Jenkins *et al.* 1988).

Ingham, B. (1991) *Kill the Messenger*, London: HarperCollins.

Jackson, R.J. and Van Schendelen, M.P.C.N. (1987) *The Politicisation of Business in Western Europe*, London: Routledge.

James, S. (1992) *British Cabinet Government*, London: Routledge.

Jenkins, K. Caines, J. and Jackson A. (1988) *Improving Management in Government: The Next Steps*, London: HMSO.

Jenkins, W. and Gray, A. (1983) 'Bureaucratic Politics and Power', *Political Studies*, Vol. 21, 177–93.

Jennings, W.I. ([1933] 1946), *The Law and the Constitution*, London: University of London Press.

Jennings, W.I. (1966) *The British Constitution*, Cambridge University Press.

Johnson, N. (1971) 'The Reorganisation of Central Government', *Public Administration*, Vol. 49, 1–12.

Johnson, N. (1982) 'Accountability, Control and Complexity', in A. Barker, *Quangos in Britain*, Basingstoke: Macmillan.

Jones, G. (1985) 'The Prime Minister's Aides', in A. King, *The British Prime Minister*, Basingstoke: Macmillan.

Jones, G. (1987) 'An Answer: Stand Up for Ministerial Responsibility', *Public Administration*, Vol. 65, No. 1, 87–91.

Jones, T. (1992) 'Judicial Review of the Independent Television Commission', *Public Law*, Autumn, 372–7.

Jordan, G. (1984) 'Enterprise Zones in the UK and US Ideologically Acceptable Job Creation', in J.J. Richardson, *Unemployment*, London: Sage.

Jordan, G. (1976) 'Hiving Off and Departmental Agencies,' *Public Administration Bulletin*, No. 1, 37–51.

Jordan, G. (1978) 'Central Co-ordination, Crossman and the Inner Cabinet', *Political Quarterly*, Vol. 49, 171–80.

Jordan, G. and Richardson, J. (1987) *British Politics and the Policy Process*, London: Allen & Unwin.

Jowell, J. and Oliver, D. (1985) *The Changing Constitution*, Oxford: Oxford University Press.

Jowell, J. and Oliver, D. (1988) *New Directions in Judicial Review*, London: Swee & Maxwell.

Jowell, J., and Lester, A. (1988) 'Beyond Wednesbury; Substantive Principles of Administrative Law', *Public Law*, 368–82.

Judge, D. (1984) *Ministerial Responsibility: Life in the Strawman Yet?*, Strathclyde Papers on Government and Politics, No. 37.

Justice/All Souls (1988) *Administrative Law: Some Necessary Reforms*, Oxford: Clarendon Press.

Kaufman, H. (1981) 'Fear of Bureaucracy: A Raging Pandemic', *Public Administration Review*, Vol. 41, No. 1, 1-9.

Kemp, P. (1988) 'Plans and Progress so far' in Arthur Young/RIPA, *The Next Steps: A Review of the Agency Concept*, London: RIPA.

Kemp, P. (1993), *Beyond Next Steps: A Civil Service for the 21st Century*, London: Social Market Foundation.

King, A. (1985) *The British Prime Minister*, Basingstoke: Macmillan.

Lawson, N. (1993) , *The View from Number 11*, London: Corgi.

Lee, J.M. (1974) 'Central Capability and Established Practice', in B. Chapman & A. Potter, *WJMM: Political Questions*, Manchester: Manchester University Press.

Lee, J.M. (1977) *Reviewing the Machinery of Government, 1942–1952*, n.p.

Lee, J.M. (1990) 'The Ethos of the Cabinet Office', *Public Administration*, Vol. 68, No. 2, 235–42.

Low, S., ([1904] 1914) *The Governance of England*, London: T. Fisher Unwin.

Lupton, T. (1971) *Management and the Social Sciences*, Harmondsworth: Penguin.

Lynn, N. and Wildavsky, A. (1990) *Public Administration*, New Jersey: Chatham House.

McGregor, D. (1960) *The Human Side of Enterprise*, New York: McGraw-Hill.

Mackenzie, W.J.M., Barker, A. and Hague, D.C. (1975) *Public Money and Private Interests*, London: Macmillan.

Mackenzie, W.J.M. and Grove, J.W. (1957) *Central Administration in Britain*, London: Longman Green.

Madgwick, P. (1991) *British Government: The Central Executive Territory*, Hemel Hempstead: Philip Allan.

Majone, G. (1989) *Evidence, Argument and Persuasion in the Policy Process*, New Haven: Yale University Press.

Mallaby, G. (1965) *From My Level*, London: Hutchinson.

Marsh, R. (1978) *Off the Rails: An Autobiography*, London: Weidenfeld & Nicolson.

Marshall, G. ([1984] 1986) *Constitutional Conventions: The Rules and Forms of Political Accountability*, Oxford: Clarendon.

Marshall, G. (ed.) (1989) *Ministerial Responsibility*, Oxford: Oxford University Press.

Marshall G. (1992) 'Ministerial Responsibility, the Home Office and Mr. Baker', *Public Law*, 7–12.

Marshall, G. and Moodie, G. (1971) *Some Problems of the Constitution*, London: Hutchinson.

Marston, J. and Ward, R. (1991) , *Constitutional and Administrative Law*, London: Pitman.

Mayo, E. ([1933] 1945) *The Human Problems of an Industrial Civilization*, New York: Macmillan.

Mellon, E., (1991) Evidence to Treasury and Civil Service Committee.

Merton, R.K. (ed.) (1952) *Reader in Bureaucracy*, Glencoe Ill.: The Free Press.

Metcalfe, L. and Richards, S. (1987) 'Evolving Public Management Cultures', in J. Kooiman and K. Eliassen *Managing Public Organizations*, London: Sage.

Mohr, L.B. (1971) 'Organizational Technology and Organizational Structure', *Administrative Science Quarterly*, Vol. 16, No. 4, 444–59.

Morgan, G. (1986) *Images of Organisation*, London: Sage.

Moskow, M.H. (1987) *Managing in the Public Sector*, Washington, DC: Center for Excellence in Government.

Murray, M.A. (1975) 'Comparing Public and Private Management: An Exploratory Essay', *Public Administration Review*, Vol. 35, 364–71.

Nicolson, I.F. (1986) *The Mystery of Crichel Down*, Oxford: Clarendon.

Niskanen, W. (1971) *Bureaucracy and Representative Government*, New York: Aldine Atherton.

Niskanen, W.A. (1973) *Bureaucracy: Servant or Master?*, London: Institute of Economic Affairs

Nystrom, P. and Starbuck, W. (1981) *Handbook of Organisational Design*, Vol. 2, Oxford: Oxford University Press.

Olsen, J.P. (1981) 'Integrated Organisational Participation', in P. Nystrom and W. Starbuck, *Handbook of Organisational Design*, Vol. 2, Oxford: Oxford University Press.

Osborne, D. and Gaebler, T. (1992) *Reinventing Government*, Wokingham: Addison-Wesley.

O'Toole, B. (1989) 'The Next Steps and Control of the Civil Service', *Public Policy and Administration*, Vol. 4, No. 1, 41–51.

O'Toole, B. and Jordan, G. (1994) *Next Steps; Improving Management in Government*, Aldershot: Dartmouth.

Pahl, R.E. and Winkler, J.T. (1974) 'The Coming Corporatism', *New Society*, Vol. 30, No. 627, 72–6.

Painter, C. (1991) 'The Public Sector and Current Orthodoxies', *The Political Quarterly*, Vol. 62, No. 1, 75–89.

Pannick, D. (1992) 'Who is subject to Judicial Review and in Respect of What?', *Public Law*, Spring, 1–7.

Part, Sir A. (1990) *The Making of a Mandarin*, London: André Deutsch.

Perrow, C. (1979) *Complex Organiszations*, Glenview: Scott, Foresman.

Peters, T.J. & Waterman, R.H., (1982) *In Search of Excellence*, Cambridge, Mass.: Harper & Row.

Pifer, A. (1975) 'The Quasi-Non Governmental Organisation', in Hague, Mackenzie and Barker, op. cit.

Pitt, D. (1980) *The Telecommunications Function in the British Post Office*, Farnborough, Hants: Saxon House

Pitt, D. and Smith, B. (1981) *Government Departments: an Organizational Perspective*, London, Routledge and Kegan Paul.

Pliatzky, L. (1980) *Report on Non-Departmental Bodies* Cmnd. 7797.

Pliatzky, L. (1985) *Paying and Choosing: The Intelligent Person's Guide to the Mixed Economy*, Oxford: Blackwell

Pliatzky, L. (1992) 'Quangos and Agencies', *Public Administration*, Vol. 70, Winter.

Pollitt, C. (1984) *Manipulating the Machine*, London: Allen & Unwin.

Pollitt, C. (1987) 'A Blockbuster from Bielefeld: Review of Guidance, Control and Evaluation in the Public Sector', *Public Administration*, Vol. 65, Spring, 105–7.

Pollitt, C. (1990) *Managerialism and the Public Services*, Oxford: Blackwell.

Ponting, C. (1986) *Whitehall: Tragedy and Farce*, London: Sphere.

Pugh, D., Hickson, D.J. and Hinnings, C.R. (1983) *Writers on Organisations*, Harmondsworth: Penguin.

Pugh, D. (1991) 'Foreword' to A. Huczynski and D.A. Buchanan, *Organisational Behaviour*, Engelwood Cliffs: Prentice-Hall.

Pym, F. (1984) *The Politics of Consent*, London: Hamish Hamilton.

Rainey, H.G., Barkoff, R.W. and Levine, C.N. (1976) 'Comparing Public and Private Organizations', *Public Administration Review*, Vol. 36, 223–44.

Rawlings, H.F. (1986) 'Judicial Review and the Control of Government', *Public Administration*, Vol. 64, 135–45.

Rawlings, R. (1987) 'In the Jungle', *Modern Law Review*, Vol. 50, No. 1, 110–17.

The Reorganisation of Central Government (1970) Cmnd 4506.

Rhodes, R. (1988) *Beyond Westminster and Whitehall*, London: Unwin Hyman.

Richards, S. (1988) 'Management in Central Government', *Public Money and Management*, Spring/Summer.

Richards, S. and Rodrigues, J. (1993) 'Strategies for Management in the Civil Service,' *Public Money and Management*, Vol. 13, No. 2.

Richardson, J.J. (1984) *Unemployment*, London: Sage.

Ridley, N. ([1991] 1992) , *My Style of Government*, London: Fontana.

Robson, W.A. (1971) 'The Reorganisation of Central Government', *Political Quarterly*, Vol. 42, 87–90.

Roethlisberger, F.J. and Dickson, W.J. (1939) *Management and the Worker*, Cambridge, Mass.: Harvard University Press.

Rose, R. (1984) *Understanding Big Government*, London: Sage.

Rose, R. (1987) *Ministers and Ministries*, Oxford: Clarendon Press.

Schwartz, B. and Wade, H.W.R. (1972) *Legal Control of Government*, Oxford: Clarendon.

Seidman, H. (1975) *Power, Politics and Position*, New York: Oxford University Press.

Seldon, A. (1990) 'The Cabinet Office and Co-ordination 1979–87', *Public Administration*, Vol. 68, 103–21.

Self, P. (1977) *Administrative Theories and Politics*, London: Allen & Unwin.

Shonfield, A. (1965) *Modern Capitalism*, Oxford: Oxford University Press.

Smith, B. (1975) *The New Political Economy*, London, Macmillan.

Simon, H. ([1957] 1961) *Administrative Behaviour*, New York: Macmillan.

Smith, M.J., Marsh, D. and Richards, D. (1993) 'Central Government Departments and the Policy Process', *Public Administration*, Vol. 71, Winter, 567–94.

de Smith, S.A., ([1954] 1980) *Judicial Review of Administrative Action*, London: Stevens.

Steel, D. (1982) 'Government and Industry in Britain', *British Journal of Political Science*, Vol. 12, No. 4, 449–503.

Stewart, J. and Ranson, S. (1985) 'Management in the Public Domain', *Public Money and Management*, Spring.

Stockman, D. (1986) *The Triumph of Politics*, London: Coronet Open Market edition.

Sunkin, M. (1987) 'What is Happening to Applications for Judicial Review?', *Modern Law Review*, Vol. 50, 432–67.

Sunkin, M. (1988) 'Judicial Review and Central Government', PAC Conference, York.

Sunkin, M., Bridges, L. & Meszaros, G. (1993) *Judicial Review in Perspective*, Public Law Project, London.

Taylor, F. (1911) *Principles and Methods of Scientific Management*, New York: Harper Bros.

Thatcher, M. (1993) *The Downing Street Years*, London: HarperCollins.

Theakston, K. (1987) *Junior Ministers in British Government*, Oxford: Blackwell.

Thomas, R. (1978) *The British Philosophy of Administration*, London: Longman.

Thomas, R.E. (1981) *The Government of Business*, Deddington: Philip Allan.

Thompson, D.L. (1985) *The Private Exercise of Public Functions*, Policy Studies Organisation Series.

Thompson, V.A. (1964) *Modern Organizations*, New York: Knopf.

Treasury and Civil Service Committee (1988) *Civil Service Management Reform: The Next Steps*, Eighth Report, HC 494, London: HMSO.

Treasury and Civil Service Committee (1990) *Progress in the Next Steps Initiative'* Eighth Report, HC 481, London: HMSO.

Treasury and Civil Service Committee (1991) *The Next Steps Initiative*, Eleventh Report, HC 496, London: HMSO.

Turpin, C. (1985) 'Ministerial Responsibility: Myth and Reality', in J. Jowell and D. Oliver, *The Changing Constitution*, Oxford: Oxford University Press.

Ulph, C. (1985) *150 Not Out: The Story of the Paymaster General's Office*, Crawley: HM Paymaster General's Office.

Wade, H.W.R. (1982) *, Administrative Law*, Oxford: Clarendon.

Wakeham, Lord (1993) 'Cabinet Government', Lecture given at Brunel University, 10th November.

Waldo, D. (1990) 'A Theory of Public Administration Means In Our Time A Theory of Politics Also', in N. Lynn and A. Wildavsky, *Public Administration*, New Jersey: Chatham House.

Walker, P.G. (1972) *The Cabinet*, Glasgow: Fontana.

Walsh, K., Hinings, C.R., Greenwood, R. and Ransom, S. (1981) 'Power and Advantage in Organisations', *Organisational Studies*, Vol. 2, 131–52.

Waltz, K. (1968) *Foreign Policy and Democratic Politics*, London: Longmans, Green & Co. Ltd.

Wass, D. (1984) *Government And The Governed*, London: Routledge.

Wettenhall, R. (1986) *Organising Government: The Use of Ministers and Departments*, Sydney, Croom-Helm.

Whitelaw, W. (1989) *The Whitelaw Memoirs*, London: Headline.

Wildavsky, A. (1990) 'Administration Without Hierarchy? Bureaucracy Without Authority?', in N. Lynn and A. Wildavsky, *Public Administration*, New Jersey: Chatham House.

Wilding, R. (1982) 'A Triangular Affair: Quangos, Ministers and MPs', in A. Barker, *Quangos in Britain*, Basingstoke: Macmillan.

Willetts, D. (1987) 'The Role of the Prime Minister's Policy Unit', *Public Administration*, Vol. 65, No. 4, 443–54.

Wilson, G. (1966) , *Cases and Materials on Constitutional and Administrative Law*, Cambridge: Cambridge University Press.

Young, H. and Sloman, A. (1986) *The Thatcher Phenomenon*, London: B.B.C.

Young, S. and Lowe, A.V. (1974) *Intervention In the Mixed Economy*, London: Croom Helm.

Zellick, G. (1985) 'Government Beyond Law', *Public Law*, Summer, 283–308.

Index